Pakistan
a travel survival kit

Pakistan – a travel survival kit

Published by
Lonely Planet Publications
PO Box 88, South Yarra 3141, Australia
Also at PO Box 2001A, Berkeley, CA 94702, USA

Printed by
Colorcraft, Hong Kong

Photographs by
Peter Campbell – 97A
Phyllis Elving (Pacific Travel News) – 32AB, 33ABC, 64B, 65C, 96BC, 97B, 129B
Pakistan Tourism Development Corporation – 64A, 65AB, 96A, 128ABC, 129AC
Alan Samagalski – cover

Illustrations by
Peter Campbell

First published
October 1981

This edition
October 1984

National Library of Australia
Cataloguing-in-publication entry

Santiago, Jose Roleo.
  Pakistan, a travel survival kit.

  2nd ed.
  Previous ed.: South Yarra, Vic.: Lonely Planet, 1981.
  Includes index.
  ISBN 0 908086 53 9.

  1. Pakistan – Description and travel –
  Guide-books. I. Title.

915.49'1045

THE AUTHOR
Jose Roleo Santiago has been 'on the road' for over two decades, travelling extensively in South-east Asia, the sub-continent, the Middle East, Europe, Africa and the Americas. He has supported himself along the way as a jack-of-all-trades including travel writing. As well as this book he has also written a new Lonely Planet guide, *Bangladesh – a travel survival kit*.

ACKNOWLEDGMENTS
This book would not have been possible without the kindness and assistance extended by the PTDC (Pakistan Tourism Development Corporation) tourist officers, by local and foreign travellers and the many hospitable Pakistanis I met on my travels in the country. In one way or another they provided information on places that I failed to visit. Particular thanks must go to the following:

Heinrich Haller (D), James Dunlop (NZ), Ruther Nielsen (Dk), Willie Bart (Bel), Hubert Binaenens (Bel), Stefan Unzicker (D), Syed Khurshid Alam (Pak), Naeem Akhtar Butt (Pak), Giovanni Pagliarin (It), Theodore Schmidkunz (D), John Armitage (NZ), J Vanlaer (F), Professor Frank E Young (USA), Syed K Hussain Shah (Mal), G Davis (A), Graeme and Debbie Miller (A) and David Stanley (Can).

For this edition, further information was provided by many people, including:

Mary Bakht-Testa (USA), Eggy Bardoell (N), Paul Butler (UK), Paul & Maree Girdler (A), Norma Glanfield (A), Harry Golding (USA), R Hee (USA), Chris Kempen, Jeffe Kaye, Anna Lenk (Can), Margaret Lesjak (A), Glen McDonnell (A), John Ovink (N), Nicholas Pierce (UK), Steffie Price (UK), Don Riggs (USA), Richard Waye (UK).

(A – Australia; Bel – Belgium; Can – Canada; Dk – Denmark; F – France; D – West Germany; It – Italy; Mal – Malaysia; N – Netherlands; NZ – New Zealand; Pak – Pakistan.)

Publisher's note The people mentioned above are just a few of the hundreds of travellers who take the trouble to write with facts about where they've been. Their letters are invaluable in helping to keep this and our other guides up to date. As well as these volunteer researchers, thanks must also go to the workers at Lonely Planet who helped produce this book, particulary Mary Covernton (editor), Graham Imeson (maps and design) and Anne Logan (typesetting).

A WARNING & A REQUEST
Things change – prices go up, good places go bad, bad places go bankrupt, and nothing stays the same. So if you find that something in this book is now dearer, worse or non-existent, don't blame the author or Lonely Planet, but do write and tell us about it. The best letters score a copy of the next edition – or another LP guide if you prefer.

Contents

Introduction

Pakistan is one of the more misunderstood countries in Asia. During the heyday of the Asia overland trip it was the country overlanders rushed through – a transit zone from the exotic colours of Afghanistan to the mysticism of India. Now with the continuing upheavals and uncertainties in Afghanistan and Iran it is almost as if Pakistan has been left out on a limb.

Although part of the subcontinent it is quite different, an Islamic country with its own cultural and historical heritage and fascinating in its own right. Pakistan was the site for some of the world's earliest human settlements, the centre of the great prehistoric Indus Valley Civilisation, the crucible of ancient empires, religions and cultures. Alexander the Great ended his long march eastward here and built Greek towns and cities which later gave impetus to the fusion of the Graeco-Roman and Indian art styles that emerged in the superb Gandhara culture.

The magnificent city of Lahore is a Moghul masterpiece, as important as any of the Moghul cities of India, while to the west is Peshawar, the capital of the swashbuckling Pathans, and gateway to the Khyber Pass, the romantic western approach to the subcontinent. In the south is Hyderabad, the metropolis of Karachi, but Pakistan saves its best for the north, craggy and forbidding but nonetheless stunningly beautiful. It is also historically significant – a museum and a gallery of prehistoric, protohistoric (archaeological designation for the earliest age of history, coming immediately after the prehistoric age), and historic rock carvings and inscriptions – particularly along the Karakoram Highway which follows the ancient Silk Trade Route from what is now known as the Grand Trunk Rd all the way to Mintaka Pass.

Places like the Swat Valley, Chitral Valley, Gilgit, Hunza and Baltistan are among the most beautiful and unspoilt regions in the world. Set against a background of the spectacular Trans-Himalayas, they not only offer a chance to see unique cultures, fascinating petro-glyphs (rock carvings – especially pre-historic rock carvings), great ranges, the highest peaks and the largest and longest glaciers in the world, but also treks through untouristed and untrammelled country – a wilderness area.

Facts about the Country

The Beginning

Until the end of the Mezosoic era, 65 million years ago, a broad, deep sea called the Tethys existed where the subcontinent is today. At that time there were only two great land masses on earth: to the north was Angaraland occupying what is now the Arctic region and in the south was Gondwanaland in what is now the Antarctic. Separating the two was the Tethys Sea.

In the Cenozoic era the sea filled with sediment, became shallow, overloaded and finally collapsed, causing the folding of the earth's surface. The cooling of the earth's interior, and probably the explosion of magma at certain centres in this part of the globe, gave rise to plate tectonics or continental drift, resulting in a large section of Gondwanaland smashing into Angaraland.

This cataclysmic collision created the mountain ranges, which rise in the north-west of Afghanistan and run across northern Pakistan, India and down through Burma. At the points of impact the earth was heaved up with tremendous force: in the north the crust wrinkled and corrugated for hundreds of km from south to north, while in the west and north-west it not only became corrugated but also cracked.

There is much evidence to support the Angaraland-Gondwanaland collision theory: the fossilised remains of a great whale have been found in the mountains in Chitral and there are other fossils to indicate that the Himalayas were once at the bottom of the sea. The geological upheavals occurred less than a hundred million years ago, but considerable seismic activity continues today involving a displacement of about three centimetres annually which corresponds to the yearly rise of 2.5 to three centimetres of the Himalayas.

For thousands of years rain, wind, snow, sun and earthquakes turned the land into what it is now: a land of greatly varying topograhpy, of arid semi-wasteland, vast, fertile plains, dry and lush plateaux, huge expanses of desert, arid, barren, hilly regions, green wooded mountains but also great, bare mountains, perennially covered with snow. It is a land criss-crossed by many great rivers, the longest and mightiest being the Indus – father of rivers – which has its source in the Manasarowar Lake in Tibet. The land is covered by innumerable streams, brooks, and rivulets, and dotted with lakes.

It was in this region that the paleolithic age began half a million years ago. On the banks of the Soan River in the Potwar Plateau, members of this early civilisation fashioned stone tools and started the movement that culminated in the great Indus Valley civilisations of Moenjodaro and Harappa (3000 BC), which occurred at the same time as those of the Nile and Euphrates. There were earlier civilisations in Sind, Baluchistan (6000 to 3000 BC), the North West Frontier Province, the Punjab, and even the craggy northern mountain area where there is evidence to indicate that Neolithic tribes were interested in astrology. And there were other similar prehistoric cultures contemporaneous with the Moenjodaro and Harappa that evolved independently of one another. They appear to have emerged at almost the same time, but only Moenjodaro and Harappa developed a highly advanced and well-organised urban way of life based on agriculture and trade, with a literary culture that has pictographic characters which still remain undeciphered.

Gandhara Culture

In 1700 BC the highly sophisticated

culture of the Indus Valley civilisation suddenly disappeared, a period which coincided with the arrival of the neolithic Aryans from Siberia and the Urals. The fine wheel-turned 'painted black on red' pottery disappeared and was replaced with a crude, primitive pottery. The art style drastically reverted back to the ithyphallic art form (representations of the erect penis) and there was a break in the cultural development of the area which was regressive and a return to the neolithic art style. The Aryans settled there and adopted much of the culture they discovered. They refined Hinduism from worship of the Brahman bull and developed a script known as *pakrthi*, considered the precursor of Sanskrit, which also remains undeciphered.

In the 6th century BC, at about the same time that Buddhism emerged, the land now known as Pakistan became the 20th satrapy of the Persian Achaemenian Empire of Cyrus the Great, and later of Darius. In the 4th century BC this region was conquered by Alexander the Great of Macedonia. Greek rule was brief. In the latter part of the same century Chandragupta founded the Mauryan Empire and during the reign of his grandson, Ashoka, Buddhism took root and flourished in the Peshawar Valley. On the death of Ashoka, in the 2nd century BC, the Bactrian-Greeks arrived, followed by the Scythians from Central Asia, who were in turn succeeded by the Parthians from Persia.

In the 1st century AD Kanishka led the Kushans from Afghanistan into the region and established an empire which extended from the Aral Sea up to the Gangetic Plains of India and spread from Sind and Baluchistan to the Pamirs and Tibet. It became one of the major commercial *entrepots* on the Silk Trade Route which linked Rome and Chang'an (now Xian) in China, with the subcontinent. During this period the Graeco-Roman and Indo art style fused and gave rise to the emergence of the Gandhara culture. Buddhism along with the Gandhara art genre swept through the Karakorams into Central Asia and influenced the Buddhist art form in China and Tibet. However, Gandhara was not merely a commercial hub, it was also a centre for pilgrims, religion and education: it was the Buddhist holy land.

Chinese pilgrims were greatly impressed by Gandhara, but in the 3rd century AD it was annexed by the Persian Sassanians and under them the Buddhist Gupta Empire emerged in the 4th century AD. The latter continued cultural and commercial links with Byzantium, Persia and China. In the 5th century AD, at about the same time that Rome entered into a 'dark age', the White Huns or Hephthalites pillaged the region, put the population to the sword and the cities to the fire, a disaster from which the Gandhara culture never recovered. Xuan Zhang, a Chinese pilgrim, who visited the region in the early 7th century AD, was greatly impressed by the cities, but by then Gandhara was already in decline.

In the 7th century AD the Arabs invaded Persia, and in the early 8th century AD led by Mohammed Bin Qasim they invaded Sind, introduced Islam, and gradually expelled the Hindus. In the middle of the 10th century Mahmud of Ghazni conquered the northern region of the subcontinent which had gradually reverted to Hinduism. In the northern mountainous frontierland the Chinese arrived in the middle of the 8th century AD. They were booted out by the Tibetans in the 9th century AD and by the 10th century it finally fell under the sway of Islam.

At the end of the 12th century Shiabuddin Ghauri occupied Delhi and the land up to the Gangetic Plains, but in 1206 General Qutb-ud-din Aibak established the Sultanate of Delhi. A few years later, however, Tartar-Mongol hordes burst onto the plains of Russia, Persia and the subcontinent and in 1249 Lahore and Delhi were sacked and depopulated. Late in the 14th century the Mongol hold over

Russia began to wane and the Mongol empire which had once stretched from the Sea of China to the Baltic began to decline, finally fragmenting on the death of Kublai Khan, the last great emperor of China. Fighting amongst the Khanates in Central Asia continued to blow up until the empire finally faded away.

The Moghul Empire

The Tartar-Mongol hordes were to reappear in the subcontinent as Moghuls under Amir Timur or Tamerlane. At this stage they had 'progressed' from being pagans and animists to adopting the tenets of Islam, but it wasn't until 1526 under the leadership of Babar that the last of the Afghan kings were defeated and the Moghul dynasty founded. This was expanded further by his grandson, Akbar (1556 to 1605).

In this period architecture took on a distinctive Moghul style, which featured exquisite designs that verged on the fantastical. Moghul art, culture and literary activity flourished and there was a proliferation of magnificent buildings, mosques, forts, palaces and gardens. Forts with battlemented ramparts were massive and resplendent palaces, beautifully designed and richly embellished with all the comforts sought after by oriental potentates. Most of the mosques were constructed along massive proportions, but somehow, at the same time, managed to appear dreamlike and delicate with slender minarets tapering up to a cupola.

This artistic, cultural and literary activity along with the construction of buildings and roads continued under Akbar's son, Jehangir (1605 to 1627) and his grandson, Aurangzeb, (1658-1707), who almost brought the entire subcontinent under his rule. However, the dynasty came to a sticky end on his death as his sons fought and murdered each other in their battle for the throne. The decline of Moslem power which followed gave impetus to the rise of the Sikhs in the

Punjab and the British in Bengal in the latter half of the 18th century. The Moghul Empire survived for some time afterwards but its power base was destroyed.

The Sikhs

The Sikhs' rise to power began with inscursions into the frontier provinces where Moghul power had weakened. They established their influence in Kashmir, further north to Ladakh, north-west as far as Gilgit and to the west as far as the Peshawar Valley in the 1840s. Meanwhile the British were moving slowly but inexorably from Bengal southward, then north-west.

The British first came to the region for trade during the reign of Akbar at the beginning of the 17th century. Akbar's son, Jehangir, received Sir Thomas Roe as the ambassador of James 1 of England and shortly afterwards the British East India Company was established in Bengal. When the Moghuls began to lose power in the middle of the 18th century the British became involved in the internecine battles that flared up in the subcontinent in their effort to protect their commercial interests. In 1757 Robert Clive defeated Nawab Sirjerdaullah at Plassey.

This victory was the signal for the British East India Company to carry out a piecemeal conquest of the entire subcontinent, overtaking the Sikhs in 1849 and superimposing their power in Kashmir, Baltistan, Gilgit and the region beyond the Punjab later known as the North West Frontier Province. The Sind was taken in 1843 before the final collapse of Moghul power. Mismanagement by 'John & Company' made the British Imperial Government take over direct administration of their vast empire after the Great Mutiny of 1857. Expansion continued. However, they failed in several mighty attempts to annex Afghanistan, the last province of the Moghuls in the west. Hunza, under the leadership of Colonel Durand, was the last bit of territory in the subcontinent to be conquered by the British. It fell in 1891.

British India

Euro-Asian trade and commerce, conducted overland along the numerous camel caravan trails of the ancient Silk Trade Route, ceased with the emergence of the Ottoman Empire in the middle of the 15th century. If there had been any likelihood of it being re-established the Portuguese navigator Vasco da Gama's discovery of a sea route to India and the East Indies in the latter part of the same century soon put an end to it. From then on Euro-Asian trade and commerce was conducted by sea. In effect da Gama's discovery resulted in the conquest of the subcontinent by the British merchants, the only invading power to arrive by sea via the Cape of Good Hope. Historically they were the only invading power to go westward against the major eastward current into Afghanistan.

With the arrival of the British, Moghul art, culture, literature and architecture were replaced along with the old Moghul monarchical governmental infrastructure. British art, culture and language were introduced and a colonial government administration from the district officer to the viceroy was established. The period saw a resurgence in the construction of public buildings, housing, courts of justice, police stations, military cantonments and churches and cathedrals, which were generally in districts of towns and cities known as The Mall. There was a fusion of Moghul and Victorian architecture in public buildings, but the churches and cathedrals retained their Norman or traditional Gothic design while a more modern architectural approach was developed for the houses.

The British began the construction of an immense network of highways, roads and rail tracks that spanned the entire length and breadth of the subcontinent from the coastal regions of Dacca, Calcutta, Madras, Cochin, Bombay and Karachi to the mountainous regions of Darjeeling, Kashmir, Baluchistan and the North West Frontier Province. Clear-cut definitions of boundaries for kingdoms or states and empires that surrounded the subcontinent from the west to the north and to the east were also introduced at this time. Explorers, travellers and adventurers proliferated, most of them going deep into the mountainous regions of the Himalayas, the Karakorams, the Hindu Kush, and beyond into Afghanistan, China and Tibet.

The subcontinent was mapped down to the last centimetre and the so-called Durand Line came into being to define its length and breadth. This generally followed the natural geographical barriers, such as the deserts, the dry, rugged offshoots of the Altai Range in the south-west which demarcate the borders with Iran and Afghanistan and the stupendous mountainous regions of the Hindu Kush, the Karakorams and the Himalayas to the north and the north-east with China and far to the east with Burma.

Evolution of a State

From the outset the Moslems were naturally hostile to the British, who applied the policy of 'divide and rule' to secure their hold on the subcontinent, which obviously further exacerbated the Moslem-British relationship. The Moslems felt deprived of the privileges they had enjoyed under the Moghuls, denied the educational and economic opportunities available under the new regime, and resented their degradation as a minority group. They knew, however, that the British were a people to be reckoned with.

Sir Syed Ahmed Khan (1817 to 1898) aspired to restore Moslem prestige in the subcontinent and thus began the Aligarh Movement out of which evolved the Moslem League. The Indian National Congress which was set up mainly for the struggle for independence amalgamated with the Moslem League. However, the

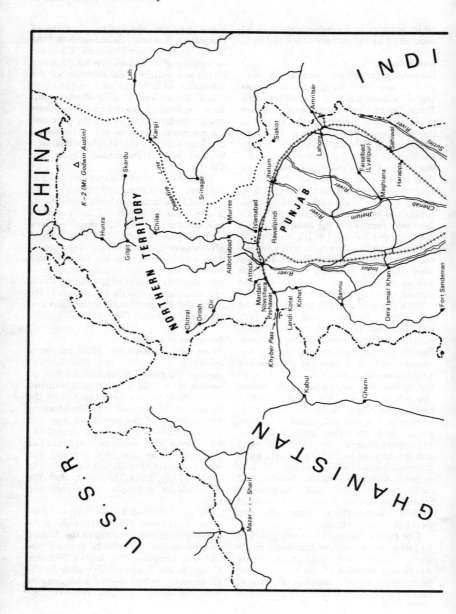

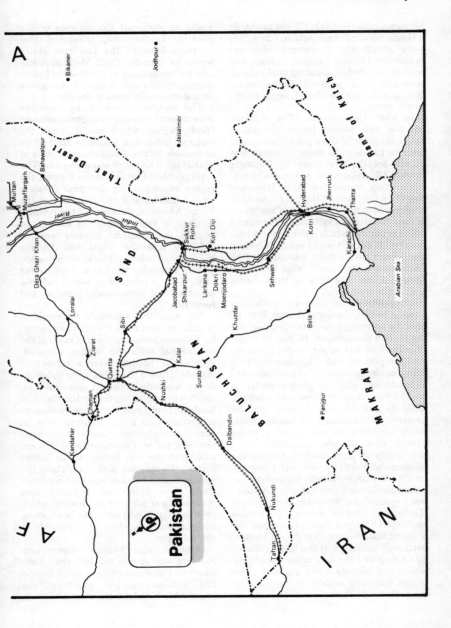

Moslems considered that it was primarily a Hindu political organisation. Since they were specifically concerned with the protection of their religion, culture and way of life, and in securing their social, economic and political rights under British rule, the Moslem League finally broke away.

In 1930 the concept of a separate Moslem state was put forward by Alama Iqbal, the great Moslem poet. Three years later in London the word Pakistan was coined for the first time by Chowdry Ramat Ali. Apparently *pak* means pure, while *istan* stands for land. It means therefore the 'land of the pure'. Another theory is that it is composed of acronyms of the first letters or syllables of the names of the provinces which make up the whole country. It doesn't really matter which is the correct theory for it was adopted by Mohammad Ali Jinnah, also known as *Quaid-i-Azam*, who took up the political goal of the poet Iqbal.

The political aspirations of the Moslem League before, during and after WW 11 posed a seemingly insoluble problem for the British government. British missions failed to find any answer to the problem, and the plan to make Moslem majority provinces in the west and east of India into autonomous Moslem states under a unified central government was rejected, both by the Moslem League and by Congress. Mohammad Ali Jinnah steadfastly objected to any other solution except that of the formation of a completely separate Moslem state for the Moslems of India to which both Congress and the British eventually capitulated.

Having decided that the only 'solution' was to partition the country into separate Hindu and Moslem states, the British appointed Sir Cyril Radcliffe to draw the dividing line. Nehru, Jinnah and Mountbatten all insisted that the line be drawn by 15 August – the date of independence which had already been decided upon before Radcliffe arrived in India. That gave Radcliffe little more than seven weeks to work out the division of the country. Furthermore, convinced that relations between the two new states would be friendly, Field Marshal Auchinleck (Commander-in-Chief of the Indian Army), authorised Radcliffe to ignore considerations of natural defence.

The decision was made to carve the subcontinent into a central, predominantly Hindu region, which would retain the name of India, and would be flanked on either side by the double-headed state of 'Pakistan'. The result was a disaster. The main problem centred on the Punjab, the region encompassing the great Moslem city of Lahore and the holy city of the Sikhs, Amritsar. Partition of the country resulted in the migration of millions of people: the Moslems heading west to Pakistan and the Sikhs and Hindus heading east to India. This mass migration was accompanied by riots and massacres instigated on both sides, which led to a bloodbath of unforeseen violence and ferocity.

Nor were the wholesale exchange of population and riots the only problems, for Pakistan ended up short of many of the commercial skills the Hindus supplied. Worse, the borders were a subject of dispute. During the build up to independence Kashmir remained undecided on which way to go , but finally the Rajah of Kashmir, Hari Singh, signed the instrument of accession to India. Subsequently an armed struggle took place with Pakistan retaining a slice of Kashmir on the western side, with the rest falling under Indian control. To this day both sides claim the predominately Moslem region of Kashmir. Each time India and Pakistan find themselves at each others throats, which over the last 30 odd years has been often, the Kashmir question is inevitably a central issue.

In the long term Pakistan's most serious problem was simply the fact that there were two Pakistans. When, on 15 August 1947, Pakistan emerged on the map it was as a double-sided nation, with one side in the extreme west of the subcontinent, the other in the extreme east. West Pakistan comprised Sind, West Punjab, the North West Frontier Province, Baluchistan and the former British political agencies in the northern region, while East Bengal and a great part of the Sylhet district formed East Pakistan. The western half was always the dominant partner despite the fact that it was the Bengalis in East Pakistan who supplied the majority of the country's export earnings. Basically the only real connection between the two halves was that they were both followers of Islam. And stretched between them was over a thousand km of hostile India.

From the outset everything about the country had an air of impermanence: things were set up with a view towards reorganisation later. Even the new country's name was tentative. In 1953 the country was renamed the Islamic Republic of Pakistan, only to be switched back to Pakistan in 1958. Initially Karachi, the port city of Sind, became the temporary capital. Then a new capital, Islamabad, was mooted to be sited on the Potwar Plateau but before it was finished the capital was moved, in 1959, to nearby Rawalpindi.

After 11 years of inefficient and corrupt 'democratic' government General Ayub Khan set up the first military government in 1958. He introduced reforms in the agrarian and industrial sectors of the nation's economy, but in 1969 he was succeeded by General Yahya Khan who proved to be rather ineffective. All this time discontent had been growing in the eastern half. The standard of living there was lower; their representation in the government, civil service and military was far smaller and their share of overseas aid and development projects was also disproportionately small.

In 1970 two events shook the country apart. A disastrous cyclone wreaked havoc on the eastern half, and the assistance the Bengalis received from West Pakistan was shamefully indifferent.

Then in December 1970 elections took place to return the country to civilian rule. A general election was held in each wing on a one-person one-vote franchise. The Awami League, led by Mujibur Rahman, won in East Pakistan with an overwhelming majority of 167 of the 169 seats, while the Pakistan People's Party headed by Zulfikar Ali Bhutto emerged the dominant political party in West Pakistan, taking 88 of the 144 seats. A constitutional dispute then arose over which political party should form a government which resulted in Mujibur Rahman being arrested and slapped into jail. This sparked off an insurrection in East Pakistan which led to the army taking over. The army's cruelty prompted bitter guerrilla opposition and finally India, flooded with Bengali refugees, stepped in and declared war against Pakistan. The Pakistan army was defeated in the east, culminating in the creation of Bangladesh.

Back in the west Bhutto came to power and governed Pakistan from that time until 1977 when he was ousted in a bloodless coup d'etat over his re-election. Controversy arose over whether or not Bhutto had rigged the votes, and whether or not there should be a re-run of the election, until it appeared that the country was on the brink of civil war. The army took over and Bhutto was arrested and imprisoned. Eventually the Supreme Court found him guilty of direct involvement in the murder of a political opponent and, despite the protests and appeals from leaders all over the world, he was hanged on 4 April 1979.

Since then General Zia-ul-Haq has governed the country under martial law. There has also been a steady swing towards a more fundamentalist Islamic rule in line with much of Islamic Asia. Today Pakistan is relatively quiet and stable, pursuing a policy of non-alignment and normalisation of relations with India. It is also trying to improve relations with neighbouring countries like China and Iran and, even more importantly, with the oil-rich states in the Middle East and the Gulf region.

Pakistan has gradually acquired a prominent, if not influential, position not only in the Islamic world but also in world affairs at large.

POPULATION & PEOPLE

Pakistan has a population approaching 80 million with a large percentage being concentrated in urban areas such as Karachi, which has slightly less than five million, and Lahore with three million. It is composed of heterogeneous racial stocks which include Dravidians, Aryans, Arabs and Mongols.

The population is far from evenly distributed due mainly to Pakistan's diverse topography. The Indus Plains of the Punjab and Sind are heavily populated in contrast to the deserts and barren hilly regions of Baluchistan, the North West Frontier and the arid desolate northern mountain zone.

The racial groups are amazingly diverse in complexion, physique and culture. The more numerous Punjabis and Sindhis who settled along the Indus River are similar to the people of India; the Baluchis and Pathans of the deserts and hilly regions in the western frontier are closer to the Turkish racial stock of Afghanistan and Iran; while, with the exception of the Baltis who are related to the Tibetans, the people of the Northern Territory are a hybrid population of the Caucasoid and Mongoloid racial stocks.

Each group or tribe retains its cultural and traditional customs, language, social system, attire, headwear and songs. Generally they are traditionally hospitable. 'Their simplicity ... is part of their charm,' wrote Camille Mirepois, author of *See Pakistan Again*, 'which has not yet, like elsewhere, been eroded by tourism.' Islam is the cohesive force which binds them all together.

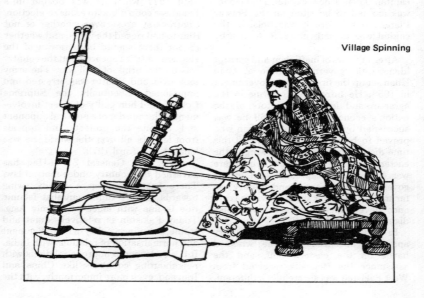

Village Spinning

ECONOMY

The land of the Indus is basically agrarian, self-sufficient in grains – mainly wheat – and is presently developing a number of light engineering and electrical industrial complexes. Pakistan produces 20% of its oil requirement and has coal mines and a tremendous quantity of gas. Its vast mineral resources remain unexplored and unexploited as yet. It exports textiles to the west, and foodstuff and technological know-how to the Middle East, but the bulk of its foreign exchange earnings comes from its overseas workers in the oil states. As with many third world countries it suffers from inflation problems, particularly now that the petro-dollars have begun pouring into the country.

GEOGRAPHY

Pakistan stretches from the Arabian Sea in the south to the Tibetan Plateau in the north, over a total area of 796,000 square km. It consists of four provinces: the Sind; the Punjab; Baluchistan; and the North West Frontier Province, plus the northern territory of Gilgit-Hunza, Baltistan and Azad Kashmir & Jammu.

In the west it is bounded by 800 km of desert along the Iranian border and by the 2200-km Durand Line drawn in 1897 to separate British India from Afghanistan. It runs from the Chagai Range up the Altai Range, the rugged Hindu Kush, to the Pamirs where a 15-km wide strip of Afghan land is all that separates Pakistan from the USSR. In the north the great Karakorams form the border with China, while in the north-east a ceasefire line demarcates the Pakistan and Indian sections of Kashmir & Jammu. From Jammu in the Punjab the border with India is clearly delineated by the Radcliffe Line drawn in 1947. It runs south for 1500 km through the Punjab and the Rajaputana Desert to the Arabian Sea. In the south of Pakistan is the 800-km long Arabian Sea coastline.

The country is divided into six geographical regions: the Lower Indus Plain; the Upper Indus Plain; the Salt Range; the Baluchistan Plateau; the Western Border Mountains; and the Northern Mountain Zone. The Indus forms the backbone of the whole country. From Tibet it crosses Ladakh close to the Chinese border and traverses the Karakorams into the plains. Other rivers like the Jhelum, the Chenab, the Ravi and the Sutlej rush down to join the Indus as it sweeps across the long plains to the Arabian Sea.

The coastline is semi-tropical, rich in marine life and has mangroves in the Indus delta. Moving north the land where the Indus flows is green and fertile, but dry and sandy on its lateral peripheries to the east and west. The plains end abruptly with the Salt Range of the Potwar Plateau where the land appears scarred and eroded. From here the land rises steeply to wooded massifs, which finally meet the convoluted glacial regions of the Hindu Kush, the Karakorams and the Himalayas. Except for the Indus Plains, which constitute about a third of the country, Pakistan is all hilly deserts, plateaux and great mountains.

FLORA & FAUNA

Along the coast there is a variety of marine life which includes shellfish, dolphins and sharks, while the Indus delta has crocodiles, reptiles and hog deer. Wheat, barley, oats, sugar-cane and cotton as well as a wide variety of tropical fruits such as mangoes, guavas, papayas and bananas are grown on the plains. Wildlife in the southern plains includes boar, deer, goats, porcupine, rodents and reptiles, while water buffalo, cattle, camels, donkeys, sheep, horses and goats are the most widely used domestic animals.

The barren sandy wasteland away from the Indus has sparse and stunted vegetation except for the oases with their date palm trees. Camels, jackals, hyenas, feral cats, panthers and leopards are to be found here.

In the more temperate areas apples,

pears, plums, peaches, walnuts, mulberries, grapes and berries are grown. The trees up in the northern mountain zone include fir, pine, spruce, willow, eucalyptus, juniper and the Himalayan *chenar*.

Some of the rarest wildlife in the world exists in this area, including the Marco Polo sheep; the markhor, a wild mountain goat, which grows to about 1.5 metres; the ibex, another kind of mountain goat; the urial, a wild sheep; the snow leopard, which is believed to be almost extinct; and black and brown Himalayan bears. Reptiles, and various species of rodents and birdlife also abound here. The latter includes the Indian roller, the crested hopoe, the kingfisher, the common kite and a number of migratory birds from Siberia. The northern mountain zone is noted for its hawks, falcons and eagles. Flowers in the glacial region of the Himalayas include the wild rose, sunflower and edelweiss among others. Numerous herbs such as alfalfa and thyme grow in profusion in this craggy country.

RELIGION

The state of Pakistan was founded on Islam, and is consequently overwhelmingly Islamic. Hindus compose only about a million of the total population, a far smaller percentage than the number of Moslems in India.

However, historically it has been the centre for a great number of religions. Hinduism evolved here from the original Aryan invaders, and Ashoka turned Buddhism into a great religion which reached its peak during the Gandhara period. Tantric Buddhism emerged in the northern highland, but this too completely disappeared with the arrival of Islam.

Other religious minority groups include a number of Christians, Pharsees and the Kalash Kafirs of the Chitral region. In Karachi there is a small but influential group of Zoroastrians who form and important, but unofficial, line of communication to their fellow fire-worshippers in Bombay in India. Even the Moslems are

divided into three major sects: the Sunnis, orthodox Moslems; the Shi'ites or Shias, followers of Immam Ali who was killed in the Karbala; and the Ismailies or Maulais. With the exception of countries like Iran where the Shi'ites are in the majority, the Sunnis predominate throughout the Islamic world.

The influence of the Islamic fundamentalist movement in neighbouring countries moved the government in Pakistan to codify Islamic tenets into the body of laws of the country. The severe penal code upheld in Saudia Arabia of cutting the hands off thieves and of flogging lovers convicted of adultery has been adopted by Pakistan.

Islam

The founder of Islam was the Arab prophet, Mohammed, who was born in Mecca in 571, and began his teachings in 612 AD. His descent is traditionally traced back to Abraham who had two wives, Hagar and Sarah. Hagar gave birth to Ismael, and Sarah had a son named Isaac. As the first wife, Sarah demanded that Hagar and Ismael be banished from the tribe. According to the Koran, the holy book of Islam, Ismael then went to Mecca, and apparently his descendants can be traced through to Mohammed.

The initial reaction to Mohammed's message was one of hostility; the uncompromising monotheism threatened the polytheism and idolatry of the Arabs – instead, Allah is the God, all-powerful, all-pervading. Mohammed's teachings conflicted with what he believed was a corrupt and decadent social order, and in a society which was afflicted with class divisions, he was preaching a universal brotherhood in which all people are equal in the eyes of God. One of Mohammed's strengths was that he did not evince supernatural powers. His claim was that he was the chosen teacher of God's message; his only prophet, charged with the divine mission of interpreting the word of God. But somehow Mohammed managed to be able to forge together an early Hebraic kind of monotheism with a latent Arab nationalism, and by 622 was beginning to gain adherents. In the same year he and his followers were forced to flee from Mecca to Medina in 622 AD, and there he managed to build a political base and an army, which eventually defeated Mecca and brought all Arabia under his control. Mohammed died in 632 AD, two years after taking Mecca, but by the time a century had passed the Arab Moslems had built a huge empire, which stretched all the way from Persia to Spain, and though the power of the Arabs was eventually superseded by the Turks, the power of Islam has continued to the present day.

At an early stage Islam suffered a fundamental split which remains to this day. The third caliph, successor to Mohammed, was murdered and followed by Ali, the prophet's son-in-law in 656. Ali was assassinated in 661 by the Governor of Syria, who set himself up as caliph in preference to the decendants of Ali. Today 90% of all Moslems are Sunnites, followers of the succession from the caliph, whilst the remainder are Shi'ites, who follow the descendants of Ali. Today, Iran is the only country where the Shi'ites form a majority.

The teachings of Mohammed are collated and collected in the scripture of Islam, the Koran, which was compiled from his oral and written records shortly after his death. It is divided into 14 chapters and every word in it is said to have emanated from Mohammed, and been inspired by God himself in the will of Allah. Much of the Koran is devoted to codes of behaviour and much emphasis is placed on God's mercy to mankind. Mohammed's teachings are heavily influenced by two other religions, Judaism and Christianity, to the point where there are some extraordinary similarities, including a belief in a hell, heaven and one true God, a creation theory almost identical to the Garden of Eden, and myths like Noah's Ark and Aaron's Rod.

The name Islam is derived from the word *salaam* which means 'peace', but it has a secondary connotation, 'surrender'. The true meaning is something like 'the peace which comes by surrendering to God' and the corresponding adjective is *Moslem.* The fundamental tenet of Islam, however, is based on the expression '*La ilaha illa Ilah*' – there is no God but Allah. Islam is a faith that demands unconditional surrender to the wisdom of Allah and means far more than a mere set of beliefs or rules. It involves total commitment to a way of life, philosophy and law. Theoretically it is a democratic faith in which devotion is the responsibility of the individual, unrestricted by hierarchy and petty social prerequisites, and concerned with encouraging initiative and independence in the believer. Neither, in theory, is it bound to a particular locale: the faithful can worship in a rice field, house, mosque or on a mountain. But in practice it is a moralistic religion and its followers are duty-bound to fulfil many restrictive rituals and laws, such as the washing of hands and face, worshipping five times a day at a mosque, constant recitation of the Koran, alms-giving, fasting annually during the period of Ramadan and saving to make the pilgrimage to Mecca. It is also a fatalistic faith in which everything is rationlised as the will of Allah.

Sufism – Islamic Mysticism

Today, Sufism is a peculiarly Pakistani form of Islam. But historically, it emerged in Persia and spread across the Middle East and to the west and east of the Indo-Pakistan subcontinent. It was brought there by believers of the Sufi saint, Shahabuddin Suhrawardy, such as Shah Abdul Latif Bhitai, Sachal Sarwart, Lal Shahbaz Qalandar and Hazrat Bahauddin Zakaria of Multan in the 12th and 13th century.

Shah Latif Bhitai is considered the greatest Sufi mystic and poet/philosopher of Sind and after him come Sachal and

Qalander. These Sufis were pirs, dervishes or fakirs, who proselytized Sufism by preaching brotherhood, love and peace. They relied mainly on their own moral and spiritual resources and were impressive for they did not condemn other creeds, but had faith in them as other avenues to Allah.

The Sufis led mystic ways of life and like the Sadhus of India were ascetic wanderers. They wandered through the deserts, renounced vanity, protested against worldliness and sought knowledge in a nomadic existence. When they did settle, like Lal Shahbaz Qalandar in Sehwan Sharif or Shah Abdul Latif Bhitai who lived in a sand dune in Hala near Hyderabad, they tended to choose caves. In Gholra Sharif near Rawalpindi there are man-made caves, now in ruins, where the *pirs* retired for months, even years to meditate on life, the universe and Allah.

They wrote verses about the love of God which they set to music and sang and danced to, first slowly then faster and faster until in a frenzy they fell into a trance. Legend has that when Sachal went into an ecstatic trance through the rhythmic sounds of various musical instruments, including his own voice, his long hair stood on end. Qalandar is remembered by his followers for his loud music and wild dancing.

Sufism influenced the literature, art, culture and music of the land and gave rise to another religion: Sikhism. Guru Nanak, founder of Sikkim, and Kabir, a Moslem saint, propagated the belief in oneness. Nanak was a Hindu but was claimed as a leader by the Moslems who called him Nanak Shah, while the Hindus regarded Kabir as their greatest teacher. This united both the Hindus and the Moslems and gave impetus to the emergence of Sikhism.

The shrines of Qalandar in Sehwan Sharif, of Latif Bhitai in Hala, of Datta Ganj Baksh in Lahore, of Immam Bari (Shiah Sufi) in Islamabad, are always

shrouded with a profound air of mysticism despite pot-smoking malangs or dervishes or fakirs, who dance in a frenzied manner to the beating of drums. The shrines are usually hung with pennants or colourful flags during *urs*, the anniversaries of saints, when hundreds of thousands of their followers gather there. At these times despite the massed crowds they mannage to retain a strict, sacred, religious festival mood.

In Baltistan the Sufis of the Valley of Khapulu, the Nurbuksh, have distinctive temples that are to be seen nowhere else in the world. They are also more liberal in their philosophy and behaviour towards others.

While Sufism is peculiar to Pakistan, like all Islamic societies, with the exception of South-East Asia, Pakistan is a closed society. Males and females are segregated in restaurants and public transport, and except in urban areas, women are usually veiled or in purdah.

Life in Pakistan

Pakistan is a tapestry of bright and dazzling oriental colours set against the sounds of plodding camels, the clip-clop of horse-drawn tongas and victorias, the sputtering and skittering of auto-rickshaws and, above all, the wail of the muezzin. That cry from the minarets is an ever-present reminder of the power of religion in this intensely Islamic country. The call to prayer, long and passionate, emanates from loudspeakers jutting out of minarets of mosques in towns and villages throughout the country. Out in the fields a tractor will stop and a Sindhi or Punjabi farmer will spread his prayer mat on the ground facing Mecca.

Except in the really remote villages purdah (seclusion of women) is slowly being put aside. In those hidden areas of Baluchistan, amongst the Pathans of the North West Frontier Province and in the high northern mountains, any local woman caught unveiled hastily slips on her purdah, or if without a veil, turns her back and hides her face. In the wilder tribal areas of the mountains, life is hard and insecure. The men walk around armed, not merely to hunt, but to protect themselves from their tribal enemies. Women seldom venture far from their houses, which are walled in and built with towers like forts.

These fortified villages are usually autonomous. They have a *jirga* – a village council of elders – where disputes are adjudicated and decisions concerning village life made. There is usually a *malik* who generally speaks Urdu and English, and acts as a kind of political agent or liaison officer between the tribes and the government. Higher up in the mountains the small groups of villages, which have emerged into mirdoms, are more peaceful and, unlike the people of Baluchistan and the North West Frontier Province, are no longer tribal.

Life for the pastoral nomads is different again. In spring and summer they load up their camels and move to the upland pastures. The men herd the cattle, sheep and goats, and the women, unveiled and unselfconscious, trudge along carrying their babies in one arm while balancing large wicker baskets on their heads. In the winter they return to the desert where young children, still only toddlers, are taught to look after the family animals. Even in these remote regions the muezzin call to prayer can be heard.

Pakistan is a land of mosques, but also one of graveyards and shrines known as *derghas*, bristling with flags where country people come to pay homage, make requests or offer prayers to those legendary saints who flew like eagles or turned the course of rivers. These legendary times are still part of every day life in Pakistan. In and around Hund the children use writing tablets and reed pens like those of the Gandhara period. The turbans, footwear and musical instruments have scarcely changed over the centuries and in the valleys of the Kalash Kafirs the way of life has scarcely changed for over 2000 years. In the Larkana region bullock carts are like they were 5000 years ago in Harappa and Moenjodaro.

People appear to be almost contemptuous of time refusing to be driven to a hectic way of life despite encroaching progress. This dichotomy between old and new is becoming increasingly obvious, impinging on all aspects of life. Islamic fundamentalism is dragging the country back into mediaeval times while modern trends are pulling in the opposite direction.

But despite the strictures of Islam, many travellers report that Pakistan can be an amazingly friendly country, and that the people are more courteous and outgoing than they are in India. But women may find the Pakistanis oppressive and overbearing. It is important to remember that women in Moslem society remain hidden in the background and that often they are still killed by their own kith and kin if discovered talking with a male stranger.

ARCHAEOLOGY

Pakistan is one of the most interesting and fascinating archaeological areas in the world. Here one can trace human development from the paleolithic, neolithic, prehistoric, proto-historic and historic ages.

Paleolithic tribes developed the Soan Pebble Culture in the Potwar Plateau 500,000 years ago; neolithic tribes probably preoccupied with the study of the stars developed their megalithic culture up in the Northern Territory; and in Amri in Sind and Mehr Ghar in Baluchistan neolithic tribes (6000 to 3000 BC) were the first to domesticate the buffalo. They also had trade relations with Persia and Central Asia.

When they disappeared the pre-Aryans, who built the Indus Valley civilisation (3000 BC), emerged on the scene. The pre-Aryans produced sophisticated artefacts which are now on show in the major museums of the country.

Their steatite seals, which display advanced artistry in the craft, are of great interest. Etched in a highly sophisticated art style, they are engraved with animals like the humped Brahman bull they venerated, or tigers, elephants, antelopes, fish-eating crocodiles and rhinoceros. A seal found in Harappa has a cross on one side and a splayed eagle with a snake above each wing on the other. The motif is similar to those found in Mesopotamia, Susa, and Tall-Brak in Syria. They are often engraved with characters believed to be the precursor of hieroglyphs, which were later developed in this region.

Moenjodaro, which means 'Mound of the Dead', has surprisingly revealed no regular cemetery, but in Harappa they have found two. The graves point north-south and were large enough to contain between 15 and 20 clay pots. Shell bangles, necklaces and amulets of steatite, paste beads, copper finger-rings, earrings of thin copper wire, lamps of clay and bones of fowls were found at the foot of the graves.

Kot Diji, now the site of a great fort, in Sind near Rohri and Rehman Deri in the southern region of the North West Frontier Province and also Taxila were other cities of the great prehistoric Indus Valley civilisation. In the valley of Peshawar and in the area of the Potwar Plateau, Alexander the Great built towns and cities, supposedly to guard the eastern frontier of the Hellenic empire.

Of the Mauryan empire of Changragupta, who superseded Alexander the Great, the only inscriptions that remain are those of Ashoka, the greatest of the Mauryan emperors. The Kushan empire, developers of the Gandhara culture, left ruins of their cities like Taxila, Charsadda and Pushka-lavati, the ancient capital of Peshawar, with their artistic sculptures, Buddhist monasteries, stupas, rock carvings and inscriptions. They are strewn all over the valley of Peshawar, Swat, Dir, Taxila and right up to the northern upper highland, particularly along the Karakoram Highway which follows the ancient Silk Trade Route from what is now known as the Grand Trunk Rd up to Gilgit and beyond the Mintaka Pass.

The upper highland of the Northern Territory is a craggy gallery and museum of rock carvings and inscriptions which date back to neolithic times. These rock records show the arrival of the Aryans, and later the Achaemenians, the Greeks, the Scythians, the Parthians, the Sassan-ians, the Hephthalites and the Chinese and Tibetans, who engraved their passage through what the ancient Chinese described as the 'suspended crossing'. They recorded the minutiae of their daily life from animals, activities, royal visits of emperors to symbols, emblems, coats-of-arms and scripts.

The 'suspended crossing' was a major section of the ancient Silk Trade Route until about the 9th century AD. The petroglyphs point to the significant role of this area in the history of Eurasia, particularly during the period of the Silk Trade Route civilisation.

HOLIDAYS & FESTIVALS

Holidays in Pakistan are generally either Moslem religious festivals or concerned with independence and the memory of Mohammad Ali Jinnah, father of modern Pakistan. The Moslem holidays are based on the lunar calendar which is at least 10 days shorter than ours each year, so each year they occur 10 days earlier.

Public Holidays

23 March	Pakistan Day –celebrates the 1940 decision to press for a Moslem nation independent of India
1 May	May Day –Labour Day
1 July	Bank holiday: other offices and businesses remain open
14 August	Independence Day– commemorates Pakistan's founding in 1947

6 September	Defence of Pakistan Day – commemorates the India – Pakistan war of 1965 over Kashmir
11 September	Anniversary of Quaid-i-Azam (Jinnah's) death
25 December	Birthday of Quaid-i-Azam (Mohammad Ali Jinnah)
31 December	Bank holiday: other offices and businesses remain open

Moslem Religious Holidays For 1984 they fall approximately on:

15 June	Start of the month of Ramadan
13 July	Eid-ul-Ftr – two-day feast to celebrate the end of Ramadan
20 September	Eid-ul-Azha – sacrifice of Ismail, this is the time for the pilgrimage to Mecca
22 October	Azhura (Muharram) – death of Immam Hussain, during this period Shi'ites scourge themselves and work themselves up into an emotional frenzy over the event
1 January	Eid-Milad-un-Nabi – birthday of the prophet, Mohammed

LANGUAGE

English is widely spoken throughout Pakistan but Urdu is the major local language. In the Punjab the people speak Punjabi, while close to the Afghanistan border, around Peshawar, they speak Pushto. Other major languages are Sindhi and Baluch: Shina, Khowari, Burushuski and Balti are the Northern Territory languages.

A relatively recent language is Urdu, which was used in the Moghul encampments by a motley collection of troops mainly from Central Asia, Persia and India. It became the lingua franca of the camps and evolved into a language spoken mainly in the north-west of the sub-continent.

A knowledge of this language will improve your chances of having a good time in Pakistan. It is also spoken in parts of India and is consequently extremely useful.

Below is a list of commonly used words and phrases.

hello	salaam
thank you	shukria
sir	jenab
yes	gee
no	ney
all right	tikka
well/OK	achah
why	quon
where	queddhar
how much?	kitna?
expensive	mengha
much	boht
little	tolla
enough	bas
stop	rokhye
difficult	taglibh
and/more	ur
or	ya
that	voh
I/we	amh
you	abh
I go	jaiga
went/going	geyah
know	malam
understand	jantha
room	kamra
bedding	bistar
bus	motor
home/country	muluk
watchman	chowkidar
trouble	muskhel
year	sal
month	mina
tomorrow/yesterday	khal
morning	suba
time	badjah
hour	tanga
half	saddah
1½	dir
water	pani
tea	chai
food	khana
hot food	garam
cold food	tanda
meat	gosht
roasted skewered meat	kebab

chicken	*murgi*
rice	*chawal/pulau*
potato	*aloe*
vegetable	*subji*
lentils	*dahl*
onions	*pear*
egg	*anda*
bread	*roti*
unleavened flat round bread	*chapatti*
Persian bread	*nun*
garlic	*tohm*
salt	*namak*
sugar	*chinni*
hot weather	*garmi*
cold weather	*sardi*
ice/snow	*baraf*
rain	*baras*

Greetings	
Peace be unto you!	*Wasallah-allaikhum!*
Unto you also peace!	*Allaikhum salaam!*
How are you?	*Abh kiah leh?*
What is your name?	*Abh khe nam heh?*
God willing!	*Inshallah*

The word *heh* is almost always added when asking a question. For example when you're asking for something to eat or drink you must say: *khana heh?* or *chai heh?*

When you're asking whether this particular bus is going to Gilgit or whether there's a room available, you use heh once again: *Gilgit bus heh?*; *Kamra heh?*

The same principle is used when asking where a specific place is. For example, 'Where is the GPO?' is translated as *GPO queddhar heh?*

If you want sugar and milk in your tea another useful phrase to remember is *chai duod-chinni.*

Numbers

1	*eek*
2	*duo*
3	*teen*
4	*char*
5	*panj*
6	*cheh*
7	*saht*
8	*ath*
9	*nou*
10	*das*
11	*yarra*
12	*barra*
13	*terra*
14	*chudha*
15	*pandra*
16	*sullah*
17	*satthara*
18	*atharra*
19	*ounis*
20	*bis*
30	*tis*
40	*chalis*
50	*pachas*
60	*sa'ath*
70	*sathar*
80	*assi*
90	*nubbe*
100	*eek sou*
1000	*ahzar*
100,000	*eek lakh*
10 million	*eek crore*
10 billion	*eek arab*

Note The difficulty with Urdu numbers is that they have different terms running in a consecutive manner. For example 25 is not *bis-panj* but *pachis*; 24 is not *bis-char* but *chou-bis*; but you can say *sathar-ur-panj* for 75.

Take care not to confuse *pachis* (25) with *pachas* (50).

Facts for the Visitor

VISAS

A passport that is valid for Pakistan is required by all visitors – Pakistan does not recognise India or Bangladesh. British Commonwealth citizens – Australians, New Zealanders and Canadians *et al* – do not need visas for visits of up to three months; nor do citizens of a number of European and Asian countries. Check with the nearest and most convenient Pakistan embassy or consul about this. Other nationalities require a visa which is issued free to citizens of some countries including the USA and, once again, is valid for three months. Pakistan also issues multi-entry visas which allow six trips within a period of one year.

Non-Commonwealth tourists/travellers are granted a one-month visa, which is considered sufficient time for sight-seeing and is not normally extendable. With the exception of Commonwealth citizens, people staying for more than one month are required to register with the police.

Visa Extensions Visa extensions are denied or granted according to the treaty agreement of the government of Pakistan with the government of the traveller. However, foreign registration officers in the hinterland are often not aware of these treaty agreements.

Tribal or special areas have different rules and regulations. Commissioners and/or superintendents of police have no authority to extend visas. They can only issue a permit allowing an extension for a certain period of time. This varies in different regions, but usually does not extend beyond a week.

Travellers seeking a visa extension in the Punjab – particularly if in Rawalpindi or Islamabad – should see Abdul Salaam of the Interior Ministry, Block R, Room 512, 5th floor, the Secretariat, Islamabad.

Karakoram Highway Permits are no longer required for the Karakoram Highway from Rawalpindi to Gilgit and as far as Baturo Bridge beyond Hunza.

MONEY

Approximate rates (1984) are:

US$1	Rs14.1
£1	Rs19.5
A$1	Rs12.3

The rupee (Rs) is divided into 100 paise but you may still occasionally hear prices referred to in annas: the rupee used to be divided into 16 annas, and in markets the term is still used occasionally. Twenty-five paise is equal to four annas. When you're changing money, always check that you have been given the correct amount and flip through the paper bills received. If you have been handed any really dirty, tatty-looking notes that have obviously been in circulation for years, try to exchange them for newer ones there and then if possible. As in India you may have some difficulty in them being accepted elsewhere if you don't.

You can bring in any amount of foreign currency or travellers' cheques but only Rs100 in Pakistan currency. Inflation has hit Pakistan rather badly and prices are spiralling. Sterling pounds and US dollars have good exchange rates, but not quite good enough to offset the effect of inflation. Deutsche marks are also good. As usual American Express travellers' cheques, which are available in any of these currencies, have the advantage of being replaceable at their offices in Karachi, Lahore, Islamabad and Rawalpindi. Offices at the latter two cities are apparently unreliable, fraught with hassles and offer service very reluctantly. Don't rely on having your money or mail sent to you here either. You will probably have to wait for ages for them, even if they are already there. If you need money from home urgently, it's better to have it sent across by bank draft as registered airmail to a specific address, preferably your embassy, consulate or a friend's place in Karachi or Lahore than to have it transferred from bank to bank via telex or cable. There are too many delays via the latter method.

If you have US dollars, Indian rupees or any other negotiable foreign currency on you when you arrive in Pakistan, hide it well. Officials – police, customs officers etc. – will have no hesitation in using threats and intimidation to relieve you of it.

On departure you can reconvert up to Rs500 into foreign currency, but you can only take Rs20 out of the country with you in Pakistan currency. Applications to the State Bank of Pakistan, or through its authorised outlets, must be made for larger sums.

CUSTOMS

The usual duty-free regulations apply to Pakistan with the exception that you should not bring liquor with you. There are generally no restrictions on what you may export, so long as you show foreign exchange receipts to the value of the items you're taking out. You are not allowed to take antiques out of the country. If you are worried about something you've purchased check with the museums at Lahore or Karachi to see whether you can export it.

Liquor SRO(1)/79 of the customs rules and regulations of Pakistan unequivocally bans the import of liquor. It should be noted however that mountaineering, trekking and scientific expeditions often bring in consumables (foodstuffs) which include a supply of liquor.

Different rules apply to different categories of travellers. People who stay more than 24 hours but not more than six months are defined as travellers not tourists.

HEALTH

You need an International Health Certificate showing you have been immunised against cholera and smallpox whether arriving from an infected or non-infected region for Pakistan. You'll also need one for wherever you're going next. If you are not immunised against cholera and find yourself at the border, you can obtain a certificate at Wagah for Rs5 – Wagah is only 27 km from Lahore. Pakistan is in the malarial area and it is necessary to take a weekly or daily dose of prescribed anti-malarial tablets.

Avoid drinking any water that you are not sure has been boiled or purified wherever possible. This is a lot easier to say than to do, but take every precaution that you can. Water is more likely to be purer and less harmful during the dry season than at any other period during the year. As in India care in where and what you eat will help protect your gut and bowels from the often savage effects of a radical change in diet.

Malaria Malaria is spread by mosquitoes which, on being bitten, transmit the parasite that causes the disease. This disease has an unpleasant habit of recurring from time to time, even if you got over it quite easily the first time – and, sometimes, it can be fatal.

So far you can't be innoculated against malaria – although the medicos have been hinting they're close to a breakthrough – but you can take simple precautions. These amount to taking either a daily or weekly tablet – depending on which your doctor recommends – which kill any parasites that manage to get into the bloodstream. You usually have to start taking the tablets about two weeks before entering the malarial zone and continue taking them for several weeks after you've left it. Another precaution is to try and avoid being bitten in the first place by using mosquito repellent, coils and nets.

Hepatitis Hepatitis is a disease of the liver

which generally occurs in countries with poor sanitation. It's spread from person to person by contaminated food, or water, or cooking and eating utensils. Salads which have been washed in contaminated water, or food that has been handled by an infected person, are possible sources of this disease.

Symptoms appear from between 15 to 50 days after infection – generally around 25 days – and consist of fever, loss of appetite, nausea, depression, complete lack of energy and pains around the bottom of your rib cage (the location of the liver). Your skin turns progressively yellow and the whites of your eyes, yellow to orange. The best way to detect it is to check your eyes and urine. The latter will also turn a deep orange, no matter how much liquid you drink. However, if you haven't drunk much liquid and/or you're sweating a lot, don't jump to hasty conclusions. Drink plenty of boiled or purified water and then, if your urine is still bright orange, it's time to panic!

However, the severity of the disease varies. It may last less than two weeks and give you only a few bad days, or it may last for several months and give you a few bad weeks. And you could feel depleted of energy for several months afterwards.

The usual protection agains hepatitis is a gamma-globulin injection, but its effectiveness is debatable – improved shots may provide protection for as long as six months, but some people believe they're not worth it. The only way to guard against hepatitis is to be careful about what you eat and drink.

Diarrhoea Diarrhoea is often due simply to a change of diet. A lot depends on what your digestive system is used to and whether or not you've got an iron gut. If you do get diarrhoea, the first thing to do is nothing – it rarely lasts more than a few days. If it persists, the usual treatment is a course of Lomotil drugs. In western countries you need a prescription to obtain this drug, so ask your doctor for a

supply. If the condition persists for a week or more then it seems likely that it's not simply travellers' diarrhoea and you should see a doctor. If you get a severe bout of diarrhoea, you'll become dehydrated, so make sure you keep up your fluid intake as well as your salt intake.

Dehydration It's easy to become dehydrated if you don't drink enough, which is one reason why it's a good idea to carry a water bottle with you. You will know you are dehydrated if you find you are urinating infrequently or if it is a deep yellow or orange colour. A secondary symptom is headaches. Remember, you sweat just as much in hot, dry climates like Pakistan's as you do in hot, humid climates. The only difference is that in dry climates the sweat evaporates, whereas in humid climates the sweat is unable to evaporate because the air itself is already moist, and you end up in a lather of sweat.

If you're sweating profusely, you're going to lose a lot of salt, which leads to fatigue and muscle cramps. Make it up by putting extra salt in your food – a teaspoon a day is enough – but don't increase your salt intake unless you also increase your water intake.

Medical Facilities There are a number of excellent hospitals in urban areas which can correctly and quickly diagnose ailments, prescribe medical treatment and even provide free medicine. Doctors specialise in local diseases and they know their business. Medical assistants in Pakistan also appear to know what they are doing, even if they simply dump pills into your lap.

CLIMATE

Pakistan has some real climatic extremes, from the broiling heat of the southern deserts to the freezing cold of the northern mountains. The summer season begins in mid-April, but it starts to get uncomfortably hot in May. June, July and August are the hottest months of the year. On the plains temperatures are generally 30°C or more, but can soar to a very uncomfortable 45°C.

The monsoon arrives in mid-July and continues till mid-September but it is not as severe as it is in India. It brings 40 to 50 centimetres of rain on the plains and between 150 to 200 centimetres to the subnorthern highland. The monsoon never reaches the upper highland, although it gets cloudy enough to make flights pretty uncertain and irregular. From mid-September until March – after the monsoon – is the best time to visit Pakistan. The days are cool, clear and pleasant during this period, but it can get cold on the plains at night. In the depths of winter in the far north the temperature can dip well below freezing and bring bitterly cold nights.

BUSINESS HOURS

On Fridays shops and offices are closed. The weekend begins on Thursday afternoon when public and private offices close at 12 noon, and other offices at 2 pm. Usual business hours are 9 am to 4 pm in winter, 7.30 am to 2.30 pm in summer. Banks are open from 9 am to 1 pm, and big stores from 8 am to 9 pm. Hours are more variable, but usually longer, in smaller shops and stalls. Post Offices keep normal business hours except during Ramadan when some are open only until 2 pm.

BANKS

All banks, with the exception of the foreign ones, have been nationalised. Nearly all the major foreign banks are represented in the major cities, so there should be no worries about being able to cash travellers' cheques. In urban areas foreign currencies and travellers' cheques can be cashed in almost any bank, but particularly the Pakistan National Bank and the Habib Bank. In some special areas like Quetta, Peshawar and the Northern Territory only the Pakistan National Bank deals exclusively with foreign currencies

and travellers' cheques. In the Northern Territory, particularly Gilgit and Baltistan, the Pakistan National Bank does not accept foreign currencies apart from US dollars and sterling pounds. It must also be noted that banks in different regions offer different rates of exchange for foreign currencies and travellers' cheques.

Never had money sent to a bank by telegraph or telex transfer, as already pointed out there are too many delays if you are in a hurry to get money from home. This warning cannot be stressed often enough. If you need to have lost travellers' cheques replaced plan to do so in Karachi and Lahore, but not Islamabad or Rawalpindi – for reasons already stated. American Express offices, particularly in Islamabad and Rawalpindi, have become notorious for inefficiency to visitors who have limited time in the country.

EMBASSIES

There are consular offices in Karachi, Quetta and Peshawar, but most of the embassies are in Islamabad.

MUSEUMS/GALLERIES/LIBRARIES

There are libraries, museums and art galleries in almost every major city in Pakistan, including small galleries and museums specialising in folk art or handicraft.

FILM

There are now photographic studios in nearly every major city that are capable of doing excellent processing of coloured films. Buying film to suit your camera is another matter, but there are specialists shops where you can get most kinds of film in Karachi, Lahore and Islamabad.

ENTERTAINMENT

The only entertainment readily available consists of television and cinemas which usually feature local, Indian and occasionally western films.

There are no massage parlours, night clubs, cabarets, bars or red light districts here. There is, of course, sport which includes cricket and hockey. Up in the Northern Territory they play polo and games like *bushkazi*, which was introduced by the Afghan refugees in the region. This is a wild, raging activity involving lots of thrills and spills, possibly what you would expect the wild, raging horsemen of the steppes to indulge in on their day off. It requires a large playing field – at least a couple of km long – some *chapandoz*, the swaggering horsemen who look like Genghis Khan (indeed, the latter would make an ideal captain were he still around) and a *boz*, the headless body of a goat. The chapandoz are divided into two teams, a marker peg hammered into the ground at one end of the field, the boz is dropped at the other end, and then all hell breaks loose. The idea is to pick up the boz, carry it up and around the marker at the other end of the field, then drop it back at its starting point. But it's not so easy to achieve when you've got a fierce team of superb Afghani riders trying to stop you however they can!

TRAVEL & TREKKING AGENCIES

In almost every major city, there are travel and tour agencies, but there are only a few mountaineering and trekking agencies, and most of these are in Islamabad and Rawalpindi.

BEACHES

There are a number of beaches where you can go water skiing and surfing, but this is usually only possible on those beaches controlled by hotels. Western women should not wear bikinis on any other beaches.

PUBLICATIONS

Dawn and *Morning News* are the major English newspapers in Karachi and the *Pakistan Times* and *The Muslim* are available in Lahore and Islamabad. All other major magazines such as *Time* and *Newsweek* can be bought at major bookstores.

ELECTRICITY

220 volts, alternating current.

TIME

Pakistan is five hours ahead of GMT. When it is noon in Pakistan it is 7 am in London, 12.30 pm in India, 5 pm on the Australian east coast, and 2 am on the US east coast.

POST/TELEPHONE/TELEGRAPH

Mail services are fairly reliable although important letters should be registered or insured. It's best to use aerogrammes where possible. The postal service in the main cities is fairly reliable, but don't count on it elsewhere. Post restante is also reasonably reliable.

The American Express mail service in Karachi and Lahore is excellent, but as mentioned earlier, is almost always frustrating in Islamabad and Rawalpindi.

Telegraph and telephone offices are everywhere, but telegrams should only be sent from the main cities. International phone calls can be made from major hotels, but as with India do not be surprised if you have to shout down the receiver.

OTHER

There's duck shooting, wild-boar hunting, fishing and bird watching on the southern plains, and trout fishing up in the Northern Territory. Hunting has been banned elsewhere in Pakistan since 1980.

INFORMATION

The Pakistan Tourism Development Corporation has its head office at the Hotel Metropole, Club Rd, Karachi (tel 51 6031/51 0234). A number of brochures on most of the interesting regions are available here. There are also offices in Lahore, Rawalpindi, Peshawar, Quetta and most other places of interest to travellers, including the Northern Territory.

In Karachi there are also PTDC

information centres at the airport and in the Hotel InterContinental.

ACCOMMODATION

Pakistan suffered a severe shortage of accommodation in the top class hotel bracket for some years, but recently a number of new hotels have been opened. Hotels of international standard are only found in the main cities such as Karachi, Lahore, Islamabad and Peshawar. The PTDC operates rest houses or motels in a number of places of interest such as Taxila or Moenjodaro or in the northern hill towns.

At the other end of the price scale are the *muzzaffar khanas* – local inns where accommodation is usually dormitory-style and consists of no more than a *charpoi* (rope bed). In most cases these local inns and the cheaper hotels will not accept foreigners, except in remote towns and villages where there is simply no alternative available. As in India there is a wide range of hotels of varying standards and prices above this basic level. In many cases you will find places of exceptional value, but it is always wise to check the rooms and toilet facilities before booking in. In towns where specific recommendations are not listed you will generally find hotels clustered around the railway or bus stations.

Pakistan has a number of youth hostels but these are very often located inconveniently a long way from the cities. In addition a great number of them have closed down. Karachi and Lahore also have YMCA hostels open to non-members on payment of a temporary membership fee. Major railway stations usually have retiring rooms with beds available for railway passengers but you have to supply your own bedding or sleeping bag.

Camping It is possible to camp in the gardens of *Dak Bungalows*, guest houses, rest houses and Youth Hostels in Pakistan. There are no official camp-sites apart from the one in Islamabad, which has apparently gone to seed, but many hotels also permit camping in their gardens. You should not camp by the roadside or in tribal areas in Baluchistan, the North West Frontier Province or in some specified areas in the Northern Territory. On a trek try to befriend the elders of the village or the teachers. Shepherds up in the upper highland are friendly, hospitable, and generally offer tourists the use of their huts and even their food.

Showers Major railway stations usually have free shower rooms, which are handy in summer if you're on the road. In urban areas or villages there are also the *hammams*, attached to barber shops, where you can have a refreshing wash in little cubicles for a small fee. They are easily identifiable by the towels hanging out front to dry. In winter they provide hot water.

FOOD & DRINK

Pakistan is a country where a variety of different kinds of foods is available. In most cities you have a choice of Middle Eastern, Indian and Afghani food. In Peshawar what you eat is similar to the Pathan food of Afghanistan – *kebab* and *nan* – while in Lahore it is Moghul – tandoori chicken. By and large food here is similar to that in India, although the curries are generally not quite so hot.

Specialities include kebabs of various types. For example *sheikh kebab* is minced and grilled meat on a skewer, and *shami kebabs* are minced meatballs. *Tikka* is a tasty spiced and barbecued dish consisting of chunks of beef, mutton or chicken. One of the great Pakistani taste sensations is a whole roasted leg of lamb called *sajji*.

Note that there are meatless days, usually on Thursdays or Wednesdays, when restaurants only serve poultry or fish.

The unleavened Indian-style bread

known as *chapattis*, or the Iranian bread called nan are usually an integral part of the meal, as is the lentil dish *dhal*. Seafood is particularly good in Karachi. Other popular dishes include *pilau*, rice cooked with spices mixed with chicken or lamb, and *samosas*, filled with meat or vegetables. Meat features much more in the Pakistan diet than in India – vegetarian restaurants are rare.

When you're in Lahore visit the Old Walled city and try *kalla pacha*, a thick soup made out of sheep or goats' forelegs, or sample *karlai gosht*, tender mutton, stewed or crispy fried; in Karachi have some *nohari*, spicy meat in gravy; and in Peshawar ask for *chapli-kebab*, another spicy meat dish shaped like the *chappal* or sandal, hence the name. In Hyderabad and Quetta ask for *sajji*.

There is a wide range of desserts, which include the popular ice-cream-like sweet called *kulfi*. Small sweet pastries are also popular as desserts, and there's a wide variety of fresh fruits varying from the tropical mangoes, pomegranate, papaya and melons of the plains to the apricots, peaches, apples, mulberries and pears of the cooler hill regions. There is also a variety of nuts available, including walnuts and almonds.

As in India the iced curd (yoghurt) drink *lassi* is very popular and refreshing. Another tasty drink is *nimbu pani*, which is made from fresh limes – ask whether the water's been boiled or purified before drinking it, if you're worried. You can also get brands of soft drinks such as Coca Cola. Generally tea is served with milk and sugar already in it – often with far too much of each. You can also get the black tea of the plains *sulaimani* and the salted tea of the northern area as well as Tibetan style tea, churned with butter. Green tea, called *shabaz chai*, is popular too and is usually flavoured with cardamom or jasmin.

Restaurants In the better hotels and restaurants western food is available, but generally local food is all that's available, except for western-style breakfasts. As with India, the railway station restaurants are good places to go for a rather bland local attempt to reproduce English food. In major towns you will also find a few Chinese restaurants. Except for the restaurants at railway stations, opening hours are generally only from 7.30 to 9.30 am for breakfast, 12 noon to 2 pm for lunch, and 7.30 to 10 pm for dinner. Outside these hours it's considered snack time, and a sandwich and tea or soft drink is about all you can find. There are a few restaurants which only serve Moslems.

Ramadan During the Moslem fasting month of Ramadan – with the exception of those at the railway stations – restaurants, teashops and food stalls are closed from dawn to dusk. In urban areas there are places which open – discreetly – but in smaller towns and villages everything is closed, even to travellers. You can eat or drink on trains and aircraft, but not in buses. Please respect those who are fasting and only drink, smoke or eat with discretion when travelling.

When the sun sets the restaurants and teashops open again. Food stores open at

Liquor Permits To have a drink you need a liquor permit which first requires a Tourist Certificate from the tourist information centre. They will direct you to the Excise and Tax Office where a Rs12 fee entitles you to six bottles of hard liquor or 60 bottles of beer in a month! You can apply for a three-month liquor permit if you wish. The Excise and the Tax Office will tell you where you can buy alcohol. The American Club is Islamabad is the place to buy foreign liquor once you have your permit.

Importing liquor is banned except for mountaineering, trekking and scientific expeditions.

THINGS TO BUY
Pakistan has a number of interesting local

handicrafts which include the fine Persian-style carpets rated by connoisseurs as being almost as good as real Persian rugs.

It also has some of the finest embroidery and leather work you will come across anywhere. Particularly fine are the leather bags, jackets and shoes, which are excellent buys. Pakistan also produces exquisite brass and copperware, as well as jewellery and other articles made of onyx, silver and gold. Pottery is another highly developed craft as is carpentry, so if you like ornately carved wooden screens, trays and furniture this is a good place to get them. Less ornate wooden products that Pakistan is noted for, but nevertheless considered by experts to be the best sporting equipment of its kind in the world, are cricket bats and squash racquets.

In major cities government-controlled handicraft shops have fixed prices. Lahore and Peshawar both have extensive bazaars where you can often find unusual articles and precious and semi-precious gems, but Karachi probably has the widest range of shops and articles. Bargaining here is essential to get good value for money.

Duty-Free Shop There is only one duty-free shop, and it is at the Karachi International Airport where foreign-made perfumes, liquor and cigarettes are available. In addition local handicrafts, such as carpets and leatherwork and gems, are on sale here.

WHAT TO BRING
As little as possible is the golden rule of good travelling. It's usually better to leave it behind and have to get a replacement when you're there, rather than bring too much and have to lug unwanted items around.

However, if you intend to go trekking, take good mountaineering or trekking gear. See section on Northern Territory for equipment and requirements.

Other useful items to bring with you are a plug for sinks and basins, a padlock for hotel doors which are often fastened with a latch, and plenty of film

Clothing Except for the coldest mid-winter nights, you will need nothing more than light clothes on the plains. A sweater or light jacket may be necessary for cold nights. But it's a different story up in the mountains where it gets icy cold, particularly at high altitudes. You will need as much warm gear here as possible. In the height of summer on the plains or in the thin air of the mountains, you will also need good sun hats and glasses for protection against sunstroke.

The usual rules of Asian decorum apply to dress standards. In particular, women should dress very discreetly, but men should also be careful about what they wear – shorts are frowned upon. In summer it's preferable to wear light cotton shirts rather than singlets or T-shirts.

OTHER
If you're arriving overland via India shawls, blankets and Nescafe from Amritsar can be sold in Lahore at a minimum 100% profit. Leather 'fez' style hats from Pakistan will sell in Srinagar at a 400% mark-up.

A
B

A Boats in Karachi harbour
B Gidani Beach near Karachi

DRUGS

Smoking dope is apparently legal in the North West Frontier Province outside Peshawar. But if you try it anywhere else, you run the risk of receiving an unlimited jail sentence or handing over a hefty bribe to get out of it.

Warning to Dope Smokers Be very wary of anyone who approaches you offering drugs. Many local dealers have connections with the police and will set you up for a 20% cut in the price of the drugs confiscated. Do not be persuaded to do any drug-running in the hope of making a quick buck, a number of unsuspecting travellers are in jail because they were induced to be 'mules', the colloquial expression used in Pakistan for drug smuggling. You may find yourself busted for very little and end up in jail with a lot of hassles and a no-money type situation.

A Japanese traveller recently had to pay $US500 to a Lahore policeman after his 'friendly' hotel owner had dropped him in it.

HINTS FOR WOMEN TRAVELLING IN PAKISTAN

The following is an extract from a letter sent to us by an Australian woman which may be useful advice for other women travelling on their own or together.

Nothing could be preparation for the actual experience of walking down the street, the culture shock was so great I spent a lot of my time in Karachi in self-imposed purdah.

The things I think should be noted by the lone female traveller are:

Buy some *Shalwar Kameezs* (local clothes) which are excellent to travel in and people appreciate that you're wearing them. They also make you 'invisible' to the local males to some extent.

Make yourself get out and walk – start with the main street. This is easy to do if you stay near the city centre and it's good exercise (if you're like me and the Aussie girl I travelled with and like the food, you will need to unless you want to put on weight). By walking you get to see all the bazaars and everyday life close up and it's cheaper.

Get some idea of Pakistani pronunciation so that when you need to ask directions they will understand you.

If you want attention in banks, post offices etc. become like a Pakistani male – aggressive.

Brush up on sport – always one way of getting into a conversation (people seem to be pleased if you know who is in their national teams). Also a good way of diverting the conversation from sex – all the men I talked to in Pakistan always got round to sex and would ask the most personal questions, and they had no hesitation in telling me how sexually frustrated Pakistani men are. Though I don't think they expected me to do anything about it. Politics is another good subject to change the subject if all the sex talk gets too much.

Getting There

AIR

Karachi is the main international access point for air travellers, although there are also some flights through Lahore – mainly to and from India – and Islamabad. *Pakistan International Airline* has a wide range of services to other Asian countries, the Gulf states and Europe. There are flights to Bombay from Karachi and to Delhi from Lahore. On departure there is an embarkation airport tax of Rs100.

Concessions

Foreign travellers staying two weeks to three months in Pakistan are eligible for a 27% discount on international flights. There are also special fares from Pakistan to Peking, which depart Islamabad, go to Peking and then on to Tokyo.

Arrival

PIA has buses between the airport and town in Karachi and Islamabad. Taxi meters will not be working, count on about Rs40 in Karachi and Rs25 in Islamabad, but rather more at night. There are quick and comfortable minibuses between Islamabad Airport and Zafar Chowk in Islamabad via Saddar. They are labelled Overseas Workers Foundation.

LAND

India

Most overlanders today will be arriving from India – there are numerous fascinating comparisons and contrasts between Pakistan and India, making it interesting to see the two countries one after the other. Since Partition the border with India has been closed everywhere except in the Punjab. There used to be a railway line across the desert from Jodhpur in Rajasthan to Hyderabad in Sind, but today this is closed. A tentative plan to open this rail route has been mooted, but it's not yet known when. Similarly the road

routes through Kashmir are also closed. Prior to Partition the main route to Srinagar in Indian Kashmir was from Rawalpindi and you could also reach Skardu from Srinagar via Kargil. Today the only access between the two countries is the Lahore-Amritsar rail link which crosses Attari and the road link which crosses at Wagah. See Lahore for details on schedules and fares.

There is a toll tax on all overland routes of Rs2.

Afghanistan

There are two road entry points between Pakistan and Afghanistan, but since the Russian invasion few travellers have been prepared to take the risk of entering this way. Nonetheless, officially the borders are still open, although in practice they are virtually closed. Previously the most popular entry point was at Torkham on the famous Khyber Pass between Peshawar and Kabul. See Peshawar for details of this route. There is also a less frequented crossing at Chaman in the south between Quetta and Kandahar. See Quetta for details.

Iran

The land route between Pakistan and Iran is now open. It is a long trip across a rugged section of Baluchistan between the Iranian town of Zahedan and Quetta in Pakistan, crossing the border at Taftan. See Quetta for full details of this route and rail route.

China

Foreigners are not generally allowed to cross the border between Pakistan and China, but the 2500 km trip from Islamabad along the Karakoram Highway to Kasghar in China's Sinkiang Province would certainly be an extremely fascinating one if you could use it. It follows the ancient Silk Trade Route from the Grand Trunk Rd through Kasghar to the modern Chinese city of Xian, built not far from the site of the ancient cosmopolitan capital, Chang'an. In the summer of 1983 the Chinese border on the northern frontier of Pakistan was opened to Pakistan and Chinese nationals, but so far not to foreigners. General consensus is that this border may be opened to travellers again in the near future.

Other

Overland road and railway lines are at Gaudasinghwallah near Lahore and Khokhrapar in Sind on the Indo-Pakistan border, but they are still closed.

SEA

India

There are boats from Bombay twice weekly to Karachi, usually on their way to the Gulf states. They are operated by the British Indian Navigation Company and McKinon & McKenzie Co. Both these shipping lines have offices on Chundigarh Rd. The fare from Karachi to Bombay is Rs475 deck class, more for berths or cabins.

Gulf States

From the ports of the Gulf states these same boats make it back to Karachi on their way back to Bombay.

Africa

There are also freighters plying between Karachi and Mombasa and Dar es Salaam via Aden.

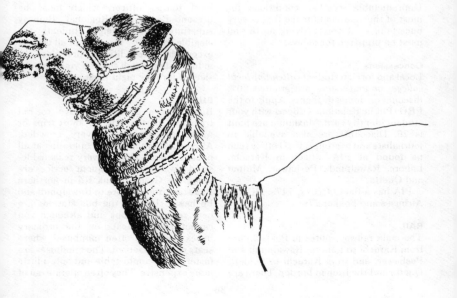

Getting Around

AIR

Pakistan International Airline has an extensive domestic network with several flights daily between the major centres: Peshawar, Multan, Islamabad, Lahore and Karachi. There are also flights to Quetta, Hyderabad, Sukkur, Moenjodaro, Chitral, Gilgit, Skardu, Saidu Sharif, Gwaddar and Pasni. The services from Peshawar to Chitral and from Rawalpindi (Islamabad) to Gilgit and Skardu will probably be of particular interest to travellers. The flight to Skardu in particular is fantastic since the mountains are often rather higher than an F-27's maximum altitude, so you weave in and out of 7000-metre peaks.

The fares on these routes are artificially low since the government wants to emphasise the links with these remote regions which are often cut off by snow-blocked passes for most of the year. Unpredictable weather conditions for most of the year could make flights very uncertain, so if you're flying north you must be prepared for delays.

Concessions

Local and foreign students *attending local colleges or universities* are granted 30% discount on domestic flights. Apply to the PRO (Public Relations Officer) with your student identity card. Maximum age limit is 26. Discounts are also available to journalists and to groups. PRO offices can be found at PIA offices in Karachi, Lahore, Rawalpindi, Peshawar, Multan and Quetta.

PIA has a fleet of 707s, 747s, DC10s, Airbuses and Fokker 27s.

RAIL

The main railway routes in Pakistan are from Karachi to Lahore, Rawalpindi and Peshawar, and from Karachi to Sukkur, Quetta and the Iranian border. There are several classes: air-conditioned first class sleepers and seats; first class sleepers and seats; and second class including express trains and ordinary mail trains. On the main rail routes there are usually several trains daily.

Trains are always overcrowded and between big cities it can be difficult to get seats. You must always reserve seats several days in advance for air-conditioned and first class seats. All sleepers also require advance reservation. If all else fails you can get a station porter to 'reserve' a seat for you for a nominal fee.

Concessions

Any foreign tourist irrespective of age – student or not – is eligible for a 25% discount for six months from normal rail fares. To get this discount you need a Tourist Certificate, obtainable from the local tourist officer, which must be presented to the Regional Railway superintendent. Foreign students are elegible for a 50% discount in all classes except the air-conditioned first class. As in India life is much easier if you can get a sleeper for long night trips.

BUSES

Buses are a good alternative to rail transport, particularly for short trips or where the trains are very crowded. Although there are buses operating at all hours between almost every reasonable-sized town the most frequent services are along the Grand Trunk Rd in northern Pakistan: from Lahore to Rawalpindi and Peshawar. Usually the bus stations are near railway stations and although you cannot reserve seats on the ordinary buses there are often minibuses where seats can be reserved. The minibuses are faster, more comfortable and only a little more expensive. They often operate out of a different station from the ordinary buses. There is a government-operated luxury bus service between Lahore and Islamabad.

Concessions

NATCO (Northern Area Transport Company) and other bus lines operating between Rawalpindi and Gilgit and in the northern area offer 50% discount to both local and foreign students and it's not necessary to be attending local colleges or universities.

CARGO JEEPS

In the upper northern region of Pakistan the usual form of transport between towns and villages are the cargo jeeps which carry cargo and passengers along the narrow and steep mountain roads. Many of these roads are simply too severe or too narrow for any other form of transport. Note that cargo jeeps do not usually run to set schedules and they are not cheap. If PIA has a flight it will probably be cheaper than a jeep.

CAR RENTAL

Consult the tourist offices for information on car and driver rental. Check with your national motoring organisation about import regulations for bringing your own car to Pakistan. For some time it was, and may still be, possible to import a car for 15 days, extendible for a further 15 days, without the necessity of holding a *carnet de passage*. Longer stays do require a carnet or a bank guarantee that you will re-export the vehicle when you depart. The Automobile Association of Pakistan, 8 Multan Rd, Samanabad, Lahore, or the Karachi Automobile Association, Oriental Building. McLeod Rd, Karachi can provide more information.

ROADS

The major roads in Pakistan are generally sealed and in good condition but minor roads are much worse. This applies particularly to the northern region where roads can be hair-raising and subject to damage by snow, landslide or earthquake. Driving in towns and cities can be a time-consuming and nerve-shattering experience due to the chaotic pedestrian, animal, bicycle and auto-rickshaw traffic. Try to avoid the rush hours in big cities, you could end up a cot case otherwise. When you're driving through tribal areas be very careful, if you have an accident you are likely to be a long way from medical treatment, on top of which you may also find yourself embroiled in a tribal conflict. Unless it's imperative, it's wise not to drive at night since very few bullock carts, bicycles or trucks have tail lights.

LOCAL TRANSPORT

For urban transport you've got a choice of taxis, auto-rickshaws, pedi-rickshaws and tongas, plus buses, minibuses and miniwagons. Fares for the latter are usually fixed: buses cost from 50p to Rs1.50 depending on the city and on the distance. Minibuses are usually a little more expensive but are faster and more comfortable. Buses are always packed.

Taxis and auto-rickshaws (a motor scooter tri-wheeler) may have fare meters but they are unlikely to be functioning. Count on about Rs2.50 per km for a taxi, half that for an auto-rickshaw. Bargain hard and always fix the fare before you start off. Pedi-rickshaws and tongas (two-wheeled horse carriages) are also subject to pre-departure fare negotiation. Since street signs are often invisible, non-existent or indecipherable, it is necessary to take a pedi-rickshaw or auto-rickshaw to get where you're going. It will prove less inconvenient, less hassle, less time and energy consuming.

Sind

It was called the 'Unhappy Valley' or the 'Land of Uncertainties' by ancient travellers such as the persians, Greeks and Arabs who marched through the scorching deserts of Persia and Baluchistan for long, wearying days and weeks towards the Valley of the Indus – seemingly a promised land – only to find it depressingly arid and barren. 'The skies are enormous. So much sheer space, so much parched land exposed under the pitiless sun, such endlessly monstrous horizons lie heavy on the spirit,' writes Jean Fairley. It is also a land of parrots that dart around; of the sheesham and pipal trees; of the brightly-plumaged kingfishers that flash along the canals and river banks; and of white herons perched on the backs of water buffaloes.

The province of Sind, the Lower Indus Plain, is almost 140,000 square km in area, and most of it dry alluvial deposits. Separated from the Upper Indus Plain by the rocky gorge above Sukkur-Rohri it slopes southward down to the Arabian Sea and from the edge of the Kirthar Range of the Baluchistan Plateau, which makes up the provincial boundary line in the west, it sprcads eastward to the Thar Desert. In the middle of this plain flows the Indus River – its life and soul – down to the delta region out into the Arabian Sea.

The climate is generally dry and hot with temperatures in summer rising to between 27° and 40°C. The coastal region does not suffer from extremes of temperature, mainly due to the sea, but does tend to be oppressively humid during the summer monsoon which sweeps up from the Arabian Sea and drops a little rain on the parched plain. In autumn and winter, when the winter monsoon wind from Central Asia blows across and over the great mountains of the north-west, the temperature can dip to as low as 7°C, but generally it stays around 20°C – a mild and pleasant climate.

Under these geographical and climatic circumstances it was only on the banks of the life-supporting Indus and its many tributaries that villages and towns sprang up. Here the beginning of civilisation emerged: Moenjodaro on the west bank of the Indus and the earlier Kot Diji on the riverside just south of the Sukkur-Rohri region. The Indus Valley Civilisation reached its peak in Moenjodaro. The region from Thatta, south of the Indus, was also once the centre of a very advanced civilisation. Its great cities were served by the port of Banbhore, believed to have been the landing site of Mohammed Bin Qasim, the Moslem conqueror of Sind, but, like Moenjodaro, these cities disappeared; exquisite burial grounds being the only trace of them.

These cities must have been contemporaneous with the historical periods discovered in Banbhore: the Scytho-Parthian (2nd century BC), the Hindu-Buddhist (1st century AD), and the early Islamic cultures (8th century AD). The prosperity they enjoyed could be ascribed to the port town of Banbhore which, at that time, must have been linked up with the great trading area which began on the coast of East Africa and extended through Aden on the Arabian Peninsula to Persia. Banbhore was also connected by overland camel caravan routes from Basra through Persia into the Makran and also from Baluchistan and the Punjab. These were minor veins that formed part of the ancient Silk Trade Route of Eurasia.

What happened to these cities? 'In this place there was a great city whose inhabitants were so depraved they turned into stones,' the 12th century Arab traveller from Morocco, Ibn Battuta, was told. And he himself saw 'innumerable number of stones in the shape of man and animals, mostly broken, disfigured.' Now they are all gone; cities and all have disappeared without a trace, perhaps buried in the sand.

In the early 18th century the Indus changed course and must have closed up the port of Banbhore which was eventually replaced by Karachi. The pace of development in the southern region faltered and it never recovered its ancient glory. Karachi and the surrounding areas did not prosper as much as the ancient and mediaeval cities that previously thrived and flourished in the Banbhore-Thatta region.

At this time Thatta, the birthplace of Akbar, on the west bank of the Indus to the south, and Hyderabad, on the east bank and to the north, appear to have developed in importance. The coastal region was simply dotted with tiny fishing villages and Karachi was only beginning to emerge as a port town. Thatta was once the capital of the Moghuls in Sind but it declined when the Moslem rulers moved the capital to Khudabad and in turn Khudabad faded away when the Indus changed its course. Hyderabad eventually became the capital of Sind.

The whole Lower Indus Plain fell into a deep lethargy that disappeared only when the British added it to their Indian empire. Once again the banks of the Indus became alive with activity. Great highways were cut, rail tracks were laid and irrigation canals and barrages were built. Unfortunately these put an end to traffic on the river itself. The plain, at once so dry and so green in patches, is interspersed with sprawling industrial cities and plant complexes, mediaeval cities, ageless villages and hamlets.

In the hot season the whole landscape shimmers and the grey, brown and even reddish colours all turn creamy-white. Dust and sand carried up by the wind create a haze which blots out the sun or turns it opaque. It is the season along the coast when fishing ceases and marriages take place, when on a full moon the

villagers in their fine bright clothes, along with the fakirs, snake charmers and musicians trudge up to the mountain shrines for an all-night feast. They sometimes put on wrestling matches during this period, but more often it is a time for music, dancing and enjoying the moon.

In autumn, when fishing is resumed, the whole coastline, particularly in the late afternoon, is suffused with colours. The sky and the sea are generally tinted with crimson.

KARACHI

The city was originally a little fishing village where Kalachi, a dancing girl of great beauty, lived. Kalachi's fame was spread far and wide by boatmen, caravan traders, poets and minstrels. Tales of her loveliness and charm bedazzled strangers from far-flung lands and since then the fishing village has been called Karachi.

Alexander the Great was believed to have set sail from here on his way back to Syria. It replaced Banbhore as a port and, though small, was a thriving harbour where pilgrims embarked on their voyages to Mecca.

Ten years before the Great Mutiny took place in India the British first showed their interest in Sind, and when General Dyer advocated its conquest, Lord Napier sent the *Wellesley* to Karachi. On the approach of the ship the Talpur rulers ordered cannons on the fortress of Manora Island to fire welcome salvoes. Whether it was intentionally misinterpreted or not, the friendly salvoes from the cannons brought about the capture of the town without bloodshed on 17 February 1843.

Richard Burton, later to become famous for his explorations of the Nile and for his literary achievements, shifted the capital of Sind from Hyderabad to Karachi. Construction works took on a hectic pace. Streets were laid and paved, highways and railways constructed, port facilities improved, and a number of buildings, of varying architectural designs, including Gothic, Victorian and contemporary, were built. Among them are Frere Hall, the Chief Courts, the Municipal Corporation Building, Cotton Exchange, the President's House, the Assembly Chambers, Port Trust Building, the Mereweather Tower, St Andrew's Church and St Patrick's Cathedral.

From then on Karachi overshadowed Hyderabad as the commercial, educational and administrative centre of Sind. It expanded into a great sprawling, bustling metropolis, and since Partition, when its population was 400,000, the population has rocketed to around five million, many of them refugees.

For the first decade after independence in 1947 Karachi was the capital of Pakistan until the new city of Islamabad was ready for use in 1965. A dry, hot and dusty city, squeezed between the desert and the Arabian Sea, Karachi has little of obvious interest to the tourist, but it is still more than simply an arrival point and travel crossroads.

Information

There are Tourist Information Centres at Karachi International Airport (tel 4 9241); *Hotel InterContinental* (tel 51 6397) in the city; and at *Hotel Metropole* on Club Rd (tel 51 0234).

The Immigration and Central Police Station of Sind, the GPO, the Telephone and Telegraph Office, and American Express are all on Chundigarh Rd which used to be known as McLeod Rd.

The best time to visit Karachi is from September until April. May and June are the hottest months of the year.

For information on fishing or hunting check with the Tourist Information Centre on Club Rd.

Consulates

India – India House 3 Fatimah Rd (tel 51 4310)
Sri Lanka – 44E Razi Rd, Block No 6, PECHS

Iran – 81 Shahrah-e-Iran, Clifton Beach (tel 53 0596)
USA – 8 Abdullah Haroon Rd (tel 51 5081)

The City

Karachi's overall features are a composite of the Talpurian, the British and the modern elements, quite different from its contemporary sister-cities in India and the Punjab as it does not have the ubiquitous Moghul features. Over the years it has acquired the usual trappings of a modern metropolis: towering hotels, banks, travel agencies, airline offices, tourist shops, cinemas, shopping centres, double-lane boulevards and an international airport. With their quaint architecture and sedate atmosphere, the buildings of the British era – contrasted against the bold, new concrete-and-glass structures – are distinctive and well preserved. Along with the Talpurian bazaars they lend the city an historical air.

Tomb of Quaid-i-Azam

The most important city monument is the mausoleum of Quaid-i-Azam, Mohammad Ali Jinnah, the founder of Pakistan, who died in 1948. Its architecture combines both the traditional and modern Islamic designs. It's about 31 metres high and is topped with a simple marble dome. It has a blue glazed ceiling, the tiles for which were donated by Japan. The glass and gold chandelier came from China and a silver handrail from Iran. It is situated just north-east of Bohri Bazaar at the end of Jinnah Rd.

National Museum

In the centre of Burns Garden it is open daily, except Friday, from 10 am to 4 pm. Exhibits include relics excavated from the 5000-year-old city of Moenjodaro, Hindu sculptures and Buddhist artefacts from Taxila and Swat, and of the Moghul period.

Art Galleries

There are numerous art galleries here including:

Art Council of Pakistan Gallery (tel 51 5108)

Faysee Rahman Art Gallery, Denso Hall, MA Jinnah Rd

Indus Gallery, 11-B/6, PECHS (tel 43 3229)

Pakistan Institute of Art & Designs, 61-N, Block 6, PECHS

Midway House Art Gallery (tel 48 1571)

Rehman Gallery, 12 Banglore Town, Main Drigh Rd (tel 41 4073)

Atelier BM, 194-A, Sindhi Muslim Society (tel 43 3867)

Pakistan-American Cultural Centre, 11 Fatimah Jinnah Rd (tel 51 3836).

Mosques & Other Buildings

Karachi is one of the largest Islamic cities and has a number of mosques. The **Defence Society Mosque**, named after the suburb, is the best known and probably the most visited. The large **Memon Mosque**, near Jodia Bazaar, is more traditionally mosque-like than the modern, low-slung Defence Society Mosque. **Frere Hall** in the peaceful Bagh-i-Jinnah gardens is imposingly Victorian.

Bazaars

Saddar is the city centre where the **Empress Market** is. It's a conglomeration of bazaars, modern shopping centres and tourist shops selling everything from carpets and leather bags to snake-skin purses and fur coats. In every direction the footpaths are crowded with stalls selling fruit drinks, newspapers, second-hand clothing, fancy jewellery, spicy cakes and miscellaneous articles from combs and mirrors to scissors and ear-cleaners. There are eating places – local, western and Chinese – and hotels of every category here. The top-notch places are clustered around Club Rd where you will find the tourist office. Along MA Jinnah and Garden Rds are cinemas featuring Pakistan, Indian and western films. This is just one block north of Empress Market, which is dominated by a British clock tower where buses and minibuses pick up passengers for Lee Market, the airport, and Hyderabad.

Westward towards **Lee Market** you pass barbers working on the pavements, while to the south-west, towards Shah-i-Iraq where the Excise & Tax Office and passport office are found, are the letter-writers. They tap away on their typewriters under makeshift lean-tos on the footpath.

McLeod Rd, now Chundigarh Rd, is an avenue with modern shops where the GPO, the City Railway Station, and the banks, including American Express, are located. From here turn north-west into **Boulton Market** where the money-changers

Statuette of the Mohenjo-daro priest.

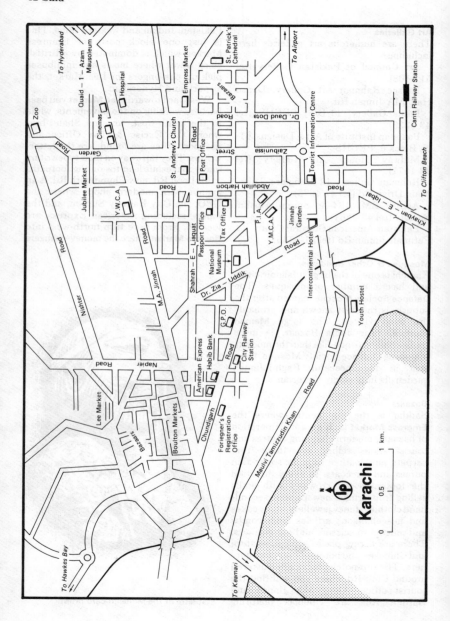

Karachi

To Hyderabad
To Airport
Cantt Railway Station
To Clifton Beach
Quaid - 1 - Azam Mausoleum
St Patrick's Cathedral
Hospital
Empress Market
Zoo
Cinemas
Bazaars
St Andrew's Church
Dr Daud Dota Road
Garden Road
Zaibunnissa Street
Post Office
Tourist Information Centre
Jubilee Market
Y.W.C.A.
Abdullah Harbon Road
Shahrah - E - Liaquat
Tax Office
P.I.A.
Jinnah Garden
Nishter Road
Passport Office
Y.M.C.A.
Road
M.A. Jinnah Road
National Museum
Dr. Zia Uddik
Intercontinental Hotel
To Iqbal
Khayaban - E - Iqbal
G.P.O.
Road
City Railway Station
Youth Hostel
Lee Market
Napier Road
American Express
Habib Bank
Chundigarh
Boulton Markets
Bazaars
Foriegner's Registration Office
Maulvi Tamizzudin Khan Road
To Hawkes Bay
To Keamari

N

0   0.5   1 km.

used to operate, then head past **Mereweather Tower** where there are some fairly decent restaurants on the right, and you finally arrive at Lee Market.

En route you pass a series of Talpurian-looking bazaars with no pedestrian pavements. They have expanded into the British area which has a more exotic atmosphere now. The bazaars are a maze of narrow lanes, and where they've spread into the British area the paved streets are crowded with stalls and tarpaulin lean-tos selling potatoes, grains, salt and sugar, textiles, second-hand clothes, hardware, porcelain, metal pots and copperware.

Outside the bazaars the streets are congested with stalls made of bits of wood, boards, tin and canvas. They sell *pan* and cigarettes or fruit drinks made from lemons, oranges, mangoes, pomegranate or sugar cane. The area is far more crowded and bustling than Saddar. The Lee Market section of Napier Rd used to be a redlight district, well known for cheap hotels and also exotic food.

Streets

Karachi has well-paved streets, broad and well-lit avenues, even two-lane boulevards where trafic is frenetic from dawn to dusk, and bedlam at rush hours. Only late in the evening does the pace slacken. There is a motely coleection of plain- painted public government buses mixed with ornately and colourfully painted private buses; white and yellow minibuses and black and yellow taxis, lavishly decorated auto-rickshaws and garishly painted lorries and cargo trucks. The ingenious auto-rickshaws sputter, skitter and trundle their three-wheeled way in and out of a maze of buses and trucks, camel wagons and donkey carts, even carts drawn by people. Karachi donkey carts all have number plates announcing which Karachi donkey cart they are. On Wednesday afternoons the donkey cart drivers hold impromptu races along Mauripur Rd, west of the city towards Hawkes Bay.

In the swirl of traffic camels plod along pulling overloaded wagons, but managing to maintain their measured gait with head high above the congestion of more lowly vehicles. It all seems chaotic but traffic flows quite smoothly except for occasional mishaps when an overloaded donkey cart or horse cart suddenly tilts back leaving the unfortunate animal dangling in the air. Apart from Saddar there do not appear to be bus stations anywhere in Karachi, people simply clamber on board while buses are still moving. Buses are always impossibly crowded, but always seem to have room for one more passenger.

Beaches

With its coastal location, Karachi has some superb beaches. There is good swimming allyear except in the June-August monsoon season when the currents can be tricky and jellyfish abound. To prevent offending the Moslem sense of decorum and avoid hassles into the bargain, bikinis should be worn only on private, hotel-controlled beaches.

Clifton Beach is as much amusement park as beach – and an excellent place for children. It has a fair ground and an amusement park with merry-go-rounds, ferris wheels, flying saucers, lindy-loops, toy trains and self-drive cars for two and four. Another recent attraction is a dolphin pool. Towards Marine Drive camels and horses can be hired by the hour. There are teashops and foodstalls dotted along the shore, which serve fried fish. There are also kiosks where you can buy soft drinks, stalls for *pan* and cigarettes, and tourists shops. Close by is the **Pidgeon Temple** where there is a fresh water spring and aquarium at the Moslem shrine. As it is an amusement park it is crowded all week. Take Bus 20 from Shahrah-i-Iraq Rd.

Manora Island is another beach resort with a lighthouse that appears not to be in use any more. It is 15 minutes by minibus to Keamari, the Karachi port, where you can get a boat to the island. At Keamari

you can also hire outrigger sailing boats –
bunder boats – complete with crew for
Rs25 per hour. A popular activity is to hire
a boat for five or six hours at Rs100 per
head. You can take the boats around the
harbour, go scuba diving, dive for lobsters
or fish. Boat trips can stretch deep into the
night, particularly in autumn when turtles
lay their eggs on the beaches, or you
decide to pig out on seafood: crabs, fish,
lobsters and shark.

Sandspit, Hawkes Bay & Paradise Point
are connected beaches, merging into one
long beach. There are saddled camels and
horses for hire, teashops, soft-drink stalls,
and even huts you can rent by the day. But
note that the currents become really
treacherous here during the monsoon
season so take care at that time.

Sandspit is almost nondescript, but the
scenery improves at Hawkes Bay, and is
really beautiful at Paradise Point. From
here the beach arches around to Hawkes
Bay and Paradise Point and is lined with
weather-beaten huts. The land rises from
the shore to semi-arable wasteland that is
patched with green and spreads back to
mountains topped with shrines. These
beaches fill up on Thursdays and Fridays.
Bikinis are really verboten then. The local
females go into the water completely
dressed! The rest of the week it is usually
deserted and it's possible to wear bikinis
then.

Five years ago Hawkes Bay was
becoming a junkies' and freaks' haunt,
and was apparently also a smuggling area
patrolled by police and coast guards to the
wee hours of the morning. Avoid going to
Paradise Point and beyond either on a
dark or moonlit night, particularly if you
are a woman or with a woman.

The beaches are 40 km from Karachi,
2½ hours by bus from Lee Market. Buses
depart Karachi at 6 am, 2 and 5 pm.
Returning buses leave at 9 am, 4 and 6
pm.

Gadani Beach is a developing resort
about 50 km from Karachi. Take a look at
the shipwrecking yard and workers'
shanties while you're here. The hulking
remains of once great ships are beached
and gradually cut into scrap iron piled
high in rusting heaps on the beach. Each
house in the fishing village has a camel
tied up outside and smuggling is said to
supplement the income from fishing. It's a
three-hour bus trip from Lee Market – an
early bus leaves at 8 am and another at 1
pm. Even on the early bus you only get a
few hours at Gadani if you're day-
tripping.

Pharsee Tower of Death
Traditionally, only Pharsees were allowed
here, but others can now visit this rather
macabre place, provided they are accompanied by a Pharsee. On Mehmudabad
Rd, near Corporation and Pharsee Gates
in the Korangi area, it consists of two
rather squat towers set in a large
compound. You can't miss it, the vultures
and buzzards circulating overhead are a
dead give-away. Hmmm!

Other
A great way to spend a few hours is
Wandering around the fish harbour on the
West Wharf is a great way to spend a few
hours. Hundreds of ornately-painted and
decorated boats, and all kinds of other
water craft, docks there daily, buying and
selling fresh vegetables and fish.
at is the colourful **dhobi ghat** where
laundry is done en masse. If you like zoos,
the Karachi **zoo** is worth going to, if only to
see an elephant collecting rupees. It's a
favourite trick of one of the elephants
here.

Once the monsoon is over crabbing,
diving for lobsters, fishing, scuba diving,
or simply boating at night, are all great
fun.

The Karachi Cultural Club puts on
programmes regularly, except during
religious festival when they are usually
postponed. There are several venues
including Adamjee Hall (tel 7 0135); Fleet
Club at the Star Hotel and Moti Mahal
Auditorium at the Taj Mahal Hotel.

Places to Stay – Bottom End

Very cheap and centrally located in the Saddar area is the *State Hotel* on the corner of Rajagazanfar Ali Rd, south of Empress Market. It's reasonably clean and popular with travellers. Singles and doubles cost Rs15 and Rs25 with fans and common toilets and showers. Another cheapie is the *Asia Hotel*, also in the Saddar area on Zaibunnisa St. It's fairly clean, just south of Empress Market, and a good place to meet travellers. There are only double rooms, fan-cooled with common showers and toilets at Rs24. The *Khyber Hotel* on MA Jinnah Rd near St Andrew's Church is reasonably clean, has attached bathrooms and costs Rs 30 and Rs50 for singles and doubles. The *United Hotel*, Dr Daud Pota Rd, Saddar, is similar and costs Rs40 and Rs70. On the same side of the street the *Salatin Hotel* is similar in standard and price. Across the street the *International Hotel* is cheaper at Rs25 to Rs40.

Hostels *Amin House* on Maulvi Tamizuddin Rd is a Youth Hostel, which accepts foreigners whether they are members or not. A dorm costs Rs15, a single with attached shower and toilet is Rs20. Recently renovated it is not too far from the Cantonment Railway Station. It is Rs3 to Rs5 by auto-rickshaw.

YMCA Hostel, on Stratchen Rd, (tel 51 6927) is opposite the PIA office. It's a modern building with *en suite* bathrooms in the majority of rooms. Non-members can use the facilities for a temporary membership fee of Rs20. There's also a Rs200 deposit, returnable on departure; singles cost Rs50 and doubles are Rs60 without attached bath, Rs80 with one. It also has family rooms, but only married couples are accepted. The YMCA is clean and comfortable and the canteen's cheap, though opening hours are unpredictable. The *YWCA* is on MA Jinnah Rd (tel 7 1662), a block from Abdullah Haroon Rd to the left heading north.

If you're just passing through Karachi try the *railway retiring rooms*. At the Karachi City Station a single costs Rs20; at the Cantonment Railway Station a double cost Rs24.

Middle

A number of hotels span the top end to bottom end gap. The *North-Western Hotel* at 26 Beaumont Rd (tel 51 0843) is better than its Rs70 to Rs115 prices for singles and doubles would indicate. Situated in a pleasant old building it has 23 rooms and the tariff includes breakfast. The *Al-Farooq* off Zaibunnisa St (tel 2 2811-2) has 35 rooms, with singles and doubles at Rs60 and Rs100. It also has an excellent restaurant. *The Palace* also on Dr Ziauddin Ahmad Rd (tel 51 1011-9) has 24 rooms at Rs133 and 188 for singles and doubles. In Saddar the *Gulf Hotel* (tel 51 5834-6-9) has singles and doubles at Rs109 and Rs172. Going down a price notch the *National City Hotel* and the *Royal City Hotel*, both near the Orient Cinema, have singles and doubles at Rs 100 to Rs 180.

Top End

There's the *Karachi Holiday Inn* (tel 52 0111, 52 2011), 9 Abdullah Haroon Rd, with singles/doubles for Rs750/870, plus additional 15% tax and Rs30 surtax per person. These taxes apply to all hotels of international standard in Karachi. The *InterContinental Hotel* (tel 51 5021) on Club Rd has 306 rooms, restaurants, shops and a swimming pool. Charges are US$60 to 80 for singles and US$70 to 90 for doubles. Opposite the InterContinental is the new *Sheraton Hotel*, then there's the *Hilton Hotel* directly across from the *Mehran Hotel*, and the *Taj Mahal Hotel* on Drigh Rd towards the airport all in the same price range as the above: the Mehran (tel 51 4739) being lightly cheaper with singles and doubles for Rs423 and Rs560. The older *Metropole Hotel* (tel 51 2051-20) on Club Rd has 134 rooms, and is now used mainly for offices which include the tourist office. Singles cost between Rs300 to 400 and doubles are between Rs350 and 450. The 3-star *Beach Luxury Hotel* on Maulvi Tamizuddin Rd (tel 55 1031) is west of the town centre and within the sight of the harbour. Built in the mid-40s it's in a state of genteel shabbiness. Nevertheless it has a pool and a pleasant outdoor garden restaurant. The 150-room hotel costs from Rs100 to 450 for singles and from Rs 350 to 550 for doubles.

Other hotels in the Rs200 and above bracket include: *Midway House*, Stargate Rd, Karachi Airport (tel 48 0371), which has 175 rooms, with singles for Rs320 to 566 and doubles from Rs645; *Hostellerie de France*, Main Drigh Rd (tel 4 9501) with 80 rooms has singles and doubles for Rs275 and Rs488; *Imperial Hotel*, Maulvi Tamizuddin Rd (tel 55 1051-55) has 56 rooms with singles and doubles for Rs332 and Rs422; *Columbus Hotel*, Clifton Rd (tel 51 1311-4), 42 rooms, singles and doubles Rs235 and Rs305; *The Inn*, Karachi Airport (tel 41 2011), 101 rooms, with singles for Rs190 to 250 and doubles for Rs310; *Palace Hotel*, Dr Ziauddin Ahmad Rd (tel 51 1010-19), 40 rooms with singles and doubles for Rs132 and Rs165 or Rs192 to Rs231 with air-con; *Jabees*, Abdullah Haroon Rd (tel 51 2011-5), singles and doubles Rs169 to Rs317.

Places to Eat

The cheaper eating places are in Lee Market, near the bus station. They have Pakistani food only and most charge Rs5 to Rs6 a meal. The best cheapie in town is close to the Mereweather Tower. It's on the right on the way to Lee Market, in a long narrow dining hall, in front of which they serve all kinds of seasonal fruit drinks at Rs3.50 a glass. Here you can get Chinese chicken sweetcorn soup for Rs3.50, egg or chicken or vegetable fried rice for Rs3.50 a bowl and have a satisfactory meal for only Rs10.

Most of the medium-class restaurants in town are run by Pharsees. You can get western-style breakfast and meals at most

of them, but the best food is Pakistani such as chicken tikka for Rs12 or kebabs at Rs4 a stick. There is a reasonable eating place in front of the Empress Market where you can eat for Rs10. You'll also find a number of Chinese restaurants here, including one on Abdullah Haroon Rd. The *South China Restaurant* on Shahrah-i-Iraq Rd is often open only in the evening. On Tariq Rd there is another, more expensive, Chinese restaurant which costs from Rs30.

Just before the Cantonment Railway Station, to the right, is a nondescript local restaurant which has good food in the Rs10 to Rs12 bracket. Clifton Beach has a number of stalls serving fried fish for Rs5. For interesting local specialties and delicacies try *Hill Park* on PECHS – difficult to get there without your own transport – it's on Bond and Frere Rds near Jubilee Cinema. Slightly more expensive is *Farooq's Restaurant* in the Al-Farooq Hotel, which is noted for its barbecued leg of lamb, a spicy peppery treat. Another good restaurant is *The Horseshoe* on Airport Rd. It has local and European dishes which cost between Rs50 and Rs70. Live music is a feature here. The *Kehkashan* (Galaxy), at Terminal No 1, International Airport, offers international cuisine for Rs50 and Rs55. It also has live music. Then there's the *Kehkashan 11* in the departure lounge, which is good for snacks and quick meals. On University Rd, Gulshan-e-Iqbal, the *Kee Chain* is excellent for all sorts of barbecues. Everything about the *Omar Khayam*, near the Sheraton and Inter-Continental is relaxing, except for its prices. But if you want to treat yourself to air-con luxury and superb seafood, give it a try. Opposite the Sheraton, *Le Cafe* has tasty snacks, burgers etc, and good music. The *Samarquand* at the West Wharf is another great place for seafood and it's cheap – only Rs10 a meal. In the Beach Luxury Hotel, *The Casbah* also has good seafood, tikkas, shasliks and Lebanese dishes.

On the ground floor of the Sheraton is *Al Bustan*, which has delicious seafood; or there's *Fanoos Lounge* for European snacks, ice-cream and fruit juices. The latter also has music. *Le Marquis*, on the mezzanine, has superb French food, and on the same floor is the *Maskada Lounge*, which specialises in pastries, capuccinos, and espresso and Turkish coffees. The main *Sheraton Restaurant* offers what it calls a 'European Express', which consists of a variety of dishes from Brussels, Paris, Prague, Berlin, Bucharest, Athens and Istanbul.

In the *Northwestern Hotel*, only about 200 metres from the InterContinental, there's *Agha's Tavern* which has good Pakistani food and some western dishes. Behind the Metropole *The Village* has cheap kebabs or you can get snacks at the nearby *Cafe Grand* and *Ampi's*. *Alfa* on Innervarity Rd has South Indian vegetarian food. Or there's *Maxim's* or the *Golden Horseshoe* at Sherheed-i-Millat and Main, Drigh. Try also *Fish Harbour* for superb seafood of all kinds. If you're into American food and music, go to *Nadia's Coffee shop* in the Holiday Inn. It's got a very pleasant atmosphere.

Liquor Getting a drink in fundamentalist Pakistan can be a difficult proposition. Generally foreigners are allowed to drink, but only in their hotel room. Most of the bars in the more expensive hotels are now closed. To get a drink apply for a Tourist Certificate at the tourist office on Club Rd. The staff here may pass you on to the Excise & Tax Office on Shahrah-i-Iraq Rd in the government complex compound, and they will direct you to where you can buy alcohol.

Getting There
Getting Around
Local

From the international airport into the city centre it costs Rs2.25 by minibus, Rs1.75 by bus, Rs20 by auto-rickshaw and Rs30 by taxi. From the Cantonment Railway Station to the city centre it's Rs0.75 by bus, Rs1.50 by minibus, Rs3 to Rs5 by auto-rickshaw and Rs10 by taxi. Around the city taxis cost Rs5 and auto-rickshaws Rs2 to Rs3. Both taxi and auto-rickshaw meters are notoriously unreliable so always agree on the fare before starting out. Cars with drivers can be hired from around US$30 a day including fuel for 100 km. City tours can be booked through the tourist office or private tour operators and start from around Rs50.

Air

A 20%-concession is available from the *PLA* office opposite the YMCA hostel on Stratchen Rd, but you must see the manager before applying. Bring the necessary documents with you. There are two flights weekly to Bombay and to Delhi in India.

Domestic flight schedules and costs are listed below:

	Flights	Rs
Karachi-Quetta	three weekly	535
Karachi-Lahore	four daily	855
Karachi-Rawalpindi	four daily	1045
Karachi-Peshawar	one daily	1160

There is an airport tax of Rs5.

Warning The international airports in Karachi and Lahore now have trained German Shepherd dogs to sniff out nefarious drug smuggling.

Trains

For concessions apply for a Tourist Certificate at the Metropole Hotel on Club Rd. Address it to the Superintendent of Railways whose office is at the City Railway Station, Commercial Department, Chundigarh Rd.

On the Karachi-Lahore-Rawalpindi-Peshawar route there are five, sometimes six trains daily. The trip takes 19 to 21 hours to Lahore; 28 hours to Rawalpindi and 32 hours to Peshawar. There is also a 16-hour service to Lahore at 6 am on the

Shalimar Express and *Super-Express* costing Rs264.

The British Indian Navigation Company and McKenzie Co are both on Chundigarh Rd. They have boats going to Bombay twice a week and once weekly to the Gulf states. The fare from Karachi to Bombay by boat costs Rs475 deck class, more for berths or cabin class.

Buses

Buses for Thatta and Hyderabad depart at half-hour intervals from 6 am to 6 pm. The Thatta service leaves from Lee Market and the trip takes two hours, while for the three-hour journey to Hyderabad the buses depart from Boulton Market.

Blue Lines has an office at the Palace Hotel Annexe opposite the Sheraton. This company has luxury air-con coaches that make regular trips to Hyderabad which take three hours and cost Rs34; to Larkana a seven-hour trip costing Rs98; and to Sukkur. The latter is a 7½-hour journey that is Rs98. The bus company, *Mirpurkhas* (tel 51 1011/51 1019) may also have regular services to Pakistani towns before long.

Note that overland routes to the Makran coastal area remain closed to foreigners, but the Karachi-Khuzdar road via Bela in Baluchistan is now paved and open. It's still apparently unsafe and, for security, tourists with their own transport are advised to travel in convoy. If you are on your own, it would be better to take another route. See section on Baluchistan.

To India Land routes to India through Sind remain closed although there is a plan to open the railway line between Bramer in Rajasthan and Hyderabad in Sind. At the moment the only routes are via Lahore and from Karachi by air and sea.

Things to Buy

Across from the Hotel InterContinental the government-run Sind Handicraft Centre has fixed prices for locally produced items ranging from embroidery work, appliqued quilts and covers to leather goods, brassware, beadwork, folk jewellery and carved wooden chests. In Saddar the shops sell embroidered Kashmiri shawls, carved onyx pieces and other Pakistani crafts. You will find most of the carpet shops along Zaibunnisa St near Bohri Bazaar. You can see carpets woven in the villages being trimmed and finished in Karachi. Visits can also be arranged to a small silk weaving factory and to a brasswork shop. The main bazaars are the balconied shops of **Jodia Bazaar** behind Boulton Market, where the atmosphere is traditional, the new **Liaquat Market** to the north, and the central **Bohri Bazaar** in Saddar.

Around Karachi

There are a number of interesting places to visit out of Karachi, accessible either by public bus service or through day tours; the latter usually organised by the PTDC. North of Karachi the land becomes dry and barren, and then gradually gets greener and more arable beyond Keenjhar Lake and Kotri Junction.

Chaukundi

The tombs at Chaukundi are archaeologically interesting, although it is not clear exactly how old the graves are. They are believed to date from the 13th to the 16th century. They are constructed out of slabs of rocks, stacked into elongated pyramids of cubical stone (chaukundi means cubical) and carved with exquisite designs, but the origins of the designs and the purpose of the eerily quiet tombs is a continuing mystery. Chaukundi is 27 km from Karachi. Buses depart regularly from Lee Market.

Manghopir

There is a sulphur thermal spring here which is apparently good for skin diseases, rheumatism, frigidity! and other afflictions. Manghopir has a shrine to the Moslem Saint Mangho, which, according to local legend, is guarded by crocodiles. It is about 40 km from Karachi and buses depart from Lee Market. There are no hotels here, only sheds for local travellers and pilgrims.

Banbhore

This ancient sea port is believed to have been the landing site of the Moslem conqueror, Mohammed Bin Qasim, in the early 8th century. It is interesting for the ruins of three different historical periods which have been uncovered here: Scythian -Parthian; Hindu-Buddhist and Islamic. Banbhore is about 64 km from Karachi and five km off the National Highway to Thatta. Buses go from Lee Market.

Haleji Lake

Situated 85 km from Karachi, 15 km before Thatta, Haleji Lake is considered to be the largest waterfowl sanctuary in Asia, and is the main reservoir for Karachi. It's 1½ km off the Thatta road from the village of Gujjo. Thousands of birds of over 70 species migrate here in winter from Siberia and stay through January and February. The birds include flamingoes, pelicans, pheasant-tailed jacanas, herons, ducks, partridges, and egrets among others. Fishing or duck shooting, which is permitted in winter, require permits obtained through the PTDC. There is a *rest house* here where you can stay for Rs30 a day. The PTDC has huts from Rs75 to Rs200 plus 15% surtax.

THATTA

At one time Thatta was important as Sind's capital city and as a centre for Islamic arts. From the 14th century four Moslem dynasties ruled Sind from Thatta, but in 1739 the capital was moved elsewhere and Thatta declined.

It was believed that this was the place where Alexander the Great rested his legions after their long march; his admiral of the fleet, Nearchus, sailed from here back to the Persian Gulf. Today most of the remaining monuments only date back to the 16th and 17th centuries.

Makli Hill – City of Mausoleums

A couple of km before Thatta is this vast necropolis which covers 15 square km and is said to contain over one million graves.

They are mainly made of sandstone, exquisitely carved with geometric and floral designs. Most of them date back to the Summas, the dynasty which ruled the Sind from the mid-14th to the early 16th centuries. Others are from the Moghul period. The carvings are so regular they seem to have to been stamped into the stones. Some of the mausoleums are being restored. Recent tombs from the Arghun and Moghul periods have beautifully glazed or enamelled tiles and bricks, which they still continue to manufacture, particularly the Thatta blue tile.

Amongst the more important tombs is that of Mirza Jani Beg. Built in 1599 for the last of the Turkhan rulers, it is made of glazed bricks. North of this is the imposing mausoleum of Nawab Isa Khan, the Moghul governor of Sind. Its design is similar to those found in Fatehpur Sikri in India. A low building similarly designed, a little to the east, houses the tombs of the women of his zenana: the part of a house where high caste Moslem women were cloistered. There is a fine view from here across the lake of the town of Thatta. The mausoleum of Diwan Shurfa Khan built in 1638 is slightly to the north-west, and is a square solid structure with squat round towers at each corner. A couple of km north the tomb of Nizam-ud-din is a square stone building constructed out of the materials of a Hindu temple.

The Town

The town is dominated by the great mosque built by the Moghul Emperor Shah Jahan. The 33 arched domes give it superb acoustics and the tilework, a whole range of shades of blue, is equally fine. This mosque has been carefully restored to its original condition. Situated on the outskirts of the new town, it is surrounded by narrow lanes and multi-storey houses made of plaster and wood which are topped by *badgirs*, the windcatcher designed to funnel cool breezes down into the interiors of buildings. They are also quite common in Hyderabad. The bazaars of Thatta are known for hand-printed fabrics, glass bangles, and the Sindhi embroidery work inlaid with tiny mirrors, one of the better known handicrafts of Pakistan.

Getting There

Thatta is 100 km from Karachi, about half-way to Hyderabad. The nearest railway station is at Jungshasi, about 21 km away. The PTDC arranges tours to Chaukundi-Banbhore-Makli Hill-Thatta but a minimum of four or five tourists are required. Public transport can be a little difficult particularly fro Banbhore. Please note that in summer it can get very hot with temperatures rarely dropping below 40°C.

Places to Stay

There are a few local hotels which take tourists, but generally the place to stay is down at Makli Hill. The PTDC has tents for hire there, and apart from this *Dak Bungalow* has accommodation for Rs30 a single and Rs50 a double.

Keenjhar Lake

Keenjhar lake is a beautiful resort surrounded by woods, and less than two hours from Thatta by bus, which goes all the way to Hyderabad. This is a good place to spend time boating and fishing and picnicking, a place to rest up before moving north to Hyderabad and Moenjodaro. In a wooded area there are *huts, motels* and *cabins* operated by the PTDC (tel 341) with rates from Rs75 to Rs 500 per day plus 15% surtax.

Jherruk

On the banks of the Indus River, 56 km from Thatta, this is another lake. Near the Jhimpir Railway Station the shrine of **Amirpir** is worth a side trip.

Getting Away

There are bitumenised roads all the way to Hyderabad in the north and Tharparkar Desert in the east. From the desert you can make a loop up to Mirpur Khas and then back to Hyderabad.

HYDERABAD

Hyderabad, 180 km north of Karachi, is the second largest city in Sind and one of the largest in Pakistan. Its population is about 700,000. Hyderabad is five km from the eastern bank of the Indus and is connected with Karachi by rail and a super-highway which goes over the Kotri Barrage.

It is one of the oldest cities on the subcontinent, dating back to the time of the Hindu ruler, Nerron. When the Indus changed its course away from Khudabad, at that time the capital of the region, Hyderabad, became the new capital. In 1768 the Kalhora ruler constructed a fort half a square km in area which still stands today. In 1843 the British arrived and defeated the Talpurs, completing their conquest of Sind.

Under the British a new section, containing their government administrative offices, was added to the old city. It was centred around the old fort and Shahi Bazaar, one of the longest in the city at 2½ km. The bazaar is a labyrinth of narrow alleys where they produce Sindhi embroidery, block prints, gold and silver jewellery. You can also buy pointy-toed shoes, perfumes and most important, the glass bangles, for which this bazaar is famous.

In the old city, buildings are topped by *badgirs* that look like chimneys on roof tops. They catch the cool breezes which blow steadily in a south-west direction for 40 days from late April each year. Hyderabad is hot for most of the year, although in autumn and winter the temperature dips down to around 24°C. In the old sections of the town cows still roam the streets giving it a distinctly mediaeval atmosphere.

On the northern side of the hill on which

Hyderabad is sited there are **tombs** from the Talpur and Kalhora periods. The tomb of **Ghulam Shah Kalhora** is one of the finest, although its dome collapsed and has now been replaced by a flat roof. The railway line used to run east from Hyderabad into Rajasthan in India but the line has been closed since Partition. At **Mirpur Khas**, 65 km east of the city, there is a 15-metre high Buddhist stupa with terracotta Buddha figures.

Places to Stay

There are cheap and medium-priced hotels around Shahi Bazaar but they don't accept foreigners. However, hotels in the Ghari Khatta area, near the railway station, take travellers. Try the *Yasrab* or the *Firdaus Hotel*. There are a number of more expensive hotels around the city. In Ghari Khatta the *Spinzer* (tel 2 3537) has singles and doubles at Rs100 and Rs170. Rooms are the same price at the *New Indus Hotel* (tel 2 5276) at Thandi Sarak, and the *Faran* (tel 2 3993) in the Saddar area. In Thandi Sarak the more expensive *Sainjees* (tel 2 7275-9) has singles and doubles for Rs140 and Rs200. Middle level hotels around Ghari Khatta, like the *United Hotel* and the *Palace Hotel* have rates for singles and doubles ranging from Rs30 and Rs50 to Rs40 and Rs75 respectively.

THARPARKAR DESERT

East of the Indus in Sind is another distinctly fascinating and extremely interesting facet of Pakistan. The Tharparkar Desert, which is over 28,100 square km in area, has an entirely different configuration altogether; its own culture, folklore, unique landscape and fauna and flora.

It is a curious combination of the ancient and modern, largely because it is a strategic defence region on the Indian border.

Major towns here are **Umarkot** in the north-west, **Naukot** to the west and **Diplo** to the south-west. There are numerous villages called *goths*, which still retain their feudal, socio-economic structure. The general atmosphere is mediaeval, but it has the modern trappings of trucks, jeeps, generators and electricity. The faithful, but often complaining, camel is still widely used, but trucks carry most of the cargo and mass transport. They ply between Naukot, Mithi and Islamkot regularly, and once a month they travel towards Sandhuri, north to the Rangers' border post, to fetch supplies.

Beyond Mirpur Khas or Thatta traffic generally peters out as you progress deeper into the desert region. At **Naukot** the 586-km metalled road from Hyderabad tapers off. About three km from the outskirts of the town are the ruins of a **fort**, now inhabited by owls, pigeons, rats and other desert animals. The **shrine** of Pir Razi Shah Likyari, though venerated by both Hindus and Moslems, is in ruins.

From here the desert spreads out endlessly in all directions. **Mithi**, 67 km from Naukot, is a prosperous place linked to the outside world by telephone. What's more, many local people own transistors. There are a number of hotels with beds from Rs3 a night here. And if you're interested in craft this is where *rillis*, colourful patchwork bedspreads, are made.

In this part of the world Hindus and Moslems live in harmony, though they retain their respective rituals and customs. The Hindus predominate with 56% of the population, while Moslems make up 44%. It is typical of the subcontinent, a kind of mini-India compromising Hindus, Moslems, Rajputs and Harijans.

Islamkot, 40 km away, has well-laid out roads lined with trees, seven restaurants, but, strangely enough, not a single hotel. The Rajputs, who were originally driven out by the Moghuls, settled here and consequently there is a strong similarity to Rajasthan. It is prosperous and clean and retains its traditional songs, dances and festivals.

Though **Khario Ghulam Shah** is a very

barren region, the tribes make do with what they've got and manage to enjoy life through dance and music. The **Kasbo** village, deep in the desert, is a fertile oasis, inhabited by pastoral tribes, the Rabaris, who are snake worshippers. In this goth there are three **Hindu temples**, now in disrepair.

En route to **Virawah**, 68 km from Islamkot, are the **Abhe Ka Thar** goth of the Bheel tribe; **Lornian** of the Samma tribe; **Bhelwah** of the Moro tribe – this area is noted for succulent fruit; and **Dano Dandal**, another fertile spot where 400 families live. Then there's **Gori** goth, which has a thousand inhabitants, a primary school and an ancient Jain temple, known as **Gori Mandar**. The latter is in disrepair but is still intact and worth seeing with its domes, tiny rooms and stone carvings.

From Gori it is 23 km to **Virawah** which also has a Jain temple with stone carvings. No Jains live here now, but nearby **Pari Nagar** also has a Jain temple. This goth is believed to have been a port for the Rann of Kutch region centuries ago.

Nagar Parkar is 23 km south of Virawah – part rocky, part sandy, part green. One of the primary products here is castor oil. It's not far from the Karonjhar Hills at the foot of which are streams that are considered sacred by the Hindus. The huts in this goth are built of local stone. Three km further on is a lake called **Bodeshar Talab** which features Hindu temples – now largely in ruins – as well as a white marble mosque built in 1436. This stands in a graveyard and dominates the whole goth.

North-east of Virawah is **Sami Ji Veri**, another Rangers' border post. Cacti in this area grow to as high as two metres. From here it is only five km to Rann of Kutch where the surface of the land is crystalline white due to salinity. En route to Chachro is the peacock region. These birds are once sonumerous when revered by the Hindus, now endangered, most of them have been devoured by the Moslems.

Umarkot, 70 km to the north-west, in the direction of Mirpur Khas, is a largish town with an urban lifestyle. There used to be yogis or fakirs here like those in the hilly area of Rawal in the Punjab, but they have vanished. It is certainly the most touristed town in theTharparkar Desert, so comercial that even the snake-charmers have become materialistic. You really know you are in the modern urban world of the subcontinent when you see the beggars here.

Beyond Umarkot, to the north, the desert commences to expand endlessly again. There are isolated villages in this region, but they are not as fascinating or interesting as the goths in the south. At Khrokhropar, the border town, is the overland route to India. There is also a railway line which begins from Bramer and goes through Mirpur Khas into Hyderabad. Agreement between India and Pakistan regarding the opening of this route has apparently been reached, but it still remains to be seen when.

SEHWAN SHARIF

On the west bank of the Indus, Sehwan Sharif is 140 km north-west of Kotri. To get there from Hyderabad you must first take a minibus or miniwagon to Kotri Junction and then a train from there. The trip takes 2½ hours and the railway line passes through fairly arid, dusty and bleak countryside.

Sehwan Sharif is an oasis in this dry wasteland and is noted for the shrine of **Lal Qalandar Shah Baz** which was built in 1274. After wandering for decades, this Moslem saint from Mervant, decided to settle on a cave here. He claimed to be the last of the true Syed or direct descendants of Mohammed. He lived here for 40 years helping villagers in times of flood or famine. There are stories of him riding a lion, using a snake for a stick, and others of him flying like an eagle. Although his real name was Sheikh Usman Ali, he came to be known as Lal Qalandar Shah Baz which means 'Divine Spirit of the Eagle.'

The shrine is the main attraction of the town and pilgrims pour into it every day of the year but most particularly during *urs*, the anniversery of his death, when they turn up in their thousands. At this time you will see numerous fakirs and malangs spiritual mendicants-garbed in long flowing robes, almost rags, and adorned with steel bracelets and beads, dancing dervishes to the beating of drums. Eventually they work themselves up into a trancelike atate of total abandonment.

Things to See

North of Sehwan Sharif is Dadu, where the large red fort of **Ranikot** is located. It is reputed to be the largest of its kind in the world and has walls 24 km in circumference. It is about 90 km north-west of Hyderabad. Get to Sani, where there is a track heading west which goes for 21 km without any human settlements. The track is passable by jeep, but it takes nearly a whole day to get there. The fort was built in the 9th century AD, probably to guard the ancient Silk Trade Route north to Central Asia. Camping inside the fort is possible.

Another archaeological site is **Amri**, near Sani on the west bank of the Indus. It is neolithic (6000 to 3000 BC) and predates the Indus Valley Civilisation. It is believed that this civilisation had trade links with Persia and Central Asia before the Indus Valley Civilisation ever emerged.

Places to Stay

There is a *Dak Bungalow* in the old fort, a *Government Rest House*, the *Shrine's Guest House*, *muzzaffar khanas* and tents for the poor, for whom board and lodging is free.

MOENJODARO

Five thousand years ago, contemporaneously with the Mesopotamian civilisation on the banks of the Euphrates, Moenjodaro began to develop as one of the great cities of the Indus Valley Civilisation. The 'Mound of the Dead' as the name means, thrived from 3000 to 1700 BC then abruptly declined, due, according to historians, to a violent invasion by the Aryans in 1700 BC.

It was certainly a thriving civilisation of a high order. Long after its demise Buddhist monks – during the Kushan period – errected a stupa over 70 metres high. It's now in ruins but it still rises above the surrounding area.

Moenjodaro looms large and darkly strange from the road. There is a mystical air about it, set in semi-wasteland consisting of thick, fine dust which rises in clouds at the slightest stirring. The whole city is made of baked red bricks and the architecture is unusual and alien. It evokes a great past and exudes a feeling of history.

The City

The city was planned on modern urban lines in square or rectangular blocks, with avenues up to 10 metres wide – some paved – which crossed at right angles, while residential areas had narrower streets. The elaborately designed buildings indicate a remarkably advanced knowledge of urban planning, architecture, engineering and sanitation. There are public buildings with pillared halls, baths, a state granary, colleges for priests, palaces, houses and shops. The highly developed drainage system compares with that of the Minoans of Crete.

It is divided into two parts: a lower area to the west and an upper area, which was probably fortified, to the east. The excavated ruins cover about 100 hectares, but there are outer parts of the city still buried.

People

The people from Moenjodaro are believed to have originated in Central Asia. Evidence suggests that they were of adverage size and brown complexion, with long heads and faces and black hair. One of the busts found indicates that the men used razors. This particular Moenjodaron is depicted wearing fine muslin, which is embroidered with floral designs.

Women wore girdled skirts, beads, necklaces, gold bracelets or amulets, nose studs – still very common today in the subcontinent – anklets and earrings. They had a fan-shaped hair style and their children played with terracotta toys, such as carts and bullocks, which had sections that could be moved, like the head and tail. There is also evidence that the Moenjodarons played a game similar to chess and gambled with dice.

Economy

The economy of Moenjodaro was based on agriculture with the main crops being wheat, barley, sesum, field peas and cotton. Objects discovered include statues, toys, jewellery embellished with precious and semi-precious stones, seals made of a steatite material and games and scales, which suggest it was a society which had thriving and diverse industries and trade links with other cultures, not merely neighbouring cities but places like Mesopotamia, Persia, Central Asia, China, Tibet and Burma.

Culture

They had a very skilled and sophisticated art style, developing a technique of fine wheel-turned pottery known archaeologically as 'black and red ware', as well as standard weights and measures for business transactions and seals with animal figures and inscriptions etched on them. Their pictographic system of writing appears to have been based on astrological and zodiacal signs and the forms and shapes on fauna and flora.

They also created kitchen utensils which were predominantly made from bronze and copper, while others were wrought from silver and lead. Weapons such as swords, knives and daggers were of bronze and their arts included sculpture in terracotta, ceramics and bronzeware. The government was likely to have been both secular and religious, based on a theocracy headed by a king-priest not unlike the present king-god, Dalai Lama, of the Tibetans.

Buddhist Stupa

In the north-west of the city this stupa dates from the time of Vasudeva (182 to 230 AD), a Kushan emperor. It was in excavating this stupa in 1922 that British archaeologists stumbled upon the far older city beneath it. The stupa is on a high mound which was the fortress of the ancient city. It commands a panoramic view of the whole city.

Great Bath

West of the stupta the Great Bath was probably built for religious purposes Twelve metres long, two metres deep and seven metres wide it was surrounded on three sides by halls, rooms and chambers. It was elaborately water-proofed and immediately west of it was the Great Granary.

Houses & Other Buildings

The better houses had courtyards reached through a side-alley gate, a number of rooms including a kitchen, bathrooms, servants' quarters, paved floors and a well. The most intresting aspect of the architecture was the chute dropping down into bins outside, which indicate that garbage was collected and dumped somewhere. There were also public buildings residential dwellings and a number of shops. A structure between the stupa and the Great Bath is believed to have been the palace of the priest-king.

Museum

The museum here, although small, contains a variety of artefacts from the archaeological site: engraved seals; terracotta children's toys; kitchen utensils; weapons; sculpture; jewellery and other ornaments. Other artefacts from Moenjodaro are distributed in major museums of Pakistan like Karachi and Lahore.

Other

Rising water due to irrigation works nearby once threatened to waterlog Moenjodaro, but UNESCO came to the rescue with funds, equipment and experts.

Getting There

Moenjodaro is 430 km north of Karachi and 168 km north of Sehwan Sharif. From the latter city the routes are dusty, dry and hot. Approaching Larkana the scenery to the right of the railway tracks begins to get a little greener. The tiny station at Moenjodaro marks the dividing line between the dry, dusty region and the more fertile agricultural region where the humped Brahman bull is harnessed to the same ancient cart it was 5000 years ago.

The station is quite deserted, lonely and a long way by foot from the centre of town. If there is no tonga waiting at the station backpackers should leave their gear there and walk to **Dokri Village**, three km away, to collect a tonga to go to the archaeological site. It is about 11 km away and costs Rs10 to 15. If you're travelling south from Lahore by train get off at **Larkana**. From there it's a 28-km taxi ride to the site. Buses also run from Larkana to Dokri.

If you arrive early in the morning you can continue on the same afternoon; a day is plenty of time to see the site and museum. There is an airport near the museum and an information centre close to the site.

Places to Stay

There is an archaeological *Dak Bungalow* here. Arrangements to stay there must be made in Karachi. Alternatively there is a *motel* run by the PTDC. In Larkana the *Sambara Inn* on Raza Shak Kabin Rd (tel 2291-3) has singles and doubles for Rs175 and Rs260. It's air-con and has a swimming pool.

KOT DIJI

Kot Diji is the site of another metropolis of the Indus Valley Civilisation, considered to be older than Moenjodaro. Prehistoric atrefacts have also been unearthed here and can be seen in museums. Kot Diji is at present the dite of a huge battlemented fort. This impressive building is obvious from the highway.

It's located between Ranipur and Khairpur on the Hyderabad road, close to Rohri, on the east bank of the Indus. Worth a side trip.

SUKKUR & ROHRI

North of Larkana the landscape becomes luxuriant, lushly green and wooded. By and large this is a highly productive agricultural area. The railway line forks up here with one line heading north to the Sukkur-Rohri Junction where it continues on to Bahawalpur, Multan and Lahore in the Punjab.

Sukkur is a large town just a few km from the huge barrage named after it. Built between 1923 and 1932, the 1400-metre long barrage crosses the Indus in 46 spans and feeds seven main canals, totalling 650 km in length. One canal alone is wider and longer than the Suez or Panama canals. The Sukkur **barrage** irrigates 2½ million hectares of previously unarable land. It is the largest irrigation project in the world.

Sukkur is a large, prosperous, industrial and agricultural centre. Just across the Indus is **Rohri**, also fairly prosperous and an important railway junction. The two towns, five km apart and 488 km north of Karachi, are linked by the Landsdowne and Ayub bridges, which are themselves architecturally extremely beautiful. In the middle of the Indus there is an island where the shrine of **Khwajha Khizar** is to be seen. It is reputed to be more than a thousand years old and is venerated by Hindus and Moslems alike. Slightly south of this island is a larger island called **Bukkur**, which has a fort with a long and chequered history. The Landsdowne Bridge connects Bukkur to Rohri. The 30-

metre high **tower** of Ma'sum Shah Bakhri, Nawab of Sukkur, provides a fine view over the town and the barrage. There is also a rock in the river on which is the picturesque temple of **Shri Sadbella** with a fine view of the Lansdowne Bridge.

Places to Stay

Although it can be uncomfortably hot in summer, the towns have a quiet atmosphere and they are good places to stop off at on the journey north or south; places where you can shake off travel fatigue, reappraise your itinerary and do your laundry. There are cheap *muzzaffar khanas* in both towns and also moderately priced medium-class hotels near the railway stations. At the top end of the price scale there's the *Inter-Pak Inn* (tel 3051-52) at Lab-e-Mehran with singles and doubles at Rs175 and Rs250.

Kushan statuary representing yakshi or tree spirits dating from AD c100.

Punjab

North of Sind is the Punjab or *Panj Nad* – Land of Five Rivers – the Jhelum, Chenab, Ravi, Beas and Sutlej, which all flow south to join the Indus at Mithankot. This region is known geographically as the Upper Indus Plain. In area it is about 196,000 square km and is bounded in the west by the Sulaiman Ranges in Baluchistan and by the Indus in the North West Frontier Province. In the north it is bordered by the Hazara district and Azad Kashmir & Jammu, while in the north east the Ravi and the Sutlej and the Rajaputana Desert in India form the boundary. To the south the rocky gorge in Sind demarcates the province.

The land rises to around 200 metres and gradually climbs up to 300 metres at the Potwar Plateau. It has a continental climate, but suffers from extreme heat in the summer when the temperature soars to 40°C, untempered by any breeze except the dry wind called **loo** which, like the **ghibli** in the Sahara, blows during the day and stirring up the dust and sand to darken the sky. This is occasionally broken by electrical sandstorms and thunderstorms accompanied by heavy rainfall, which usually causes a slight drop in the temperature. The region between Sibi in Baluchistan and Jacobabad in Sind is considered to be the hottest in Pakistan. It was in the latter area that the highest recorded temperature – 51°C (126°F) – was recorded. In winter the temperature drops to a much more pleasant 24° to 30°C.

The Punjab is not only the granary of the country, but also an important industrial region. So amid grainfields of wheat, barley, rice and maize or fields of cotton, sugarcane and bananas there are industrial villages with modern plants and factories, all new and starkly alien to their surroundings. It is the only region which has diversified industries and many major industrial centres such as Faisalbad, Sargodha, Lahore, Sialkot, Rawalpindi, and Jhelum and Campbellpore, both oil-producing towns.

The land traversed by several rivers is lush green and fertile; a hospitable region where, half a million years ago, the Paleolithic Age flourished along the banks of the Soan River as it flowed down the Potwar Plateau across the Salt Range. Here the sister-cities of Moenjodara – Harappa and Taxila – emerged to be wiped out later by the arrival of the pastoral Aryans, who adopted the culture they discovered here.

This was the region that Cyrus the Great (6th century BC) of the Achaemenian Empire conquered, and his successor, Darius, turned into a satrapy of the Persian Empire, only to be superseded by the Hellenic Empire of Alexander the Great in the 4th century BC. Alexander found the rulers of Taxila friendly and was able to make treaty agreements with them. This was consolidated by the marriage of a Greek princess with Chandragupta, who later set up the great Mauryan Empire.

Along the banks of the Jhelum River, Alexander fought and won his last great battle, but it was here that Bucephalus, his faithful, charger died. It was also here where Alexander, weary of endless military campaigns, finally decided to turn homeward. His coming and going strongly influenced the emergence of the Buddhist Gandhara Culture of the Kushan Empire which had its capital in Taxila, once visited by Saint (Doubting) Thomas on his way to the coast of Malabar. It was this great 'Holy Land' of Buddhism that was to influence – through the ancient Silk Trade Route – the historical development of Central Asia, particularly of Chinese Turkestan and of Tibet.

The northern part of the Indus Plain developed faster than the southern region, not only because of its great rivers but because the main camel caravan route of the ancient Silk Trade – now making up the Euro-Asian Highway – runs through it from the Khyber Pass through the Valley of Peshawar to Lahore. This important overland trade route gave impetus to the development of villages into towns, towns into cities and cities into kingdoms. It is a very rich region, which nonetheless suffered greatly from the depredations of the Mongols, other invaders and conflicts. Its rich, natural resources have always allowed it a quick recovery.

It was only when the Moghuls invaded and had established their empire and secured the frontiers that this Upper Indus Plain began its 'golden age'. Huge forts, splendid palaces, mosques and other public buildings proliferated along the whole length and breadth of the land. Great and beautiful cities like Lahore, Rawalpindi, Bahawalpur and Multan emerged. When Moghul power began to decline in the late 18th and early 19th century the Sikhs came, only to be superseded by the British in 1849. The British similarly established their empire, secured the frontiers and continued the construction work begun by the Moghuls.

NORTH OF SUKKUR
North of Sukkur and Rohri in Sind the land, cut by the Indus and the thin, black highway, turns greener. A little beyond Ubauro a side road leads west to the Guddu barrage – about 60 km away – which bridges the Indus. This road continues on to Sui in Baluchistan to the west and then splits off to Dera Ghazi Khan in the north.

A short distance north – toward Rahimyar Khan – a road leads to Sadiqabad, while to the west the **Baung Mosque** is 26 km off the highway. Described as a 'jewel of a mosque', it has mosaics of tiny mirrors on the walls. This is now the land of the Srikis of the

Bahawalpur region, renowned for their valour as warriors. Until 1962 this area remained an autonomous kingdom. Ahmadpur East, the former capital of Bahawalpur, is about 140 km further north. It is reminiscent of the fabulous maharajas and nawabs and their lavish way of life during the British Raj era.

The land is flat and fertile for most of the way to the Salt Range, although some sections are wasteland and desert. West of the Indus the barren land is spiked with oases, while north-west of the Jhelum River most of the Thal Desert has been reclaimed for agriculture. East and south-east of Bahawalpur are the Nara, the Cholistan and the Thar desert. In this wide expanse of deserts, where nomads still live, are forts in Dewar, Muzzaffargarh, Abbas and Binot, separated from each other by hundreds of km of sand. It requires a special permit to visit the nawab's palace and the forts out in the deserts.

The old city of Bahawalpur, 50 km to the north, seems to live in the past but also has a national park, a game sanctuary and 29 km to the east, a lake. East of here the Bikaner Desert stretches for hundreds of km into India.

MULTAN
Multan is a prosperous city of bazaars, mosques, shrines and superbly designed tombs – 'one of the most splendid memorials ever erected in honour of the dead' in the words of an Englishman. There are five of these mausoleums in the old fort, the most famous being that of Saint Rukni-i-Alam, also known as Rukn-ud-din. The tomb was originally built by the Emperor Tughlag Shah (1340 to 1350) for his own use, but his son decided it should be for the saint. The dome of the tomb, which is built on high ground, is visible for many km away. One of the supporting towers was destroyed during the siege of 1848, but it was later carefully restored. This tomb is decorated with glazed tiles with patterns in *bas relief*.

Other tombs include those of Baha-ud-din Zakharia (also known as Baha-il-Haq), which was very badly damaged in 1848 and the tomb of the Sufi, Shams-i-Tabriz, who was murdered in 1247. The old fort is called Ibn-i-Qasim Bagh and there is also a Hindu temple dedicated to Shiva's 'Narsingh' or lion-man incarnation, now in disrepair. The Chowk Bazaar in the centre of town is also a fascinating place to visit.

Places to Stay
The *Mahmood Hotel* on Sher Shah Rd between the GTS bus stand and the cantonment station is not bad at Rs10, or there's a *Youth Hostel* about 2½ km from the station and directly opposite the Moslem high school. At the other end of the price scale is *Shezan Residence*, Kutchery Rd (tel 3 0253-4-5-6) where singles cost between Rs120 and 150 and doubles are Rs200; plus taxes.

NORTH OF MULTAN
To the north of Multan is a region called Choti. The native tribes in this area, the *Lagaris*, have an entirely different culture. In the district of Sanga are the *Hurs*, also unique culturally.

Climbing up onto the Potwar Plateau the land stands out to the south where the Salt Range begins and continues towards Peshawar Valley. Just before reaching the valley, the range turns south to Bannu and Dera Ismail Khan. Superfically, this is an unappealing stretch of land with its scarred red earth and sandstone rocks dissected by ridges, troughs, gulleys, crevasses and salt and coal mines. But it's also an area with some attractive historical spots.

HARAPPA
This was the first of the Indus Valley Civilisation sites to be discovered, but in size and condition it is inferior to Moenjodaro. Located 186 km south-west of Lahore, Harappa is reached via the station at Sahiwal, formerly known as Montgomery. Situated beside an earlier course of the Ravi River, Harappa was discovered in 1920-21, but through the ages the site was quarried for bricks and most of the buildings so far excavated are in poor condition. Like Moenjodaro the excavations have revealed a series of cities, stacked one upon another. The site, with its citadel and great granary, seems similar in many ways to Moenjodaro and like its southern sister-city appears to have thrived around 3000 to 1700 BC with an economy based largely on agriculture and trade. The Harappan society seems to have been egalitarian, pursuing a rather simple way of life.

Things to See
There is a **museum** here which exhibits numerous artefacts discovered on the site: terracotta toys, chess boards, utensils and pieces of jewellery indicate that they may have had trade relations with Burma!

LAHORE
Situated on the east bank of the Ravi River, Lahore is very old. Legend traces its origin to Loh, the son of Rama Chandra, the hero of the *Ramayana*, but history records that it began as a dependency of the 8th century AD Hindu ruler, Lalitiditya. In the early 11th century it came under Moslem rule and evolved as a centre of Islamic culture and learning as well as trade and commerce. In the 13th century it was depopulated and razed to the ground by the Tartar-Mongol hordes of Genghis Khan. Tamberlane and his Moslem Turks also arrived and destroyed the city.

Subsequent invaders were more peaceful in their intention. Babar, founder of the Moghul Empire, along with other Moghul emperors from Akbar down to Aurangzeb, turned it into an important city, fortified it and built spectacularly big and beautiful buildings. The Sikhs held power briefly in the early part of the 19th century and enhanced it with more stunning buildings. They were followed by the British, who

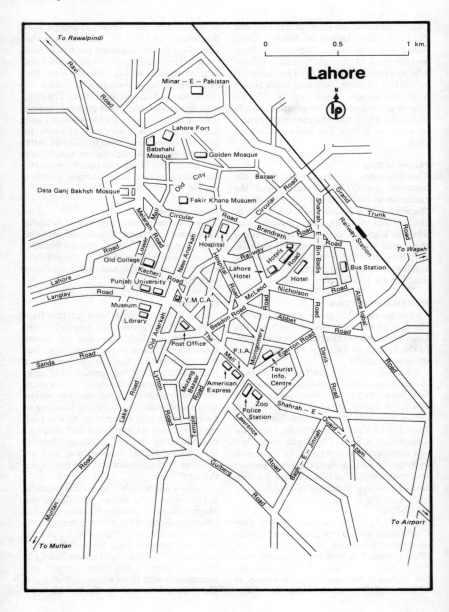

Lahore

To Rawalpindi

Ravi Road

Minar – E – Pakistan

Lahore Fort

Babshahi Mosque

Golden Mosque

Old City

Data Ganj Bakhsh Mosque

Bazaar

Fakir Khana Musuem

Circular Road

Circular Road

Brandreth Road

Grand Trunk Road

Railway Station

To Wagah

Meleram Road

Mall

New Anarkah

Hospital

Hospital Road

Railway

Shahrah – E – Bin Badis Road

Hotels

Bus Station

Lower Mall Road

Old College

Kacheri Road

Lahore Road

Punjab University

Lahore Hotel

Hotel

Nicholson Road

Alama Iqbal Road

Langlay Road

Y.M.C.A.

McLeod Road

Museum

Beadon Road

The Mall

Abbet Road

Library

Old Anarkah

Post Office

P.I.A.

Egerton Road

Davis Road

Sanda Road

Lyton Road

Mozang Bazaar Road

Montgomery Road

Tourist Info. Centre

American Express

Zoo Police Station

Shahrah – E –

Lake Road

Temple Road

Lawrence Road

Quaid – I – Azam

Gulberg Road

Bagh – E – Jinnah Road

Multan Road

To Multan

To Airport

0   0.5   1 km.

N

added still more magnificent buildings as well as enlarging the city. Lahore went through further rapid expansion following Partition.

Lahore was a cultural and intellectual centre during both the Moghul and British eras, and it's an atmosphere which is still pervading today. But it is the diversity and contrast of the different sections of the city which make Lahore interesting. Except for local tourists with their blaring transistors you could almost be back in the Moghul era.

Lahore is 213 metres above sea level and has a population of over 2½ million. The temperature here drops down to 10°C in winter, but in summer can soar to 40°C or over. The best time to visit is straight after the monsoon period when the weather is cool and pleasant.

Warning

This town gets a lot of bad press and is undoubtedly the worst place in Pakistan for rip-off merchants. Beware of buying dope from anyone, as it appears the 'conspiracy theory' is no myth here. Everyone but everyone – from dealers to hotel managers – is a police stooge, and they all work together to take your money from you. Very few hotels are safe. Don't leave money in your room if you're not there, even if you're only intending to be gone a few minutes.

Information

The Tourist Information Centre is at Lahore Airport, Transport House, Egerton Rd (tel 5 8948). The staff here are helpful and polite, and you can pick up good maps and brochures from here. But note that it is closed on Thursday afternoon and all day Friday. The PIA office, American Express, GPO, Telegraph & Telephone Office and the police station are all within walking distance along the Mall. There are no consular offices in Lahore; they are all in Islamabad.

Moghul City

Lahore is actually three cities in one. The old Moghul City is walled in by a 10-metre high brick rampart overlooking its surrounding moat. The moat is now dry and the walls dismantled in certain places to make openings for streets and roads. Within the ramparts are shrines, mosques, bazaars and workshops where craftspeople still weave textiles and do traditional copper, silver and brass work in an age-old, timeless way. The city itself is ringed by Circular Rd.

Badshahi Mosque

The mosque at one corner of the walled city is imposing, both externally and internally. Built by Aurangzeb, it has huge gateways, tall towering minarets, vast domes and a spacious courtyard. Take a look at it at dusk when the dark red bricks are fiery with the setting sun. Make sure you don't wear shorts or mini-skirts – bare knees are not appreciated here.

Lahore Fort

Like any of its contemporary forts, the great Fort of Lahore was also a palace. It was originally built by Akbar and later improved by Jehangir and Shah Jahan, both of whom gave free rein to their flair for architectural extravagance. The older gates are no longer used but inside the *Hathi Pol* – Elephant Gate – you can still see the *kashi* tile mosaics which date from the time of Shah Jahan. They were badly damaged during the Sikh wars but have now been restored. The mosaics show elephant and camel fights, polo games and scenes of court life.

The **Pearl Mosque** or *Moti Masjid* still stands in the fort and was restored in 1903-04. The *Diwan-i-Am* or Hall of Public Audience and the *jharoka* or balcony throne was the place where the emperor used to appear daily. Another interesting building is the **Shish Mahal** – palace of mirrors – which is decorated with glass mosaics and stands to the north of the square. Then there's the **Naulakha** which gets its name from its construction cost of nine lakhs (Rs900,000). The north wall has fine kashi tilework. Also worth seeing here are the *choti khwabagh* or lesser bedchamber and the *arzgah*, where noblemen would gather each morning to pay their respects to the emperor. Aurangzeb, the last of the great Moghuls, added the *Almiri Gate*. On his death the city began slide into a decline.

On Mondays, Thursdays and Saturdays there is a *son et lumiere* show in English at the fort. Entrance to the fort is free for students.

If you're interested in collecting postcards there's a good selection of high quality cards available for Rs1 each from the shop near the gate at the main entrance. The next best selection is at the Lahore Museum – same price.

Other Old City Buildings

Between the fort and the Badshahi Mosque is the **Gurudwara Arjun Singh**, a quaintly beautiful Sikh temple which is dwarfed by its large neighbours. The *samadh*, facing the east wall of the fort, contains the ashes of Ranjit Singh, the Sikh ruler of Lahore who died in 1849. Seven concubines and four wives became *satis* at his cremation, burning themselves to death on his funeral pyre.

The **Sonehri Masjid** – Golden Mosque – has three gilt domes and dates from 1753. Its builder, Bokhari Khan, is said to have died in a rather unusual fashion, kicked to death by the female attendants of a widow he had displeased or scorned! The **Mosque of Wazir Khan**, also in the old city was built in 1634 by the Governor of the Punjab during the reign of Shah Jahan. It's well worth seeing as it's very beautiful and not only has some fine kashi tilework, but also offers an excellent view of the city. There's a slight problem of finding it though. If you're coming from the direction of the railway station try to persuade one of the scooter drivers to take you. They don't like going to the bazaar area as the streets are troublesome, so you

may have to ask quite a few before finding someone prepared to take you. But if you're patient one of them will drive you there – eventually – for a cost of Rs5.

Just beyond the Circular Rd in Iqbal Park is the **Minar-i-Pakistan** – a monument to the conception of Pakistan – designed like a flower bud just beginning to open with a long stamen jutting out to the sky. There is a lift up to the top of the sightseeing tower. Inside the Bhati Gate of the old city is the **Faqir Khana Museum** which contains a collection of paintings, carvings, manuscripts, old china, carpets and numerous other objets d'art. Outside the old city is the beautiful mosque of **Data Ganj Baksh** built on a high platform.

British City

The British built their city adjacent to the old Moghul city. It begins with the **New Anarkali Bazaar**, named after the famous courtesan of Akbar, off Circular Rd to the south. Anarkali – pomegranate blossom – was entombed alive by the emperor for smiling at Prince Salim, who later became Emperor Jehangir. Her tomb is near the bazaar, which is a paved street with narrow alleys off each side. It's lined with traditional shops now crowded with stalls selling everything from glass bangles to transistor radios, beaten gold to tape recorders and refrigerators – most of it at bargain prices!

The Mall

From here the Mall runs south-east towards the airport. It is the most modern section of the city where the government buildings, big hotels, churches, modern mosques, restaurants, cafes, banks, airline offices and travel agencies are. Lined with shady trees, it's quiet, sedate, well-paved, neat and clean and has a completely different atmosphere from the rest of the city. Most of the imposing government buildings like the **High Court**, the **Punjab University** and the **Museum** are of Moghul-Victorian design, while the churches and cathedrals are either

Norman or Gothic. There are also modern structures here such as the **Shohada Mosque**, the **Islamic Summit Minar** and the **WAPDA** building.

From the Mall, streets and alleys branch off towards the British-built railway station. It is here that the section of the old Moghul city merges with the modern part of Lahore. The railway station, of Moghul-Victorian design, is surrounded with bazaars, cheap and medium-class hotels, cafes and eating places. The central bus station is just a block away and nearby are minibuses, buses, auto-rickshaws, taxis and tongas all waiting to pick up passengers. It's chaotic, crowded, confusing and dusty.

Close to the police station and opposite the Lahore Hilton in a wooded section of the Mall is the **Jinnah-i-Bagh zoo** which contains peacocks, Bengal tigers, giraffes, ostriches, Bactrian camels, elephants, deer and other animals.

Lahore Museum & Kim's Gun

Opposite the Punjab University on the Mall the **Lahore Museum** houses collections from various historical periods of Pakistan, from the paleolithic age to the Indus Valley Civilisation, the Gandhara culture and the Moghul and British periods. it's a smallish museum, but is noted particularly for its Gandhara sculptures – the most famous of which is the *Fasting Siddartha* – and for its Moghul paintings. You are not allowed to take bags inside. From 1875 to 1893 Rudyard Kipling's father was the curator of this museum. On an island in the Mall in front of the museum is **Kim's gun**, the *zamzama*. This huge, menacing-looking gun, known as the 'lion's roar', was immortalised by Kipling as Kim's gun – last used in the Battle of Panipat in 1761. A Persian inscription indicates that it was cast in 1760.

Other Museums

Faqhir Khana Museum in the Old Walled City, **Shaker Ali Museum** and **Chugtai Museum** are all worth visiting.

Tombs of Jehangir & Nur Jehan

Five km north-west of the city is the quiet secluded village of Shaddara. From here it is two km to the mausoleums of the Moghul Emperor Jehangir and Empress Nur Jehan – Light of the World. In their serene setting, they are separated only by a canal. Nur Jehan's tomb is in an open garden but Jehangir's is huge and enclosed by high walls. The building has four 30-metre high minarets; the cenotaph is inlaid with *pietra dura* work like the Taj Mahal in Agra; and on the east and west side of the tomb the 99 names of Allah are finely carved. You can see across the Ravi River to Lahore from the minarets. Close to the tomb of Nur Jehan is the tomb of Asaf Khan, her brother, but unfortunately most of the kashi tilework has been stripped off this beautiful Persian-style tomb.

Entry fee to all three tombs is Rs2 which you pay at either Jehangir's or Nur Jehan's tomb. It's about a 10-minute walk from the bus stop to Nur Jehan's tomb, and the shortest way from there to Jehangir's tomb is to jump the back wall, cross the tracks, find the break in the loose rock wall – it's easy – then follow it along the right side and you'll come to the entrance to the compound. You are not allowed to climb up via the minarets to the roof.

Shalimar Gardens

Laid out by Shah Jahan in 1642, the Shalimar Gardens are typical Moghul gardens. Designed along the lines of the imperial Persian gardens, they are an imposing 32 hectares in area. The gardens are 10 km east of the city and are built in three tiers with pools, fountains and pavilions. Entrance fee to the gardens is Rs2. The best times to visit them are between 11 am and noon or 4 to 5 pm in summer or from 11 am and noon and 3 to 4 pm during winter when the fountains – some of them anyway – are turned on.

On the way to the gardens you will pass the gate of the **Balabi Bagh** or rose garden which was designed and planted in 1655. Notice the exquisite, coloured tiles decorating this gate. Close to the Shalimar Gardens is the tomb of Ali Mardan Khan, who built them.

Around Lahore

Sheikhpura, once known as Jehangirabad, is 42 km from Lahore. Here there is a building once used as **a** hunting lodge by the emperor, now occupied by the Pakistan police. Nearby is the **Hiran Minar**, a large stone sculpture built by Jehangir in memory of his pet antelope, *Manaraj*. Sixty-seven km out of Lahore, is the **Changa Manga Forest** which has a lake

and a miniature railway that meanders through and around the forest.

Things to Buy

Most handicraft shops are along the Mall and expensive. The APWA Cottage Industries and Pakistan Handicrafts shops have fixed prices. Anarkali Bazaar, Gulberg Market, Shah Alam Market and the Old City bazaars have lower prices, and you can bargain here.

Places to Stay – Bottom End

Warning Beware of rip-offs and set-ups in Lahore. Avoid cheapies near the railway station, particularly along McLeod and Badrenath Rds. There are lots of hassles here ranging from stolen travellers' cheques to planting evidence such as

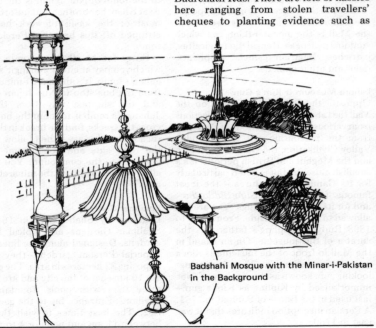

Badshahi Mosque with the Minar-i-Pakistan in the Background

A   Rajah Bazaar, old city, Rawalpindi
B   Jehangir's Tomb, Lahore

hashish in rooms in order to blackmail tourists. In particular, avoid staying at *Santana, Friend's Lalazar, Royal City* and *Chiltan hotels.* They are notorious rip-off joints. They have been investigated and warned already, but the rip-offs and scams still go on. Others to give a big miss are *Sicility, Picnic, Chilton, Tourist* and *Butterfly hotels.* Also avoid touts at the railway station for the same reasons.

If you have to stay in a cheapie check all the windows, doors and the ceiling for possible ways of breaking into it. If you're offered tea or a smoke it's wise to refuse, otherwise you might find yourself falling asleep suddenly, and wake up without your money belt, travellers' cheques and cash.

If you're in transit try the *railway retiring rooms* where singles cost Rs20 and doubles Rs30. If you're on your way to India and are passing through Wagha head straight for the border. There's a *PTDC Motel* right there with dorm accommodation that's clean and pleasant and costs Rs30 for a bed. It also provides a good breakfast.

One of the safest cheapos is the *Youth Hostel* at 110 B Firdous Market, Gulberg 111 (tel 8 3145). Dorm beds cost Rs8 and Rs10. Many travellers recommend this place, but its biggest disadvantage is being too far out of town. Not only that but it's a long and complicated way out there. You have to take bus 25 or wagon 15 south from the terminus at the end of McLeod Rd near the railway station.

The *YMCA Hostel* on the Mall is next to the GPO in a section of a large building and is easy to miss, so keep your eyes open for the entrance. It's a popular place (tel 5 4433) with dorm beds for Rs10 and

singles at Rs20. The *Salvation Army Hostel*, 35 Fatimah Jinnah Rd, also has singles for Rs20. All rooms have showers and toilets.

Campers can put up their tents or park their vehicles in the gardens of the YWCA or in the grounds of the Sally Army Hostel. Camping is also possible at the Youth Hostel, though it's not a place I would suggest for reasons already stated.

Middle

Both the *Orient Hotel* and *Lahore Hotel*, (tel 5 4051-9), which are adjacent to each other on McLeod Rd have rooms with fans and attached toilets and showers for Rs60 to Rs100. The *Asia Hotel* near the railway station is cheap for a hotel with air-con. Medium-class hotels near the railway station are always crowded and usually unpleasant.

Top End

Lahore's international hotels are mainly along the Mall, now officially renamed Shahrah-i-Quaid-i-Azam but rarely referred to as such. The *InterContinental* (tel 6 9932) has 200 rooms, modern conveniences and costs from Rs680 to 750 for singles and Rs880 to 950 for doubles. The *Hilton International* (tel 6 9971 and 31 0281), 87 the Mall has 190 rooms with singles from Rs530 to 630 and doubles from Rs660. The old-style *Faletti's* is on Egerton Rd (tel 5 3861) and has 67 rooms with single and doubles at Rs300 and Rs500.

Then there's the *International*, the Mall (tel 37 0191-6) with 110 rooms and singles and doubles from Rs200 and Rs300 respectively. A smaller hotel, *Zonobi's*, 25E Gulberg (tel 88 0015-17) has 24 rooms and costs Rs160 a single and Rs200 a double. There are also the *Hotel Indus*, 56 the Mall (tel 5 2856-8) with 20 rooms, singles/doubles Rs150 and Rs250; the *Ambassador*, Davis Rd (tel 5 4751-8), which has 24 rooms and singles and doubles for Rs160 to Rs200; and the *Country Club Hotel*, 105 the Mall (tel 31 1361-2), with 14 rooms at Rs150 a single and Rs250 a double.

Places to Eat

The cheaper eating places are near the railway station or in alleys off the Mall. One near the railway station that is recommended is the *Hotel Zaminar*. The slightly more expensive *Shishan Restaurant* on the Mall has good local and western food. *Kebana Restaurant* on Jail Rd has probably the best Pakistani food in town for Rs20 and Rs30 per meal. For spiced and grilled chicken tikka the Mozang Bazaar is the place to go at Rs12 per piece. The Gamal Mandi area, towards the old city, is good for fried fish at Rs10 and Rs12. Try *Malik Snack Bar* on the Mall for sandwiches and ice cream. The *Cathay Restaurant* opposite the American Express on the Mall is a real food trip with excellent and inexpensive priced Chinese food. Lakshmi Chowk is recommended for local dishes of every kind.

Getting Around

From the airport to the city centre costs Rs10 by taxi; Rs1 by bus. Tongas or auto-rickshaws to the town centre cost Rs3 to Rs5 repectively from the railway station or to any point around the city. Make sure you fix the fare with the driver before setting off. Fare meters usually don't

Bus Below is a list of buses which may be useful for getting around the city.

Number	Time	Starting Point & Destination
17	20 minutes	Railway Station to Shalimar Gardens
6 & 23	20 minutes	Railway Station to Jehangir's Tomb
118		Between Jehangir's Tomb & the Mall
14		Lahore Museum to Railway Station
6		Railway Station to Lahore Fort

Getting Away

Lahore is a rail, road and air junction on the great Euro-Asian Highway which spans Peshawar and Amritsar to Delhi. Railways connect Lahore with the major cities in the south and west, and the line continues via Attari into India.

Rail Get a Tourist Certificate from the Tourist Information Centre and apply for railway concessions at the office of the railway superintendent. **To Karachi** There are four trains a day that make the 19 to 21-hour trip from Lahore to Karachi. Express trains like the **Shalimar Express** and **Super Express** service depart from Lahore at 6 am and arrive in Karachi 16 hours later at 10 pm. The fare is Rs264.

Other fares	
Air-con	
sleeper	Rs605
seat	Rs305
First Class	
sleeper	Rs242
seat	Rs145
ordinary	Rs108
Second class	
mail	Rs87
ordinary	Rs78

To Rawalpindi There are two shuttle trains now from Lahore to Rawalpindi, one in the morning, the other at 3.30 pm. The trip takes five to six hours and is quicker, easier and more comfortable than the bus, which is slightly cheaper than the train.

To Quetta There are four trains a day making this 22-hour trip.

Fares:
Air-con
sleeper	Rs566
seat	Rs286

First class
sleeper	Rs225
seat	Rs135
ordinary	Rs103

Second class
mail	Rs71
ordinary	Rs51

To India You can get to India by train or bus. The train departs at 2 pm and you should be there at least half an hour before departure for immigration and customs clearance. The Indian immigration and customs check post is at Attari and it takes at least two hours to be checked and cleared. You have to buy your ticket on to Amritsar at Attari. The leg from Lahore to Attari costs Rs4.10 and from Attari to Amritsar it's Rs4.75. It's also a good idea to change some money here for your initial expenses in Amritsar. You could be up shit creek without a paddle if you don't as you won't get another chance to change money until the following day, because the train is not scheduled to arrive in Amritsar until 6 pm. As it is, it's almost invariably late. Going the other way, the train departs Amritsar at 9.30 am and is supposed to arrive in Lahore around 2 pm.

This is one couple's experience using this service:

In Amritsar you can't buy a ticket until the morning of departure – no seat reservations in either class and tickets available on the platform. It's best if you get there very early, one person barges in and gets seats and luggage space, while the other queues up for tickets. Good rate for Pakistan rupees from money-changers on the platform but not for Indian rupees coming the other way. Passport required to change money and you get a form to fill in stating how much you have changed but no-one wanted to see ours. The train is usually

an hour late and there's a long wait at the border for the Indians' luggage to be checked – the Indians hand over their passports with rupees carefully tucked inside. They carry so much stuff you will soon be snowed under and have to keep your pack on your knees if you don't get a space early. We had no hassles with officials – Indian or Pakistani.

The old road to India is open. You can get a minibus near the general bus terminus to Wagha, then walk across the border, and catch a bus to Amritsar. It costs Rs2.50 by bus and Rs3 by minibus. The border closes at 3.30 pm.

Accommodation in Wagha is available at the *PTDC Motel* where dorm beds are Rs30 and doubles Rs86.

Air Apply to the *PIA* office in the Mall for concessions. There is a daily flight from Lahore to New Delhi. Domestic flights cost:

	flights	Rs
Lahore-Quetta	three daily	855
Lahore-Karachi	four daily	645
Lahore-Rawalpindi	five weekly	215
Lahore-Peshawar	every Saturday	480

Bus The general bus terminus is on Badami Bagh. Buses leave here in every direction every half-hour from 6 am to 6 pm. The Lahore-Rawalpindi bus costs Rs28.50 and by minibus it's around Rs30. The trip takes five hours by bus, four by minibus. De-luxe buses – the 'Flying Coach' – cost Rs60 for the four to five-hour trip.

Money
If you have any local currency left change it on the Pakistan side of the border for Indian currency. You get much better rates. Apparently this is also true for your Indian currency: you get five rupees more for a hundred rupee note than you do on the Indian side of the border.

LAHORE-RAWALPINDI
The Grand Trunk Rd is presently being

turned into a double-lane superhighway in stages. On the way from Lahore to Rawalpindi the landscape becomes more arid and dusty, then gives way to expansive grainfields followed by a sprawling industrial area. After the industrial region you pass through a number of towns and villages with attractive, small mosques usually painted white, yellow and green. Traffic on the Grand Trunk Rd is fairly heavy and you will see ornately-painted trucks and buses glinting with chrome from front to back.

Roads split off to the south and to the north. To the south is Faisalabad, formerly known as Lyallpur, which was laid out at the turn of the 20th century in the pattern of the Union Jack. It is an important centre for higher education in the field of technology and is also a major market for agricultural produce. To the north is Sialkot, the site of another religious shrine but also the centre for the manufacture of sports equipment, surgical tools, rubber and plastic products, ceramics and light electrical devices.

A village which used to be a military cantonment during the British period is presided over by the forlorn spire of an English church. The bus passes through numerous villages and towns and stops at a teashop and restaurant where ice-cream and soft drinks are available. The stops make it more interesting than the train trip, apart from which it is less crowded and you see more of the landscape.

At Jhelum the land begins to ascend to the Potwar Plateau. It becomes undulating and rolling, then hilly. The lush green countryside is occasionally broken by rugged terrain and dry mountains. As you approach Rawalpindi it becomes green again. There is a sealed road to Islamabad but buses by-pass it and take the route straight to Rawalpindi.

Jhelum is a nondescript town, but the road which forks off the Grand Trunk Rd here leads north to Muzzaffarabad in Azad Kashmir. For places to stay here try the *Green Bar, Paradise* or *Garnata hotels*,

all of them have rooms – usually doubles – for Rs25 and up and the latter has air-con. Other towns on the north side of the Grand Trunk Rd are Kharian where the *Shahzad Hotel* and the *Guluf Hotel* have doubles for about Rs15 to Rs20, and Gujrat where the *Imran Hotel* has rooms for Rs15 and the *Hotel Nashiman* has air-con rooms for Rs25 and up.

Things to See

Twenty-one km from Rawalpindi and over 200 km from Lahore is **Manikyala**, an ancient Buddhist site with a stupa which rises to above 60 metres. The main structure is well preserved but there is nothing much left of the rest.

About 10 km before you reach Manikyala on the Grand Trunk Rd is **Rewat Fort**, a fortified village of the early Islamic period. It's east of the road, and has six gates, a mosque and a mausoleum.

Rohtas Fort built by Sher Shah Suri, architect of the original Grand Trunk Rd, is to the right of the town of Dina, 98 km from Islamambad. On the left is Mangla Dam and the fort is seven km to the right. It's a rough track over sand and streams. The fort itself is five km in circumference with battlemented ramparts. Along the riverside the walls are doubled. It's an impressive, little-known structure, which once guarded the precursor to the Grand Trunk Rd which ran through it.

RAWALPINDI

On the Grand Trunk Rd between Peshawar and Lahore, Rawalpindi, with a population close to a million, is not of great interest in itself. It is, however, an important transit point, as it was a couple of millennia ago when it formed part of the main artery of the ancient Silk Trade Route with trails projecting from it in every direction – south to north and east to west – as it still has today.

It is one of the oldest settlements along the Khyber-Peshawar-Lahore route which, even before the ancient Silk Trade Route was developed, must have formed a

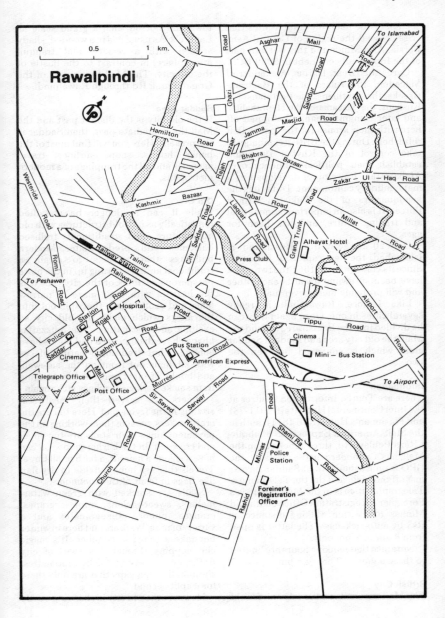

section of the neolithic trade routes that criss-crossed the region of Central Asia, Persia, Asia Minor and this western part of the Indian subcontinent in 6000 BC.

Cyrus the Great, Darius, Alexander of Macedon, the rulers of the Bactrian-Greeks, the Scythians, the Parthians, the Kushans, the Sassanians, the Hephthalites and later Genghis Khan, all stopped off here with their armies for the 'pause that refreshes'. During the British campaign to take control of the Khyber Pass and establish their political influence over Afghanistan, Rawalpindi developed as a major military cantonment. Today it is the headquarters of the Pakistan Armed Forces. It is also an important commercial and trading centre, and has been for ages.

Only 20 km away from Rawalpindi is Islamabad, the new capital of Pakistan. Since its conception in 1961 the two cities have been sprawling towards each other and will probably merge eventually.

Like Lahore, Rawalpindi is really several cities in one. Once again they can be divided into the British area around the Mall, the old city area and modern Saddar area, which is squeezed between the two.

Information

There are Tourist Information Centres at the InterContinental Hotel (tel 6 6011-74) and Flashman's Hotel (tel 6 4811), both in the Mall. American Express, on Shahrah-i-Reza Pehlavi Rd, three blocks from the Mall, has a signboard on the roadside; the GPO is on Kashmir Rd in Saddar Bazaar just off the Mall; and the the Telephone & Telegraph Office is in the Mall. There is a Foreigner's Registration Office on Rashid Minhas Rd, within walking distance or Rs3 by auto-rickshaw. The latter is open from 8 am to 2 pm only.

Note also that banking hours are limited to three a day – 10 am to 1 pm.

British City

The Mall was built on the edge of the old town and not on such a grand scale as Lahore's. As usual it is in a wooded, shady section with a relaxed and tranquil atmosphere, in contrast to the hustle of the old city. The Mall forms part of the Grand Trunk Rd through Rawalpindi.

Saddar Area

If the old city is the distant past and the Mall the immediate past, then Saddar is the present. Here you will find most of the banks, hotels, shops, airlines, travel agencies and all the trappings of a modern metropolis.

Old City

While it can no longer be classified realistically as old, old structures with old architecture and traditional trellised balconies still predominate. Modern buildings that manage to attain a traditional air have sprung up in the more prosperous sections of the city, but it is the bazaars with their maze of narrow lanes and exotic wares that spill out into the alleys which make the old city so exciting and fascinating. The muzzaffar khanas have disappeared and hotels have emerged, but traditional eating places with kitchens out front on the sidewalk and hunks of meat and chicken hanging from smoke-darkened ceilings still remain.

Diners are served their meal still sizzling in the frying pan. Here too are the craftworkers, most of them working on the pavement since their stalls are too small and crowded. In the barbershops you can have a shave, a haircut, a bath or all three. Towels that are hung outside to dry flap like flags in front of the *hammams*.

Stalls are stacked with green water-melons, sweet-melons, apples, grapes, oranges, plums, pomegranates and a variety of nuts. Walk around here in winter but take a tonga in summer. It's magic clip-clopping through the swirl of city traffic, missing everything by centimetres, slipping through gaps that are only there for a split second.

However the old city is changing subtly

with sections of the bazaar slowly being demolished and renovated.

Other

South of the city is the 900-hectare **National Park** which has a lake, an aquarium, an *al fresco* restaurant, a Japanese garden, several km of road and a bridle path for horse riding. The *Youth Hostel* is here, but it's just a bit too far out of the way to be convenient. Since 1963 Rawalpindi has been expanded in all directions, particularly towards Islamabad where, at that time, there were only a few buildings in Aabphara. Today they stretch all along the route between the two cities.

Places to Stay – Bottom End

The hotels in Rawalpindi are often full because Afghani refugees have long-term bookings. As usual the cheapies are near the railway station, but many of them won't accept foreigners. Try the *Shalimar* (Al-Shams), about 500 metres left of the station; it's good value for Rs25 a single, Rs45 a double with fan and attached bathroom. It's biggest drawback is noise. Don't confuse it with the *Hotel Shalimar* near the Mall or you'll find yourself paying top end prices when you don't intend to. Beware of police hassles in this area. Prices of most hotels around the railway station are in the range of Rs20 a single, Rs30 a double and Rs10 a dorm bed. Slightly more expensive hotels with fans and attached bathrooms are along Hatti Chowk, Massey Gate and off Kashmiri Rd. Places such as the *Shah Taj Hotel* and the *Al Hamra Hotel* are reasonably clean, with doubles for Rs30 and up.

In the old city along College Rd in the Rajah Bazaar area are the *Majesty* and *Royal hotels* with fans and shared toilets/shower for Rs12.50 a single and Rs 25 a double and over. The *Arosha Guest House* in Satellite Town, another fairly clean hotel, has singles for Rs25 and doubles for Rs45. Take a minibus and get off at Rahimabad bus stop. *Al-Hayat Hotel* on the Grand Trunk Rd costs Rs35 for

singles and doubles are Rs55 or more.

The *railway retiring rooms* cost Rs10 a single and Rs20 for doubles, but that's bed only. Bring your own sleeping bag.

Also in Pir Wadhai is the *Al-Aziz Hotel*, which has singles for Rs23, doubles for Rs31 and dorm accommodation for Rs6, all with attached bathrooms. Recommended is the *Corner Hotel*, which is new and clean, and has singles and doubles with fans and attached toilet/shower for Rs20 and Rs40 respectively. There are other cheapies in this area with dorm beds for Rs5 and singles for Rs15 and above. The latter are better, particularly if you arrive late at night.

The *Youth Hostel*, 25 Gulistan Colony, is too far out to be worthwhile. It's in a boy scouts' building near the Ayub National Park. From the Grand Trunk Rd you walk right through the park, keeping a little to the right. Ask around for it. Otherwise take bus 10 from the GPO and walk back from the garden restaurant. It costs Rs10 a night. The *YWCA Hostel*, 65A Satellite Town is rundown and takes women only. Dorm beds are available for Rs4 here.

Middle

On Murree Rd at Liaquat Bagh only the *Al-Hayat* has rates below the Rs60 and Rs120 rate of the *Park, National City, Chiltan, Sands Hills* and *Shangrila Hotels*, but it's new and has better facilities. On Hatti Chowk, Massey Gate, the *Hotel Al-Azam* is new and modern with fans and attached bath and has singles for Rs35, doubles for Rs60 and family rooms for Rs185. In the same area, a price notch down are *Hotel Lalazar, Shah Taj Hotel and Hotel Al-Hamra*, all of the same standard and rates at Rs20 a single and Rs35 a double. Off Murree Rd on Liaquat Rd are *City* and *Savoy hotels*, which are much of a muchness with singles for Rs24 and doubles for Rs40. In the Saddar area on Hussain St is *Hotel Al-Mehr* with fans and attached bathroom for Rs20 a single, Rs35 a double and dorm beds for Rs16.50. There's also the *Prince Hotel* and others of the same standard and rates. The *Pakeeza Hotel & Restaurant* on College Rd, Rajah Bazaar has singles for Rs30 and doubles for Rs50.

Top End

The *InterContinental Hotel* (tel 6 6011), in the Mall has 268 rooms with singles at Rs750 and doubles at Rs890. *Flashman's Hotel* (tel 6 4811-6), at 17/22 the Mall has 58 rooms and is operated by the PTDC. Rooms here cost Rs225 to Rs275 for singles and Rs325 and Rs425 for doubles.

Other hotels include the *Potohar*, on Murree Rd (tel 6 8701 and 7205), 34 rooms with singles and doubles for Rs180 and Rs220, the *Silver Grill*, 8 the Mall (tel 6 4729-4719) with 18 rooms at Rs270, and the *Hotel Shalimar* (tel 6 2901), off the Mall which has 100 rooms with singles from Rs360 and doubles from Rs450.

Places to Eat

The inexpensive eating places are in the Saddar Bazaar area where you can buy really good Pakistani food for Rs8 to Rs12 per meal around Rajah Bazaar in the old city. The *Pakeeza Hotel & Restaurant* is a traditional Pathan eating place on Liaquat Rd near Savoy Hotel. There are Chinese restaurants on Murree Rd and the Khyber Rd, which offer the usual Chinese menu with generous helpings for Rs25 to Rs30 a meal. The top-notch hotels have restaurants with western bill-of-fare. Try the *Kamran Restaurant*, Bank Rd, just behind London Books on Saddar St for snacks, ice-cream, coffee and other western food. It's a bit pricey but good.

Liquor The Excise & Tax Office is just off Liaquat Bagh Rd on College Rd, next to the *City Hotel*. The monthly allocation is two units or two bottles of hard liquor or 32 bottles of beer. Fee for the two units is Rs11 – mainly in stamps bought and pasted on the application form. Liquor is also available at the tourist 5-star hotels like Flashman's or the InterContinental.

Other

To cool off in summer the *InterContinental Hotel* allows non-guests to use the swimming pool for a fee of Rs34.50. The pool is open from 8 am to 7 pm. *Flashman's Hotel* has a smaller swimming pool which is open at the same times. Admission there is Rs24.50.

Getting Around

Taxis cost Rs10 within city limits; auto-rickshaws Rs3 to Rs5; rickshaws Rs2 to Rs3 and tongas Rs3 to Rs5. The government bus to Islamabad is Rs1.25; private buses are Rs1.75 and minibuses, Rs2.25. Make sure of the fare first before setting off, particularly if the metre isn't working.

Getting Away

Rawalpindi is 274 km west of Lahore, 166 km east of Peshawar, 1570 km north of Karachi and about 375 km south of Gilgit.

Trains Services are rather crowded and slow. Going by bus or minibus to either Peshawar or Lahore is more comfortable and faster.

Air *PIA* on the Mall, just off Saddar Bazaar has flights from Rawalpindi-Peking-Tokyo every Sunday. There are three domestic flights weekly to Quetta for Rs1100 and four flights daily to Karachi for Rs1160.

There are one or two flights daily to Skardu depending on weather conditions. Tentative departures are at 6.30 am and 9.30 am and the fare is Rs150. The same weather conditions apply to flights to Gilgit. Usual departure is at 10.30 am and 12.30 pm. The fare is Rs150 plus Rs5 embarkation airport tax.

Bus The general bus station is in Pir Wadhai which is a fascinating place to go. Here are some of the most ornately and garishly painted and decorated buses in the world, all shiny chrome and gleaming deep, bright colours. Most often, they have geometrical designs and Islamic calligraphy painted on them and are covered in scenes of mosques against backdrops of desert and date palm trees. Bristling with antennaes and ribbons, the buses look almost extra-terrestial on the road. They leave every half an hour in all directions.

Natco offers a service to Gilgit, which departs three times a day at 9 am, 7 pm and 11 pm. *Kohistan* also has a daily service to Gilgit at 8 am, 5 pm and midnight. The fare is Rs86, and there is a student concession of 50% on both lines.

There are some minibuses operating out of Pir Wadhai to Gilgit nowadays. They are faster, cleaner and more comfortable, but so far the service is irregular and the fare is Rs110.

The main minibus stations are off Tippu Rd and at Murree Rd behind the Moti Mahal Cinema. To Lahore by bus costs Rs25 and takes five hours or more; by minibus it's Rs28 and takes from four to five hours. The *Flying Coach Company*, (tel 57 4291), on Murree Rd near the Shangrila Hotel has de-luxe coaches to Lahore every two hours for Rs50. To Peshawar it's a three-hour trip and the fare is Rs15 by bus; Rs17 by minibus.

Speedway Buses, (tel 7 2781), at the Inter-Pak Hotel and *Rakaposhi Buses*, (tel 7 4130), at the Modern Hotel, have minibuses and wagons from Rawalpindi to Gilgit. They are near the Novelty Cinema in the vicinity of the Rajah Bazaar in the old city. Departures are between 3 and 4 am, 2 pm and 8 pm. The trip takes 14 to 16 hours or more and costs Rs70. it is several hours longer by bus from Pir Wadhai but Rs30 cheaper.

RAWALPINDI – ISLAMABAD

A well-paved double-lane superhighway links the two cities. Buses and minibuses usually wait till they're full before leaving. The last sound you'll hear when you leave Rawalpindi is the call of the muezzin echoing from the mosques. It is a sound that will ring in your ears all the way to Islamabad. Mosques – their usual mini-minarets topped with cupolas in a variety of brilliant colours – are jostled next to each other along the whole stretch.

ISLAMABAD

This modern capital of Pakistan, planned like Brasilia or Canberra, was only begun in 1961 and is still far from complete. Laid out over undulating and rolling land it used to be a barren plateau with a few scraggy trees and tufts of green at the foot of the Marghalla Hills. From one or two long, low buildings – the offices of the *Pakistan Times* at Aabphara in 1963 – it has grown into a whole, new city designed by planners and architects of world reputation.

It is divided into residential, business, recreational, industrial, government and religious sections with buildings painted in clean, clear lines that are solid and neat, yet blend harmoniously with the environment. The huge Islamabad Secretariat complex is made up of a series of blocks of long, multi-storey white buildings against a backdrop of green hills, while the State Bank of Pakistan rises in solitary splendour, almost like a tower. Other impressive buildings are the Holiday Inn and the British and American embassies.

The city has numerous high-rise apartments of about 12 to 14 storeys like those in Singapore. The streets and avenues are paved, clean and lined with flowering shady trees that flash with colour in spring. Islamabad is lush and green with many parks and gardens. All the embassies of countries which maintain diplomatic relations with Pakistan are located in this city, as is the University of Quaid-i-Azam. Like any other city in Pakistan there are numerous mosques and shrines, varying in architecture from modern to traditional. One of the most outstanding and one of the largest mosques in the world, the Shah Faisal Masjid, is in the process of being built

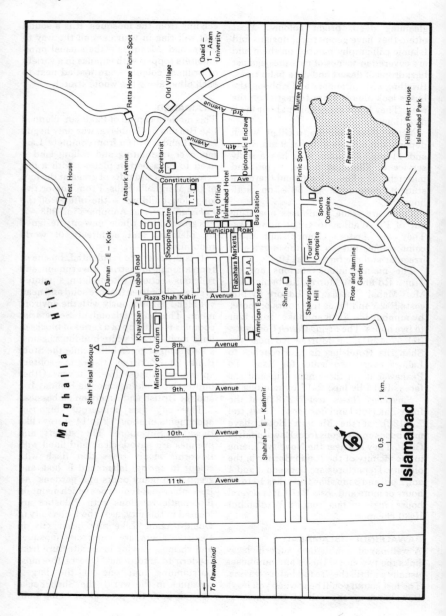

Islamabad

Marghalla Hills

Rest House

Daman – E – Kok

Ratta Hotae Picnic Spot

Old Village

Quaid – 1 – Azam University

3rd. Avenue

4th. Avenue

Diplomatic Enclave

Ataturk Avenue

Secretariat

Constitution Ave

Islamabad Hotel

Post Office

T.T.

Bus Station

Municipal Road

Shopping Centre

Khayaban – E – Iqbal Road

Rabahara Markets

P.I.A.

Raza Shah Kabir Avenue

American Express

Shah Faisal Mosque

Ministry of Tourism

8th. Avenue

9th. Avenue

10th. Avenue

11th. Avenue

Shahrah – E – Kashmir

To Rawalpindi

Muree Road

Rawal Lake

Hilltop Rest House
Islamabad Park

Picnic Spot

Sports Complex

Tourist Campsite

Shakarparian Hill

Shrine

Rose and Jasmine Garden

0   0.5   1 km.

here. Nestling at the foot of the Marghalla Hills on rising land, its gleaming white, tent-like design is extraordinarily arresting. But unlike most other cities in Pakistan, Islamabad has no tongas or bullock carts.

Also noteworthy is the shrine of Bari Immam near the Marghalla foothills. Just across Aabphara, in the wooded area near the Rose & Jasmine Gardens, is Bari Imman's father's shrine. Here fakirs, malangs and pilgrims flock during the saint's *urs* when a *mela* is held. The smell of marijuana hangs heavily in the air and drums (*tabblas*) beat out a frenzied dancing tune that becomes faster and faster. Islamabad would be a quiet place were it not for this local colour.

With its patches of vacant land and streets and roads ending in cul-de-sacs, the city still looks unfinished.

Information

The Tourist Information Centre is in the Islamabad Hotel, Municipal Rd, Ramma 6, and American Express is at Aabphara on the Grand Trunk Rd.

Note that the American Express offices in Rawalpindi and Islamabad have a bad reputation for inefficiency and poor service. The mail service is also unreliable and the wait for replacements for lost travellers' cheques seems endless. It appears that in many instances both mail and travellers' are often there, but staff will not hand them over even if your visa is about to expire the following day, causing a great deal of delay and inconvenience.

The GPO is on Municipal Rd in the Civic Centre, while the Telephone & Telegraph Office is at Shalimar 5. Foreigner's Registration takes place in the office near the GPO at the F-8/3 area near Peshawar Mor. The Ministry of Tourism is on College Rd, F-7/2. Mountaineering and trekking permits are obtained here. Take minibus 1A behind Aabphara Market to get there. Almost all the embassies are in the Diplomatic Enclave on Consitution Avenue.

Visas

India Usually you get your visa the day after you apply for it; sometimes on the same day. Note that the Indian Embassy and consular section are closed on Saturdays.

Iran It takes two weeks to get a reply to your application. Note that it is only in Islamabad that you can apply for a visa for Iran – you cannot get one in Quetta or Peshawar any more. Also the office is closed on Fridays.

Things to See

Among the culturally informative and interesting places in Islamabad are the **Institute of Folk Heritage**, G House No 6, Street 63, F-7/3 with its library of folk music and a museum of musical instruments, folk costumes and jewellery; and the **Pakistan National Council of Arts** on H-4, Street 11, F-7/2, which has an art gallery on Sher Shah Rd.

For sightseeing and relaxation **Daman-e-koh**, on Marghalla Hills, is a terraced garden which offers a scenic view of the whole city. Just off the Grand Trunk Rd is the Shakaparian Hill behind which are the **Rose & Jasmine Gardens** offering a sweeping panorama of both Islamabad and Rawalpindi. Further to the east is **Rawal Lake**, a waterfowl sanctuary where you can go boating and fishing or swimming. Behind the Secretariat Block is the old village of **Nur Shahan** and southeast of this village is the **university**.

Around Islamabad

The **shrine of Bari Imman** is east of Islamabad at the foot of the Marghalla Hills in a wooded, hilly place, usually crowded with pilgrims. A meeting place for townspeople and travellers, it has a completely traditional and mystical atmosphere. Adorned with Shi'ite flags, it reverberates with the beat of drums and dancing, and the smell of dope is almost overpowering. Numerous hawkers and stalls sell tea, food and religious objects.

About eight km west of Rawalpindi is the **shrine of Pir Syed Mir Ali Shah** in the village of Gholra Sharif. In this shrine are man-made caves, now in ruins, where the saint spent much of his time in devotion to Allah. You can stay here free of charge. The site of the shrine is warm but it's often windy. It's situated on hilly ground overlooking distant villages, and offers a great opportunity to see a fascinating, traditional aspect of Pakistan.

You cannot miss seeing the new mosque, **Shah Faizal Masjid**. Like a gigantic white tent at the foot of Marghalla Hills, it dominates the city and is visible from the highway from Rawalpindi.

Also in the foothills, 32 km from Rawalpindi, is the picturesque village of Saidpur with its jumble of stone huts and narrow alleys. The local people are Potoharis, who have developed a unique technique in wheel-turned pottery. Their pottery is aesthetic rather than practical and is engraved, embossed, painted and then glazed with melted, glass powder. If you like pottery buy some here: the output is not great but the quality is magnificent.

Other interesting areas to go to are the **Misriot** and **Mangla** dams. The former, popular for boating and fishing, is 19 km away; while the latter, near Rohtas Fort, is one of the largest dams in the world, and a pleasant place to have a picnic.

North-west of Rawalpindi, 102 km away, is **Hasanabdal**, and north of there is **Tarbela Dam**, the largest earth-filled dam in the world. Permits are required to visit this area but they are available immediately from the Water & Power Development office in Tarbela.

Places to Stay – Bottom End

There are no inexpensive hotels in Islamabad, but there's a *Tourist Camp* opposite the Rose & Jasmine Gardens for Rs5 per person. However, it has recently been used as a 'refugee' camp and has gone to seed. If you do stay here, make sure you don't leave any of your gear unattended, we've had reports that anything not nailed down disappears only to reappear mysteriously later on payment of a substantial fee.

Middle

The *Silk Road House*, 34, Street 4, F-6/3, Islamabad, near the Indonesian Embassy, (tel 2 2495) has singles at Rs60 and breakfast for Rs15, lunch for Rs20 and dinner for Rs25. Two km down Murree Rd from the Tourist Camp and the city centre is the *Garden Inn*, which is modern, has attached bathrooms and air-con, but is a little too far out to be convenient. A price notch up is the *Blue Star Hotel* in the G-8/1 area, which is new and has a pleasant atmosphere. To get there take the bus to Zero Point, then get a Suzuki wagon for Peshawar Mor. If you're near the Islamabad Hotel, British Council Library or the GPO you can get Suzuki wagons to Peshawar Mor for Rs 1. There's a direct bus, 17, to Pir Wadhai from the Blue Star Hotel.

Top End

The *Holiday Inn* on Agha Khan Rd (tel 2 6121) has 122 rooms with singles and doubles for Rs700 and Rs790, and the *Islamabad Hotel* in the Civic Centre (tel 2 7311), has 135 rooms with singles and doubles at Rs400 and Rs475. Just above the American Express on Shahrah-i-Kashmir Rd, the *Ambassador Hotel* has similar rates.

Places to Eat

The cheapies are just behind Aabphara where you can get a meal for Rs5 to Rs8 per person. In front is the *Danbar Restaurant* which has the TV going in the evening, and just round the corner is the *Kamran Restaurant* with local and western food for between Rs20 and 30. There are also Chinese restaurants at Aabphara and the Shalimar Shopping Centre.

Liquor Without exception all bars in all hotels have been closed. If you're thirsty get a Tourist Certificate, then go to the Excise & Tax Office for a permit to buy alcohol. You could also try the American Club.

Getting Around
See Rawalpindi for fares.

Getting Away
See Rawalpindi for details.

MURREE

Fifty-nine km north-east of Islamabad, the hill resort of Murree is one of the most important and most accessible in Pakistan. Murree is 2295 metres above sea level and marks the spot where the Kashmir Himalayan Range begins to descend to the wide Indus plain.

From Islamabad the surfaced road winds up through grassy plains and then through terraced and wooded hills to Company Bagh where it starts to climb steeply to Ghora Ghali. The scenery becomes more mountainous and the hillsides terraced and dotted with mud-stone huts and farm houses. Approaching Murree the mountains which, for most of the way, are bare at the top where they are not terraced, begin to be covered with pine, fir and spruce trees and flowers.

The higher you get the cooler the temperature becomes and the more the architecture changes, having a distinctly mountainous style. The atmosphere of the British era pervades, most buildings generally being post-Victorian red-bricks. To overcome lack of space the majority of buildings are two to three-storeys high and very picturesque with small windows and gabled roofs. They are stacked one on top of the other almost all the way up the hillside.

Murree is only about two km at its longest and half a km at its widest. During the British period living was literally split level, with the British ensconced higher up the hillside than the locals. Today the distinction still holds true, the upper section of town is being more

expensive than the lower one. There are places in Murree which have commanding views of the entire countryside below. In the distance the mountains are such a light blue that they almost merge with the sky. There are some excellent hiking and trekking trails around Murree.

Information

The Tourist Information Centre is near the GPO on Jinnah Rd (tel 2420) and is only open during the season.

Places to Stay

Being a popular tourist resort, Murree tends to be expensive. Guest houses have singles and doubles for Rs30 to Rs120 and Rs60 to Rs200. During the off-season these rates are halved and in early spring rooms are available for only Rs10. *Cecil Hotel*, on Mount View Rd, one of the top places (tel 2257) has singles from Rs225 to 350 and doubles from Rs400 to 525. *Brightlands* on Imtiaz Shaheed Rd, (tel 2 1120), has singles and doubles for Rs200 and Rs300.

Then there's *Abbasi Hotel & Restaurant* which has dorm beds for Rs10. It's in Jhika Ghali, three km north of Murree. Seven km further on at Burbhan is a *Youth Hostel*.

Getting There

Buses leave Rawalpindi at 8 am and Islamabad at 9 am. The trip takes about two hours.

Around Murree

Though part of the Punjab, Murree is an offshoot of that part of the Himalayas that rises to the North West Frontier hill stations of **Ayubia** and **Nathiagali**. There are other lovely resorts – smaller, greener and wooded – but with fewer facilities. These hills are known as *ghalies*, and in the spring there are numerous beautiful walks through the woods and up the slops – all with fine views of the Himalayas.

Stations in the ghalies include **Ghora**

Dhaka, Khanspur, Changlagali and **Khairagali**, the latter having *guest houses* and *rest houses*. Another excellent place to stay is at the *Galliat View Hotel* in Nathiagali. The service here is good and doubles cost Rs30. If you want a splurge you could try the *Pines International*, also in Nathiagali, which has singles for Rs180 and doubles at Rs225. Further north, near the Tourist Information Centre, is *Dine's Hotel*, (tel 505), which has rooms for Rs275.

ABBOTTABAD

North of Murree, at an altitude of 1223 metres, this popular hill station is a transit point for Muzzaffarabad in Azad Kashmir & Jammu to the east, the Kaghan Valley to the north, the Swat Valley to the west and Taxila and Rawalpindi to the south. It was named after Major Abbott, the British officer who 'pacified' the area between 1849 and 1853. This is where Kakul, the West Point or Sandhurst of Pakistan, is located.

Places to Stay

The *Palm* on the Mall, (tel 2241), has 16 rooms with singles and doubles for Rs95 and Rs150 plus 15% tax. Both *Sharban Hotel*, (tel 2376-78) and *Spring Field*, (tel 2334), have doubles only for Rs175.

The *Youth Hostel* is five km north of town on the way to Balakot near Burn Hall Senior School. It costs Rs1 by Suzuki wagon to get there. In the centre of town the *Pine View Hotel* has singles and doubles for Rs25 and Rs35. If you've got a sweet tooth, the *Modern Bakery*, opposite the post office, has a selection of cakes and pastries.

Getting There

The railway line from Taxila terminates about 15 km before Abbottabad at Havelain, leaving you in the middle of nowhere. It's much more convenient to catch a bus as there are regular services between Murree, Taxila and Rawalpindi to Abbottabad.

TAXILA

This famous archaeological site thrived from around 3000 BC to the 16th century. Situated 35 km north-east of Rawalpindi, it is on the railway line, just off the Grand Trunk Rd. Buses are faster than the trains. At an altitude of 500 to 700 metres, Taxila is girdled by the foothills of the Himalayan Kashmir Range. It's flat, semi-arid, and in summer can get uncomfortably warm and dusty. The best time to visit the area is in spring and autumn.

Archaeologically impressive, its structures are made of dry baked mud bricks with cubicles for rooms. Taxila is not a place to spend a few hours before rushing back to Rawalpindi or moving further north. Set aside a day or two, because it is scattered over a wide area. Located north-east of Bhir Mound, the museum alone needs several hours to see.

The remains of Taxila were discovered in 1852 and so far the excavations have

Fasting Buddha Statue,
Taxila Archaeological Museum

revealed three distinct cities. Bhir Mound is the earliest of the three and dates to around 180 BC. To the north-east is Sirkup originally built by the Bactrian Greeks who were followed by the Scythians, who grafted onto it their own structures. The Scythians were in turn followed by the Parthians and later by the Kushans, who transformed it into a great centre of the Gandhara Culture. It eventually became the Buddhist 'Holy Land'.

The excavated site reveals a wide street, south-north in direction, lined with buildings – usually two or three storeys high – with walled-in open courtyards. The most recent, Sirsukh, was founded around 130 AD during the Kushan period, has only been partially excavated. It is surrounded by a five-km long wall.

Things to See

Structures reveal successive waves of invaders settled here. The **Temple of Jandhial**, north of Sirkup, is 2500 years old, and appears to be Zoroastrian – a fire worshipping place – but is built like a Greek temple. Buddhist monasteries and stupas are scattered at **Mohra Moradu**, **Kalwan** and, at the far end, **Jaulian**, which is considered to be the most interesting. The **Stupa of Kunala**, the prince whose eyes were gouged out at the order of his step-mother whom he had scorned, and the **Dharmarajika Stupa**, also known as Chir Tope, are worth seeing.

A visit to the **museum** is a must. Just opposite the PTDC motel, it was opened in 1928 and has a priceless collection of Gandhara busts of the Buddha, the period which produced a style of art which evolved out of the fusion of Graeco-Roman and Indian art forms. Earlier, it must have been neolithic, then a site for the prehistoric Indus Valley Civilisation, then Aryan, followed a millenium later by the Achaemenians and the Greeks. The rulers in this area had enough wisdom not to be antagonistic to Alexander the Great when he arrived.

Other exhibits include **bas reliefs** of the Buddha's life story; gold, bronze, silver and copper coins; kitchen utensils made of copper and bronze; pottery and earthenware jars and utensils; jewellery made of gold and precious and semi-precious stones; a primitive, two-piece condenser made of clay; manuscripts on bark; a marble slab with Aramaic inscriptions; carpenter's and surgical tools and instruments; weights for scales and terracotta children's toys, similar to those discovered in Moenjodaro and Harappa.

Places to Stay

The *Youth Hostel* only accepts card-holding members at Rs8 dorm class, Rs12 a single and Rs20 a double. It's reasonably clean and provides breakfast. If you wish to have lunch or dinner you must let the manager know in advance. A little further on is the *PTDC Motel* where the Tourist Information Centre is. Rooms here cost Rs100 and over plus 15% tax.

Getting There

Taxila is three km off the Grand Trunk Rd to the north beyond the rail tracks. A paved road leads to it and a tonga for six should be about Rs1.50 each. From this direction the Youth Hostel is on the left, surrounded by a high wall and gate.

Around Taxila

About 13 km west of Taxila is a **Sikh Temple** at Hasanabdal. It houses the sacred rock on which Guru Nanak, founder and religious leader of the Sikhs, is said to have left his handprints. The Sikhs call it Panja Sahib; the Moslems know it as Baba Wali. Near here is the tomb of **Lalla Rookh**, and two km away is the **Wah Garden** built by Akbar. The Tarbela Dam is just to the north-west of here and further west the Grand Trunk Rd continues to Attock, Campbelpore and Peshawar.

The Salt Range

A little known, seldom visited area, the Salt Range records 600 million years of the earth's geological evolution and is often described by geologists as the 'Museum of Geology'. Desolate, barren and bleak, even in summer, despite the fact that parts of it are green and fertile with fruit orchards and trees, it was here that the Paleolithic age and pebble culture emerged. It is also the site of Hindu temples, Buddhist monasteries and, more recently, Moslem mosques. This was where the earth cracked and the ocean stagnated until it dried and solidified into salt.

The Salt Range starts at the edge of the Potwar Plateau with the town of Jhelum, heads off south-west, then snakes north-west, turning south just above the Kalabagh towards Bannu and Dera Ismail Khan. Here it reaches an elevation of 600 to 1500 metres. Although superficially not terribly attractive, it is geologically, archaeologically and historically important and has some pleasant spots to visit.

Not far out of Rewat, the road follows the river south to Pind Dadan Khan, 105 km away. About midway along and just off it is **Jallalpur Sharif**, plonked on the edge of the plateau at an elevation of 1100 metres. From here you get a commanding view of the range and the Jhelum River. This was climbed by al-Biruni, a Central Asian Moslem scholar, in the 11th century. Immediately to the south is **Misar Shah**, where a shrine in the style of the Taj Mahal can be seen. This is the area where Bucephalus, Alexander the Great's famous white horse, is believed to have been buried. Lower down and south-west is an ancient fort which overlooks and guards the range and the river.

From **Mandra**, a small town 45 km north-west along the Grand Trunk Rd, a road and railway line turn southward to **Chakwal**, the transit point here. It is five hours by bus from Rawalpindi to here and though the road is surfaced it's still bumpy. The railway line continues to **Bhaun**, but the road turns south-east towards **Choa Said Shah**, a lovely, little town, six km away from **Kutas**, once the site of Buddhist and Hindu temples. Nothing much remains today. About half-way to Kutas is **Dhok Tahlian Dam**, which has a *rest house* and fishing boats for hire.

The road descends for nine km down a steep escarpment with suspension bridges over gorges into **Kewra** where the biggest salt mine in the world exists. The salt seams span the whole length of the range and in some places are crystal clear, while in others are pinkish red. Certain areas, which have been mined, are like huge caves; others are filled with amazingly clear, pure water; still others have stalactites.

If you're going on a tour, check at the Pakistan Mineral Development Corporation here and get a visiting permit. It's advisable to take a torch with you.

The road goes to **Pind Dadan Khan**, site of a Hindu shrine, then crosses the Jhelum River and continues to Sargodha. South-west of Chao Saidu Shah, immediately below Bhaum, is **Kallar Kahar**, a town originally built by Babar. There is a salt lake here, not unlike the Dead Sea, which is the site of the **Buddhist Mahot Temples**, circa 10th century AD. From here the road continues towards Sargodha via Katha and Khusab.

In Khusab it forks into two: one road leading west to Talagang and Fatehgang on to Campbelpore, while the other leads off towards Mianwali. From the Salt Range you can go north to Jhelum, south to Sargodha, east to Lahore or west to Kohat and Peshawar Valley.

Places to Stay

There are medium-priced *hotels* in Chakwal, *rest houses* in Jallalpur Sharif, Choa Saidu Shah and Kewra, and a *Youth Hostel* in Kutas. To get to Kutas take a bus from Chakwal for Chao Saidu Shah.

North-West Frontier Province

Of Pakistan's four provinces, the North West Frontier Province is the smallest with an area, excluding the federally adminstered tribal areas, of only 49,400 square km. The province is almost entirely made up of tribal areas with a few political agencies, that in reality are also tribal, the difference being that they were consolidated into one political entity during the British period and still retain this status. While tribal areas are autonomous, political agencies although they have their own tribal laws are administered by the federal government.

The central government has jurisdiction along the sealed Khyber Pass in the Khyber Agency, but to the north and south of the highway tribal law prevails, as it does south of the Peshawar Valley from Darra to Waziristan. To the north, Bajaur – with the exception of Dir – the Malakhand Division, the Swat Valley, the Hazara district and Chitral, remain tribal. Gradually, their status will be transformed and inevitably they will fall within the jurisdiction of the general law of the land.

All tribal areas are off-limits to westerners as protection cannot be assured them for political reasons which include Afghani refugee encampments, smuggling and others.

Landi Kotal on the Khyber Agency Highway is now closed to foreigners indefinitely due to US pressure to stop the outflow of narcotics. It remains a nexus of smuggling with feuding tribes vying to control the smuggling business. Foreigners are only allowed as far as Jamrud. The Khyber permit beyond Jamrud is available to accredited journalists, diplomats and UNO officials and is not normally extended to anyone else.

The Darra gun factories are also closed to foreigners – again due to US pressure – but you can still travel to Bannu, Dera Ismail Khan and down to Quetta by direct bus. You still need a permit for Loralai from Dera Ghazi Khan. The journey to Quetta has been shortened, but takes time nonetheless.

There are tribal police checkposts at Jamrud on the Khyber Highway and others before Darra on the Peshawar-Kohat Rd.

In some restricted areas, travellers can get to Landi Kotal or Darra – and can make it to other tribal areas – dressed in local garb with woollen cap or turban. But it is too risky here, despite the fact that travellers are often invited by the chiefs of tribes or by Afghan refugees; sometimes to cross the border into Afghanistan. You would be ill-advised to attempt this now, it's far too dangerous. Russian troops have gradually taken control of the border, and in the spring of 1983 they pursued mujahadeens right across the Kurram Agency in Parachinar, took them back into Afghan territory and allegedly executed them.

Although the province is small, it has the most variegated topography, climate, history, social and political set-up in Pakistan. In the south at the border of Baluchistan the land is flat and barren with oases where villages and towns have sprung up. The Indus River forms the natural boundary with the Punjab to the east, while to the west the mountains here form the border with Afghanistan. Higher up the terrain continues to be as barren and forbidding as that of Baluchistan. This is where the Salt Range ends. It continues north and just below the Peshawar Valley it turns south-east skirting the Potwar Plateau.

Beyond the lush valley of Peshawar and the Kabul River the mountainous forest belt rises up from 1000 to over 4000 metres where snow-capped mountains and deep valleys are dissected by bubbling streams. Most of the southern part of the province is out of the monsoon belt and is therefore generally dry and hot. This is the native terriory of the swashbuckling Pathans, a people given to fiercely defending themselves against any invaders as well as to fighting amongst themselves. None of the conquering nations, the Moghuls; the Afghans; the Sikhs and the British were ever able to unite them. They were able to hold onto the Peshawar Valley to safeguard the strategic Khyber Pass, but were forced to leave the Pathans to administer their own laws and fight their own battles.

The North West Frontier was the centre of early civilisations such as the Grave Culture of Dir and Swat, quite different from the Indus Valley Civilisation. Conquered by Cyrus the Great it became a satrapy of Darius in the 6th century BC and later a part of the Hellenic Empire of Alexander the Great in the 4th century BC. The Mauryan and Kushan empires also rose in this region, giving impetus to the development of the Buddhist Gandhara Culture. These civilisations were swept away by successive waves of barbarian invasions: the Bactrian-Greeks, the Scythians, Parthians, the Sassanians, the Hephthalites and the Tartar-Mongol hordes. The establishment of Pax Britannica brought some stability to the region.

There is a theory – unproven – that the Pathans were among the lost tribes of Judea who migrated eastward after Moses, their leader, had been denied the right to settle in the 'Promised Land'. Somewhere, some time along the way, they became Moslems and finally settled in the valleys where they must have became assimilated with the Greeks already settled there. In the isolated valleys these people, and successive invaders, fragmented into different, independant tribal domains.

In the south the Waziristan region is divided into two agencies: the southern and northern political agencies. The southern agency is inhabited by the Mashuds and the Ahmadzais, with the former being dominant. Their principal town of Wanna is connected by sealed road with Tank and Dera Ismail Khan. The northern agency is populated by Utmanzais and Ahmadzai and the capital, Miram Shah, is linked to Bannu. In the upper region are the Kurram Agency and the Peshawar Valley. To the west the Khyber Agency up to Landi Kotal and Torkham is inhabited by Afridis and Azakzais, while in the Malakhand Division and the Hazara district are the Yussufzais and Kohistanis.

Generally the Pathans speak a language called Pushto, but in the isolation of their remote valleys they developed different dialects and fought with one another, tribe against tribe, clan against clan. In the border regions the tribes became professional thieves and lived in a state of continual warfare which was finally halted, and then only partially, with the arrival of the British. Some powerful tribes actually carved out tiny kingdoms or mirdoms, which were to become political agencies during the British era.

The western frontier areas to the south had far easier mountain passes than in the north: some of these were actually used by invaders more often than the northern passes, such as the Khyber Pass. Alexander the Great led his Greek legions over Kot Kala Pass, which is just below Chitral into the region of Dir. In the Parachinar area is the Kurram Pass, while to the south the Tochi and Gomal passes were used by invaders, traders and nomads alike. To a degree these passes contributed to the instability of the region and its continuing poverty. Women are often unable to afford purdahs and simply turn their backs when they come across strangers. Like Baluchistan the women you are likely to see here are invariably nomads. They are treated with the deepest respect and reverence and men automatically move out of their way. Try to observe this yourself if you meet up with one when you're out walking.

In the upper northern region of Chitral the same kind of development of tiny kingdoms or mirdoms took place, but the process went even deeper with the major mirdoms of Chitral attaining some kind of control or influence over other minor mirdoms. The Moghuls did not penetrate as far as this, and the isolated people developed their own peculiar culture, temperament and architecture. The whole of the upper northern region is characterised by their Central Asian influence.

This region has tougher mountain passes which are open only during the summer. From the north, the Tartar-Mongols were the only ones able to scale the passes and penetrate the region, while the Afghans were the sole invaders able to get in from the west. In many ways Chitral belongs to the upper northern mountainous area rather than to the North West Province; it was largely its political evolution that made it part of the latter. After Partition the government of Pakistan took over and continued the process the British had begun, although in many ways the 'restless ... difficult to lead and impossible to control' Pathans seem almost impermeable to alien culture.

Afghan Refugee Camps

Formerly these used to be open to foreigners so long as they had a visiting permit from the Afghan Refugee Commission on Grand Trunk Rd: nowadays you must apply to the State & Frontier Region Division, Civil Secretariat, (tel 2 0624), Islamabad. However generally permits are only issued to accredited journalists, diplomats, UNO or Red Cross officials and members of other charitable voluntary institutions. If a tourist group does get a permit, it is likely that the visit merely means an official guided tour around the camp, and it is most unlikely that a single traveller would get such a permit.

Most of the large Afghan refugee camps are along Jamrud and Charsadda Rds. If you wander into the area you may get invited in by the Afghans themselves, particularly if they are interested in doing business – selling carpets and other items – and talking about their plight. However, care should be taken that no problems arise out of an unofficial visit as the political repercussions are endless. Problems that have arisen in the past which have caused trouble are disagreements over prices of goods, political arguments and hassles with the authorities. The subject of Afghan camps is a potentially explosive political situation which must be treated with great care otherwise many people will be put in jeopardy.

PESHAWAR

The capital city of the North West Frontier Province is a place in transition: some districts are ultra modern; others cling to the romantic past. Historically, this has been the gateway between Central Asia and the subcontinent. It has never quite developed into a great metropolis, although for centuries it was the centre of remarkable civilisations, such as the Gandhara Culture of the Kushan Empire headed by Kanishka (60 AD). This highly sophisticated civilisation had diplomatic, cultural and commercial links with Rome, Persia and China through the ancient Silk Trade Route.

Peshawar is affected by the monsoon and can be warm and uncomfortably humid for part of the year. In winter the atmosphere is completely different, although cold, the landscape is charming and attractive.

Peshawar's strategic location meant that innumerable destructive hordes came, trampled upon it and left it in ruins for the Khyber Pass, though narrow, was not easy to defend. Unlike Lahore, which was able to survive ruinous attacks, recover and prosper, Peshawar was not so resilient. Peshawar's frontline position – the name actually means 'Frontier Town' – contributed to its style of development. It was always a frontier guardpost or a commercial trading place; a place where camel caravans loaded and unloaded; a transit town on the way to Lahore, Delhi or Multan. It was really only with Babar, founder of the Moghul Empire and builder of Peshawar's Bala Hissar Fort, that the city developed a kind of security.

With the decline of the Moghuls the Sikhs came, saw and conquered the region, and then in turn were followed and supplanted by the British, who also had a tough time with the Pathans, but somehow managed to subdue the whole region. Since then it has evolved into what it is now – City of the Pathans – though it remains a dispersal point, a strategic region and recently, a watching post over the troubles afflicting Central Asia.

Information

There is a Tourist Information Centre at Peshawar Airport, and another at Dean's Hotel, (tel 2428), on Shahrah-e-Reza Rd. The Foreigner's Registration Office is on Police Rd; the banks and the GPO are on Saddar Bazaar. The Telegraph & Tele-

phone Office is in the Mall. If you want to visit the tribal areas you should consult the Regional Tourist Officer at Dean's Hotel. The Afghan Consulate, (tel 7 3418) on Sahibzada A Qayyum Rd is still open, but no longer issues visas to foreign tourists, particularly to westerners. Borders have been closed and roads are unsafe. The Iranian consulate, (tel 7 3061) in the same road is open, and it's possible to get a visa for Iran here, but it takes three weeks. Far better to apply for one in Islamabad. There is a British Courier Office, (tel 7 2562), on Khalid Rd.

There are three libraries in Peshawar: the British Council Library, the Mall off Arab Rd; the National Central Library, Cantonment area, opposite the GPO and the Peshawar Municipal Library on Grand Trunk Rd, just a short distance from the Bala Hissar Fort.

Money

The State Bank of Pakistan in Peshawar does not deal in foreign currency. If you

A bakery in Peshawar

need money changed try the National Bank of Pakistan or United Bank Ltd among others.

At Quissa Khani Bazaar there are money changers who will change any currency including Arab and Iranian rials, but for hard currencies only large notes are accepted.

Things to See & Do

If you arrive in Peshawar between the end of April and around mid-May, you're in for a treat. This is festival time, the Khyber Jashne (mela), an almost month-long celebration.

Old City

Just like its counterparts in the Punjab or Sind, the old city of Peshawar is a maze of narrow lanes, buildings with overhanging trellised balconies, bazaars, local inns, eating places and mosques. It is the busiest and most bustling area of the city and is usually crowded with gun-toting Pathans, colourfully clad in turbans and long flowing quamis and baggy shalwars that resemble pyjamas. It is here that you sense Peshawar's exotic frontier atmosphere most strongly.

An extension of the old city continues behind **Saddar Bazaar** where the familiar old buildings, muzzaffar khanas, mosques and bazaars have cropped up. The alleys here are narrow and local eating places have their kitchens out front with hunks of meat hanging from smoke-darkenened ceilings, large frying pans sizzling with ghee, baskets filled with red tomatoes and fresh onions and everything reeking of curry powder. It's only a few steps from here to the main Saddar Bazaar, the really modern section of the city.

The city is surrounded by the ruins of a wall which used to have 20 gates. Within these walls are bazaars with twisting streets that have trading quarters for businesses as esoteric as sword-making. The Kabul Gate leads to one of Peshawar's most famous streets, the **Kissa Kahani** – Street of Story-Tellers –

where all the tall tales are supposed to be swapped over endless cups of green tea and hookahs. Nearby is the **Bater Bazen** named after the bird market that used to be here, but now a centre for copper and brassware. Also in this area is the **Mochilara** – the shoemakers – **Bazaar**, the place to go for an exotic pair of embroidered Pathan chappals. Near the **Gunj Gate** is a 2nd century BC stupa, a wooden building with 13 tiers crowned by an iron steeple, called **Shahji-ki-Dehri**. Close to it are the ruins of a large Buddhist monastery built during the Kushan period by King Kanishka.

British City

The British left the old city intact, just as they had done elsewhere, and grafted on a new section which began as a military cantonment. Eventually the ubiquitous Mall emerged, typically lined with large, shady trees behind which are the government buildings, the churches, official residences, the banks, library, travel agencies and now Chinese restaurants. The **Saddar Bazaar** has become the city centre and a buffer zone between the old and the new where the shops, cinemas, local modern hotels, cafes and restaurants are. A block away is the Mall which is beginning to lose its Victorian style as new buildings emerge. Like other malls in Pakistan it has a sedate and quiet atmosphere and hints of the British era still live on in the old military buildings with their cannons. There is also a little of the Moghul period to be found in the architecture of old buildings and in the Moghul gardens, such as the **Khalid Bin Walid Garden** and the **Shahi Bagh**, which is on the Charsada Rd.

Museum

On the Grand Trunk Rd in the Cantonment area the museum was originally the Victoria Memorial Building. It has a particularly fine collection of objects from the Graeco-Buddhist Gandhara period. In the north-east of the city is the **Mahabat**

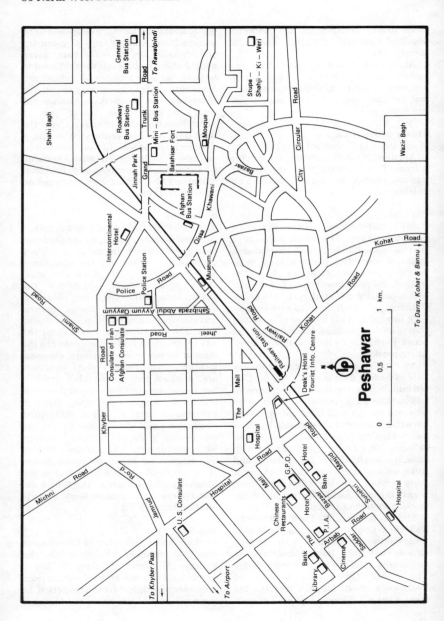

Peshawar

Khan Mosque. There is also an art gallery, **Abasin Art Gallery.**

Bala Hissar Fort

Originally built by Babar in 1519 on the north-west edge of the city. In its present form it dates from the Sikh period (1791-1849) when they controlled the Peshawar Valley. Today it is being used, once again, as a military fort. While no tourists are allowed in, the Bala Hissar Fort is clearly visible from most parts of Peshawar and occasionally you will see tanks and heavy military trucks surrounding it.

Around Peshawar

Jamrud Fort, 15 km from Peshawar, is a rambling collection of towers and walls, and a major landmark on the Khyber Pass. It's now military property and also off-limits to foreigners. **Charsada,** 29 km north-east of Peshawar, captured by Alexander the Great in 324 BC, has been identified as the pre-Kushan capital. Apples, pears, peaches and apricots grow in profusion in this region. The **Warsak Dam,** 29 km north of Peshawar, deep inside tribal territory on the banks of the Kabul River, is upheld as a symbol of changing tribal attitudes.

Places to Stay – Bottom End

The cheapies are generally in the bazaar area, but the *Rainbow Hotel* and the *National*, Khyber Bazaar, are reasonably clean, have fans and dorm accommodation with four to six beds for Rs12.50, singles for Rs15 and doubles for Rs25. *Kamran Hotel*, nearby is better and has reasonable food. Then there is the *Khyber Hotel*, Saddar Bazaar, which has fans and share bathrooms – hot water – and costs Rs12.50 for a single and Rs24 for a double. *Al Kharim* is also popular with travellers. Slightly more expensive is the *Moonlight Hotel & Restaurant* on Saddar St – the food here is also OK. There are other hotels around with rooftop beds that are fine in summer for Rs5.

The *Youth Hostel* on the university campus on Jamrud Rd is too far out of town to be convenient. There is a camp site about 100 metres from Jan's Hotel which costs Rs10 for a car and two people.

Middle

Jan's Hotel, Islamia Rd (tel 7 3006), just off Saddar Bazaar, is across from the bus stop and has singles and doubles at Rs60 and Rs85. Rooms with air-con are also available. The *Habib Hotel*, Khyber Bazaar, is next to *Rainbow Hotel*, with similar prices to Jan's, but it has a higher standard, better food and for a small fee you can have a long, relaxing soak in a nice bath. Nearby is the similarly priced, *Park Hotel*. The *Neelab Hotel* in Khyber Bazaar (tel 7 4255) has singles and doubles at Rs25 and Rs50.

Gul's Hotel, Saddar St, previously International Hotel, has singles at Rs21 or doubles for Rs34, while *Hotel Shahzad* down the same street is modern and has the same rates. *Sabir Hotel*, just off Saddar St on Chowk Fewara, is similar with singles for Rs21, doubles for Rs40 and family rooms for Rs50. It also has an excellent restaurant, particularly good for traditional Pathan food, but offers a western-style breakfast as well.

Top End

The *Hotel Khyber InterContinental*, Khyber Rd, (tel 7 6361) has 150 rooms; singles cost Rs460; and doubles Rs520. It has everything from a coffee shop to a swimming pool and tennis courts: but the bar is now out of business. The PTDC-run *Dean's Hotel* is at 3 Islamia Rd (tel 7 6481-4), and has 47 rooms with singles and doubles for Rs200 and Rs350 plus taxes. There is also *Green Hotel* on Saddar St which has single rooms at around Rs150 and the *Hotel Galaxie* (tel 7 3041), in Soekarnu Square with singles for Rs75 and doubles for Rs150.

Places to Eat

The cheaper eating places are along and

behind Saddar Bazaar and in the old city in the bazaar area. You can get good food here for Rs6 to Rs8. Cheaper still are the Khyber and Quissa bazaars where you can get kebabs, burgers, nan, fish and tea. Try the *Salatin Hotel* for a splurge on excellent Pakistan dishes. For western food go to *Dean's* for a meal costing between Rs25 and Rs35. There are two Chinese restaurants in the Mall, the *HongKong* and *Nanking*, with the usual Chinese menu for Rs35 and over. On Arbab Rd near the cinema there is a good ice-cream parlour.

Liquor Peshawar is not a 'dry' city. You can get alcohol in any of the 5-star hotels, but get a liquor permit from the Excise & Tax Office first.

Getting Around

Taxis within city limits are Rs7, while auto-rickshaws are generally around Rs5. The meters on the latter usually aren't working, so get the fare sorted out before you take a ride. Tongas are Rs2 to Rs3 between bus stations and the bazaar area. Numerous buses ply between Saddar Bazaar, bazaars in the Old City and bus stations on Grand Trunk Rd for Rs0.75 and Rs1.25.

Getting Away

Rail Travellers usually take buses for Torkham or Rawalpindi since they are more comfortable, less crowded and faster. You don't need a tourist certificate for rail concessions in Peshawar, just present your passport. This is only true of Peshawar, no other Pakistan city.

Air The *PIA* office is at the corner of Arbab Rd and the Mall: concessions are available here. From Peshawar to Chitral there are one or two flights daily for Rs130, while from Peshawar to Saidu Sharif there are three flights weekly for Rs95.

Embarkation airport tax is Rs5.

Bus There are a number of bus stations around Peshawar: *Soekarno Chowk* has buses going to Landi Kotal, Torkham, Jallalabad and Kabul; *Broadway House* on the Grand Trunk Rd has buses for Darra, Kohat, Bannu and Dera Ismail Khan. There is a minibus station near Bala Hissar Fort, which has services to Mardan, Swat, and Dir, while the *Central Bus Terminus* on Grand Trunk Rd, opposite the Royal Hotel, has buses for Attock, Hasanabdal, Taxila and Rawalpindi. Buses depart to most destinations almost every hour between 6 am and 6 pm.

Peshawar-Rawalpindi	Rs15	three hours
Peshawar-Torkham	Rs 8	two hours
Peshawar-Dir	Rs20	seven hours
Peshawar-Mingora	Rs18	six hours

THE KHYBER PASS

This famous historical pass is in the Sulaiman Hills in the Western Border Mountains. About 1000 metres high, the pass is 1-1/2km at its widest and only 16 metres at its narrowest. It's reckoned to begin at Jamrud Fort and end at Torkham, 58 km away.

In the Khyber Agency, this is the only Afghan outpost to be annexed by the British. Its recorded history is long and colourful and begins with the arrival of the Achaemenians, followed by the Greek legions of Alexander the Great, who were in turn succeeded by a series of invading hordes who thundered through on their way to the lush valley of Peshawar, tapering off with the British-Indian expeditionary forces who marched in so bravely and stumbled out so disastrously. Numerous memorials were carved on the rock faces to the British-Indian regiments who gradually wrested the pass from the Pathans and the Afghans.

Looking toward the pass from Afghanistan, the scene is one of dry, barren mountains, a dark-reddish brown, slashed with dashes of green on the slopes, and desert stretching shimmering white under the clear blue sky. The road, twisting between narrow granite walls, seems in a hurry to get to Peshawar.

The are immigration and customs posts at Torkham, the border town here, which has shops, hotels, cafes, restaurants, banks, bakeries and government offices. Most of the buildings are low-roofed and seem to huddle together as if for security. It's quite unlike Taftan, the border town for Iran in Baluchistan, where the buildings are scattered. Landi Kotal, the next town along towards Peshawar, is very much the same. Beyond this everything is dry, barren and flat, but there is not the sense of desolation there is on the Salt Range. Landi Kotal is famous for its smuggling and items from all over the world are openly on sale here at astonishingly low prices.

This is now the Khyber Agency, a tribal political agency, where signboards begin to appear by the roadside warning motorists not to wander off the main highway. Only along this metalled highway do the laws of Pakistan apply: tribal laws take over on either side of the road.

The buildings here all look alike: walls are usually made of mud mixed with straw and clay – sometimes cement – and they are the only structures you can see from the outside. You will rarely see any women, apart from the nomadic tribeswomen, who are usually dressed in red or maroon. The black and grey tents of the nomads hug the sand, while camels wander around grazing on the sparse vegetation. You will also see children, young shepherds and shepherd-esses and their little flocks of sheep and goats. Except for the nomads, all the men appear to be literally armed to the teeth.

As you approach Peshawar the land becomes greener and less wild, and the turbans, guns and bandoliers give way to urban denizens in western attire.

The Afghanistan border is still officially open but in practice it's virtually closed. Likewise the Afghan consulate is, in theory, open for business as usual, but in fact is closed. There used to be a daily bus from Peshawar to Kabul, but the service has been reduced to one bus a week now. A barrier consisting of a waist-high barb-wire fence with an opening is now part of the scenery at Landi Kotal. There are also numerous signs including a 'Welcome to Pakistan' sign, a warning to get to Peshawar by nightfall and a small board on the Afghani side with a few propaganda posters plastered on it in Urdu. If you make it to Torkham, you can spend the night at the *PTDC motel* there, although it seems rather a dubious proposition as Afghani rebels reportedly took Torkham over for a short time in late 1983. If you intend returning to Peshawar on the same day, take the train back from Landi Kotal at 2.20 pm. It arrives in Peshawar at 5.50 pm. Check the train schedule before you start out for Landi Kotal as it's a once-weekly service.

DARRA

Only 42 km south of Peshawar, the town of Darra is in a tribal area, on the main highway to Kohat and Bannu. Recently, foreigners have been banned from visiting this town, but this could change – the restriction may be lifted at any time. Ask around before you attempt to go there.

If you do manage to find your way there, it's an attractive little place with one main bazaar lined with shops, local hotels and places to eat. At first glance it looks like any other small town, but when you take a look at the shops you will be struck by display after display of a surprising commodity: guns and weapons of all types both locally manufactured and imported (smuggled). Darra is the arms capital of the North West Frontier Province and here even pens and walking sticks may conceal lethal weapons. It has been manufacturing guns or making perfect replicas of foreign firearms and supplying the warring tribes for over a century. Despite this, Darra doesn't seem to have prospered as much as one would expect, and is still a smallish town.

Apart from guns and heavier weapons, the local people seem to deal in every kind of contraband you can think of, including marijuana and heavier drugs and not merely in kilograms but in tonnes. On this scale even illegal businesses acquire a kind of legitimacy and deals are made quite openly, without fear of any interference from the authorities. Strangers, however, are likely to find themselves hassled by the police should they try to dabble! Darra is not a sinister place, despite its nefarious businesses. Hot and dusty though it is, Darra has become something of a tourist attraction.

SOUTH TO DERA ISMAIL KHAN

On the way to Dera Ismail Khan from Peshawar, you will go through Kohat, a largish, bustling township, and Bannu 189 km away and 4½ hours by bus. Eventually you will arrive in Dera Ismail Khan, 340 km south of Peshawar. If you don't have a permit to travel through the Waziristan area and Fort Sandeman in Baluchistan, you cannot take the direct route to Quetta from here. An alternative is to head directly south to Dera Ghazi Khan in the Punjab, but from there you again need a permit if you want to head west through Loralai to Quetta.

Parachinar in the Kurram Agency is another tribal area where a special permit is required. Apparently the restriction is not merely because it is a tribal area, but because of its proximity to Kabul, which is less than 100 km away. Kohat, Bannu and Dera Ismail Khan are all fairly large towns with moderately priced hotels, but they are generally only transit towns with tongas and rickshaws for getting around.

Although the country is green just out of Peshawar, it gradually becomes dry again and is dominated by barren hills and mountains. The route passes through the scenic Darra Pass with mountains to one side and wide plains below. A little beyond Kohat you will see the craggy, jagged Salt Range in the distance. In summer the dry, white powdery salt looks almost like wind-blown snow. The bleak, desolate landscape is wholely alien, grim and forbidding, but

has its own fascination, and once again becomes greener and flatter towards Bannu.

Bannu is smaller than Kohat, a peaceful place. Beyond the town the land remains flat and green most of the to Dera Ismail Khan, 145 km further on and 3½ hours by bus. But slowly it becomes dry again and sandy with the horizon shimmering in the distance. Dera Ismail Khan is a fairly large, sprawling oasis, the last major town in the south of the North West Frontier Province. Immediatley south is Baluchistan and to the south-east is the Punjab. About 20 km before Dera Ismail Khan is another Indus Valley Civilisation archaeological site known as Rehman Dheri. It is built to the same design and in the same materials as the other cities of Moenjodaro and Harappa.

The next nearest town is Dera Ghazi Khan, 256 km away in the Punjab, and six hours by bus. Usually buses go to Multan, but you can get off at Taunsa and from there take another bus. Dera Ghazi Khan is another fairly largish town, more developed than Bannu or Dera Ismail Khan, but still quite provincial. From here you can either proceed to Multan back to Lahore or continue straight to Karachi, Jacobabad and then to Quetta, or alternatively through Loralai to Quetta if you have a permit.

Note that tribal areas are generally restricted to tourists. Waziristan in particular is semi-wild, a place where feuding continues and kidnapping for ransom is still practised. Houses here are generally fortified with towers and men are always suspicious and armed.

Southward to Dera Ismail Khan there is a small-gauge train to Bannu, but it's virtually unused and most of the stations along the way are closed. The road leads down from Peshawar to Kalabagh where you can either go into the Salt Range in the Punjab or down to Mianwali, a small town, similar to Dera Ismail Khan. From Mianwali travelling further south is generally by bus or train, both of which are irritatingly slow, particularly in the hot season when you would probably prefer to explore on your own along the banks of the Indus on this side of the Punjab.

Exploration of the banks of the Indus is also possible on the North West Frontier Province side, where you may encounter tribes that sill live on the islands in the Indus River. There is a ferry that plies between towns along the river as well as pontoon bridges that span it, which allow you to travel from one little-visited village to another.

Try to avoid travelling around here during the summer and monsoon period up to October as its scorchingly hot on either side of the Indus then. It's semi-wasteland, mottled with desert scrub, flat at times, undulating at others, with a sparse covering of trees and interspersed oases. During the winter from December to February you'll find it a lot easier to move around and observe the culture of the different tribes. Further south you may even come across tribes with unique cultures.

NORTH TO CHITRAL

From Peshawar you can travel north, visiting a number of interesting archaeological sites to the Swat Valley or Chitral via Dir. The north-east of the Peshawar Valley has a concentration of archaeological sites of the Gandhara period, like nowhere else in Pakistan. Along the road to Chitral via Dir is **Charsada** (2nd century BC) and nearby is **Pushkalavati**, the Lotus City, capital of the Mauryan Empire. Originally this consisted of three cities: Bala Hissar founded in the 6th century BC; Shaikhan Dehri, the second city founded by the Bactrian-Greeks in the 2nd century BC; and Prang, the third city, which is still to be excavated. Charsada has an ancient Buddhist stupa known as the **Eye Gift**, and near this are the remains of an ancient Greek town.

Takht-i-Dehri, 44 km away from Mardan, is a well preserved Buddhist monastery with monks' cells, halls of stupas,

assembly halls and meditation rooms below. Uphill is a marvellous view of the plains of Mardan to the south and to the north is the Malakhand Pass. Three km from here is **Shari Balelol**, a village which, when excavated, revealed a walled city and a Buddhist monastery with well preserved Gandhara sculptures. Local people here make a living producing perfect replicas of the stonework. **Kotlang**, 24 km away, is known for pink topaz and is another archaeological Buddhist site.

On the road to Swabi is Shahbaz Ghari, the site of Ashoka's rock inscriptions, which reveal his remorse for the destruction and terrible slaughter in the Kalinga Kingdom of eastern India. One of the trails of the Silk Trade Route passed through this area. At Swabi, the road forks off to the left to Tarbella and to the right to Attock. Not far away is Hund.

The road continues on to Mardan, 65 km away. The ruins of a Buddhist monastery at **Chanaka Dehri** are interesting and really worth a visit. Up a hill on the same Malakhand Rd is another Buddhist site. This is the region described by Churchill as a land with 'savage brilliancy' and it was here where, impatient to get into action, he is said to have developed a taste for whisky. The Malakhand Pass begins at Dargai and the drive is particularly scenic. There is a fort at the top of a hill on the left, and on the other side is **Bhat Khela**, which has a Hindu fort perched just above it.

The Malakhand Rd splits up at Chakdara; one fork leading to Chitral via Dir, the other leading towards the Valley of Swat. The landscape from the foothills to the top of the Hindu Kush is scarred and eroded and the road runs through wide, flat valleys which narrow further north through the Malakhand Pass, then widen again to Chakdara and the Swat Valley. It continues to open out until you reach Dir, a transit town and gateway to Chitral via the 3125-metre Lowari Pass. There are some reasonable clean, medium-class hotels around the bus station in Dir if you want somewhere to stay overnight.

Further to the east is Hund, formerly known as Udabhanpur – City of Waterpots. The Indus was once crossed here with the aid of huge waterpots. It was here that Genghis Khan finally caught up with Jallaludin, emperor of the Khwarzem Empire, who had murdered the Mongol emissaries. One of the routes of the ancient Silk Trade went through this region and it was also once a Buddhist centre of pilgrimage. While crossing the Indus on his way back to China, Xuan Zhang (643 AD) lost every one of the irreplaceable Buddhist manuscripts he had collected in India. Further up on the way to to Buner and Butkhara there are other archaeological sites of neolithic, primitive rock shelters, carvings and inscriptions.

PESHAWAR TO RAWALPINDI

If you loop north from Peshawar, you rejoin the Grand Trunk Rd at Nowshera, a reasonably large town, and just across the Indus is Hund, which is difficult to get to unless you have your own transport. This ancient route is now sealed, and is not only of historic importance but also scenic. The old fort here with its great battlements and ramparts guards the route to Lahore and Delhi. Built by Akbar in 1583, it covers the crest of a hill and slopes down to the banks of the Indus. A few km east, where buses usually stop for tea, is an old Moghul structure right in the middle of the highway. It was erected to John Nicholson, a slightly strange British officer, who died in the assault of Delhi following the Indian Mutiny.

The road continues through Hasanabdal, another fair-sized town, and the rest of the way to Taxila. The sandstone hills on the south side of the highway are honeycombed with holes which are actually doorways dug by cave-dwelling gypsies. They live here much in the manner of the gypsies of Andalusia in southern Spain.

Taxila is the next stop after Hasanabdal and you can get buses from either of these places to Abbottabad in the Hazara district. From there make your way up to the Kaghan Valley or to Muzzaffarabad in Azad Kashmir & Jammu, then loop back down through Murree to Rawalpindi.

Marco Polo Sheep

Baluchistan

West of the Indus Plains is Baluchistan, the largest province in Pakistan with an area of about 343,000 square km. But though it's bigger than the British Isles, it only has a population of about one million, due mainly to its daunting arid geography.

In the south of the province, Makran is almost entirely desert with low, dry hills rising from 300 metres to 2500 metres in the north. In the west there is a large salt lake, Hammum-i-Maskhel and more expansive, desert plains. This is where the Chagai and Toba Kakar Mountain Ranges form the borders of Iran, Afghanistan and Pakistan. Around Quetta and Ziarat are fertile plateaux, but to the east tracts of desert and semi-wasteland are dissected by the Sulaiman Ranges which stretch south-north through the Khulu Agency up to the Waziristan area of the North West Frontier Province. There are four reasonably big rivers here which include the Zhob, Porali, Hingal and Dasht – all flowing south.

Baluchistan is outside the monsoon zone and has, with the exception of the hilly and arid mountainous regions, a pleasant climate. In winter the temperature falls to as low as $-30°C$ while in summer it soars from $18°$ to $30°C$. The province has been influenced by the civilisations in the Indus, Dir and Swat Valleys. One of the oldest neolithic sites (6000 BC) is to be found at Mehr Ghar, just south of Bolan Pass. This culture faded away in 3000 BC about the same time that the Indus Valley Civilisation emerged.

The Indus Valley influence emerged in the Kutli Culture of Sind in the south of Baluchistan while the Dir and Swat Culture (grave culture – 1500 to 600 BC) emerged in the Red Ware or Zhat Culture and the Buff Culture of northern Baluchistan. Along with Sind, the Punjab and part of the North West Frontier Province, Baluchistan fell under the sway of the Achaemenian Empire in the 6th century BC. Archaeological findings indicate that in the 1st century AD the Kushan Empire also had some influence and that Buddhism thrived and flourished in Baluchistan until the re-emergence of Hinduism in the 5th century AD. The latter endured until Islam burst into the region in the 7th century AD.

The Baluchs are believed to have formed part of the armu of the Achaemenian emperor, Kaikhurso – Cyrus the Great (558 to 530 BC). A thousand years on they re-appeared in history as part of the standing army of the Sassanain king, Nausheran (531 to 578 AD), marching towards Hindustan in the 5th century AD. In the 7th century AD, they appeared as supporters of Imman Ali, and after the Karbala they were again on the march towards Persia, only to turn up in the 10th century AD with Mahmud of Ghazni. After that they attached themselves to every conquering Moslem horde of the subcontinent and finally settled in this region when Barbar appeared on the scene.

Fiercely independent Baluchistan never really became part of the Moghul Empire, but effectively remained an autonomous frontier tributary. In India they fought the Hindus and gained some influence in the Punjab and Sind. In order to survive they expediently changed their loyalty and allegiance when necessary: now with the Moghuls, then the Persians and the Afghans, but their constant was the fight for Islam. When the Moghul power declined they took on the Sikhs, the Marathis and finally the British, who arrived in 1841.

When they were not fighting wars to prop up Moslem empires they pursued brigandage in the same manner as the Khanjuts of Hunza, waylaying camel caravans or plundering villages in the deserts. They were later described as 'races of barbarous people who inhabit the mountains ... whose employments are fighting and shedding blood'. Due to these 'wild tribes on the banks of the Indus' who were 'war-like' and 'good arches', the Baluchistan desert region became a 'no-man's land belonging to no province where robbers from every district found shelter and where permanent villages, except in three instances, were conspicuously absent'.

Makran, once a thriving region with its capital in Panjgur and a commercial entrepot in Tiz with 'great warehouses, palm groves and a beautiful mosque, with people of all nations', simply dried up.

When the British came in 1841, the Baluchs gave them the toughest fight they ever had on the subcontinent. They were reckless fighters, often throwing away their matchlocks to attack with the sword, only to fall to bullets and bayonets. Since their defeat they seem to have lived in a non-existent world, isolated in their inhospitable land, they reminisce about their romantic exploits of the past, and cling desperately to a tribal way of life.

In the war of independence in 1947, they supported the political goal of Quaid-i-Azam for a separate Moslem state, never quite being able to surrender their autonomy and independence, and consequently giving the Pakistan government a hard time for quite a while. Despite continuing problems, Baluchistan is an integral part of the country, fairly prosperous, and potentially immensely rich in mineral resources, which so far remain in the ground. Today, while Baluchistan is largely tribal from the Khulu Agency up to Fort Sandeman in the north and Kalat to Las Bela and the Makran coast in the south, it is gradually being weaned away from tribalism and drawn into the orbit of modern civilisation.

When the British finally defeated the Baluchs, they found that there were no cities or towns in the province, just villages and tribes. And to this day the majority of the people are nomads who migrate to the hills in spring and summer with their cattle, goats, sheep, camels, donkeys and horses, where they set up tents-*khizdis*-and huts-*jhuggis*-made of twigs and branches of trees, grass, reeds

Camel Caravan in the Baluchistan Desert

or straw. In the winter they retreat to mud huts on the plains. All the towns in Baluchistan – Quetta, Ziarat, Sibi, Fort Sandeman, Loralai and others – were built by the British. Except for these strategic areas, the British left the region alone.

They blasted tunnels through the mountains for rail tracks to Quetta and from here to Taftan in the west, Chaman in the north-west and Fort Sandeman in the north. In the main, they only set up military cantonments and tentative administrative centres. Even now Baluchistan appears to be a place where progress is almost an aberration. Apart from Quetta most places are still really villages or towns, most of them around oases and separated by hundreds of km of sand. Basically, the villages are hidden deep in the valleys of the mountains, while the plains are left to the nomads.

Baluchistan is where the alternative route of the Euro-Asian Highway passes from Zahedan in Iran to Taftan in Baluchistan and on to Quetta. Another alternative road turns south from Kandahar in Afghanistan into Chaman in Baluchistan: this is the route for freight bound for Afghanistan arriving through Karachi harbour. Apart from its importance as a transit area, there are mineral resources which are just beginning to be tapped. The Sui district has one of the largest gas deposits in the world.

Baluchistan is a province of contrasts. It has some of the bleakest landscape in the country with grim, jagged mountains, barren and arid land where the the sparse greenery shrivels and wilts, but hidden away are some stunningly beautiful places.

QUETTA – CITY OF THE BALUCHS

The capital city of Baluchistan has none of the Moghul features of other major cities of the subcontinent, no ancient bazaars, grand forts or beautiful palaces. Nor does it have the spectacular structures of the British era. Its history begins with the arrival of Islam in the 10th century with the Chakkars laying the foundation of the city, but it declined largely because of internecine fighting, and in 1730 came under the ruler of Kalat. In 1935, a disastrous earthquake virtually wiped out the city and all the present buildings date from that time. Today it has a population of over 100,000 and although it is of no particular interest in itself, it is an important crossroads with routes leading into Afghanistan and Iran. Situated at 1700 metres, the city is a pleasant escape from the heat of the plains in summer, but it gets extremely cold in the winter. Its name is derived from the Pushto word *kwatta*, which means fort.

Information

The Tourist Information Centre (tel 7 3223, 7 3011, 7 2053) is at Quetta Airport, Jinnah Rd. There is an Afghani Consulate (tel 7 4160), in the Mall and an Iranian Consulate (tel 7 5054) on Hali Rd. The office of the Deputy Commissioner is on the corner of Shahrah-e-Iqbal and Club Rds. The main banks are on Jinnah Rd in the town centre and the GPO is in the Mall.

Liquor permits are available from the Excise & Tax Office on Alandar Rd where all the licensed liquor shops are.

City

Originally the fort was all there was to Quetta which guarded the overland approaches to the western frontier for at that time the capital was at Kalat in the south. The British-built city was laid out in blocks with the Mall, which they could never do without, set in a quiet, attractive area. Around this administrative centre the rest of the city clustered.

Today it is spacious and, unlike most cities, does not suffer from traffic congestion. Apart from the bazaars, which are bustling and colourful, the city is quiet and the houses spaced well apart with walled-in compounds and lawns. There are many shady trees which emphasise the quiet and sedate atmosphere. Today

Quetta is prosperous and flourishing, partly because of its continuing military importance, but mainly because it is a transit point and commercial centre for Iran and Afghanistan.

Things to Buy

Baluchistan produces some of the finest carpets in Pakistan as well as the most beautiful embroidery works, usually in strong, vibrant colours with geometrical patterns inlaid with tiny mirrors.

Around Quetta

Chiltan Hill on Brewery Rd is a good vantage place for a view of the surrounding country. Ten km out of town the greenish-blue waters of **Lake Hanna** encircled by brick-red hills is a pleasant place to visit. A further 11 km brings you to **Urak Tangi**, which is enchanting with its mass of flowers and delicious fruit. **Pishin**, 50 km away, is another region noted for its fruit; apples, peaches, plums, apricots and grapes. Then there's **Bund Khusdil Khan**, 18 km away, which is a sanctuary for migratory birds in winter.

Places to Stay – Bottom End

The *Allah-Wallah Hotel*, MA Jinnah Rd has singles and doubles for Rs30 and Rs50 and nearby is the *Muslim Hotel & Restaurant*, which is fairly clean, modern and has singles and doubles for Rs25 and Rs45. You can also get a *charpoi-bed* in the open for Rs5.

There are other places on the same street. Close to the New Adda bus station and handy for Taftan is the *Osmani Hotel*, run by an English-speaking Afghani. Dorm bed accommodation costs Rs15 in a new building which, unfortunately, seems to be riddled with mosquitoes. On Shirki Rd also near the Taftan bus terminal, the *Mohammed Tanzabee Hotel* has attached toilet/shower and dorm beds for Rs10, Rs15 a double and a family – four-bed – room for Rs30. This is a practical place to stay overnight if you're on your way to Iran via Taftan or if you have just arrived from Zahedan. It is open till 11 pm and so is the restaurant, which has reasonable food for Rs5. There is also an interesting bazaar in the area, seldom visited by tourists.

If you want to camp, Lourdes, has a camping ground for Rs10 per vehicle.

Middle

Shabistan Hotel on Shahrah-e-Adalat St has attached bathrooms, singles and doubles for Rs25 and Rs35, while the *Hotel Zufaqhir* is clean and has a pleasant courtyard and a good restaurant for almost the same rates. The *Asia Hotel* is also clean, has share bathrooms and costs Rs25 for a single and Rs40 for a double. Most medium-class hotels are along Shahrah-e-Adalat St, just off MA Jinnah Rd.

Top End

The *Lourdes Hotel* (tel 7 0168-9) on Staff College Rd has 27 rooms with singles and doubles for Rs116 to Rs185. There are additional charges for heating in winter. Other hotels with the same or higher standards and rates are along MA Jinnah Rd.

Warning In winter, Quetta is snowy and cold, but there are no problems about accommodation – there's plenty around. However, in summer while the weather is not over-bearingly hot, accommodation

A Pathan man
B In the bazaar in Peshawar
C Gilgit

can be a problem because many Pakistanis retreat to Quetta from the lowland heat of Sind and the Punjab. *Hotels* – from the cheapest to the most expensive, including the *railway retiring rooms* – are often fully booked. The only alternative available is the *charpoi-beds* in the open. Lock your luggage in a storeroom for Rs5.

Places to Eat

All the cheaper restaurants are along MA Jinnah Rd between the railway station and the city centre. A meal costs about Rs5 and there is a cinema where you can get kebabs with nan for Rs4. Good, cheap local food can also be found in the bazaar area for Rs5 to Rs8. In the city centre in an alley next to the PTDC Tourist Information Centre there are food stalls which have legs of lamb – *sajji* – roasting from early morning until evening for Rs25 apiece.

More expensive places can be found in the upper-medium class hotels on MA Jinnah Rd in the city centre where western-style meals are the go. On the same road near the PIA office and the Pakistan National Bank is *China Cafe*, if you want a Rs25 to Rs35 splurge. There are other expensive places on Princes Rd.

Getting Around

Local There are a few taxis here, but the most common method within the city limits is by auto-rickshaw for Rs2 or rickshaws and tongas for slightly less. Generally there are no hassles about fare payments here, but it is still advisable to negotiate payment before getting on.

Getting Away

Rail Railway concessions are available from the superintendent's office in front of the station. From Quetta to Karachi there are four trains daily and the trip takes 16 to 18 hours.

Fares:	
Air-con	
sleeper	Rs500
seat	Rs277
First class	
sleeper	Rs215
seat	Rs121
ordinary	Rs94
Second class	
mail	Rs64
ordinary	Rs50

Air *PIA* office is on Jinnah Rd. Concession is also available here if you're entitled to it. Fares are:

	flights	Rs
Quetta-Karachi	four weekly	535
Quetta-Lahore	four weekly	645
Quetta-Rawalpindi	three weekly	680

Bus There are hourly buses in the morning from the Sariab Rd bus station to Taftan. Fares are from Rs60 to Rs100. For Chaman and Ziarat buses depart almost every hour from the General Bus Station on Circular Rd. The fare to Chaman is Rs8 and it's Rs16 to Ziarat.

Road The Quetta-Zahedan road, segment of the alternate Euro-Asian Highway via Taftan, is being improved and has recently been turned into a federal

A	
B	

A   In a Peshawar cafe
B   Road up the Khyber Pass

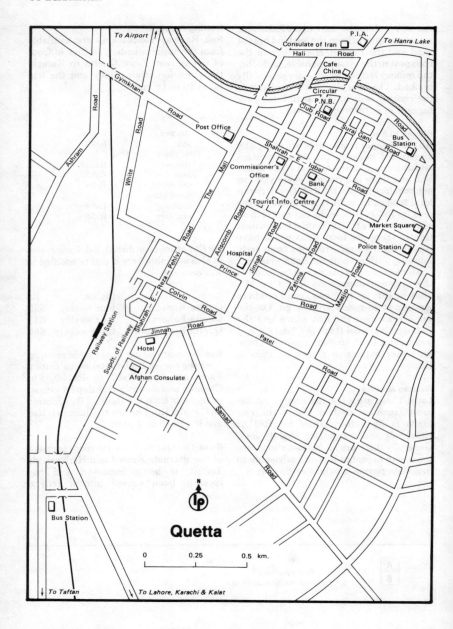

Quetta

highway. Other federal roads are the Karachi-Khunzdar-Quetta, Quetta-Chaman and the Quetta-Zhob-Dera Ismail Khan highways. All these highways run through restricted tribal zones, but it is possible now for foreigners to travel through these areas on public transport. For security reasons, if you have your own transport, it's better to follow public transport all the way.

QUETTA TO IRAN

There used to be trains to Zahedan in Iran twice a week on Wednesdays and Saturdays, but the continuing instability in the region has resulted in the Wednesday service being suspended. The train stops at every station en route and takes about 45 hours. It's a cheap way to get there – Rs38 – but it's a slow, boring trip and you must be sure to take food and water with you.

Due to widespread smuggling the train no longer goes all the way to Zahedan, stopping six km short of the border. This means you either have to take a taxi or walk to Taftan and from there find your way to Mirjaweh, the Iranian border village.

Alternatively there are buses that cover the 720 km between Quetta and Taftan. Buses depart regularly from Shirkhi Rd. The trip takes 24 hours with an overnight rest either way in the *muzzaffar khanas* in Nukundi. Cost is Rs85. The road is sealed as far as Yarmach and recent reports suggest it may be sealed all the way to Nukundi. It has been designated a federal highway and improvements are constantly being carried out.

In the opposite direction – from Taftan to Quetta – buses usually depart at 2 pm. It's quite a spectacular trip. The desert is flat and vast with undulating sand dunes looking like rolling waves, and the mountains, sky-blue in colour, seem very distant. You reach Nukundi around midnight and stop for a rest and something to eat. The following morning the bus leaves early and arrives in Yarmach before noon for lunch. From here the road is sealed and flat until just before Quetta. The bus is always stopped and searched for smuggled goods on the mountain road, and if it's a perfunctory inspection, you should arrive between 4 and 6 pm. A longer search may delay you until 8 to 10 pm.

Visas & Exchange Rates The situation in Iran, though calmer, is still volatile and, as it is unpredictable, could change suddenly. You can apply for a visa for Iran in Quetta – Japanese nationals do not require one – but it's better to do so in Islamabad as it takes three weeks to come through from Quetta. Don't forget to check with the Iranian Consulate on Hali Rd in Quetta about the border situation and the prevailing conditions in the country. Although consular officials may not have much information about what is really going on because communication is slow and poor, at least they have a feel for the situation. For your own safety keep your eyes and ears open all the time.

There are persistent rumours that there is a movement employing terrorist tactics against the Khomeini regime. Nonetheless, traffic in this region seems almost normal and reasonably regular at the moment. But don't count on it continuing to stay that way.

The immigration and customs posts are at Taftan which used to be a caravanserai, but there are no longer camel caravans going to Panjgur – buses and trucks have replaced them. Taftan's mosque, bank, hotels, eating places, teashops and houses are spread over a wide area. If you arrive on a Friday the banks will probably be closed, but there are money-changers here, who prefer US dollars, pounds sterling and Deutsche marks. In Iran US dollars fetch a fairly high premium nowadays, so save your hard currency until you get to Tehran. There's a blackmarket on Istanbul St where you can get 350 rials or more to the US dollar compared with the legal rate of 85 rials.

QUETTA TO AFGHANISTAN

There is one train daily to Chaman but buses depart almost hourly from the General Bus Terminus on Circular Rd and Suraj Rd. It's nearly 130 km from Quetta to Chaman, and the road runs across flat, dry plains, then descends a few km before climbing to the mountains. Although the road is surfaced it is in bad condition in certain sections. It twists and turns through the Khozak Pass over dry, dusty country, and although it is less than 80 km from here to Chaman, it takes three hours to cross the pass, stopping frequently to pick up passengers and cargo. In the opposite direction the bus is stopped and checked thoroughly for smuggled goods.

Eventually you descend into flat, desert and reach the small town of Chaman, which used to be just a little border village 20 years ago. There are still *no* hotels here, only *muzzaffar khanas* where you can spend the night if you arrive late. It's walking distance from Chaman to the Afghan border check-point, but I strongly advise you not to try getting there alone after dark, and even in the daytime, take care if you are alone. In any case there are no buses to take you over the 10 km to Spin Boldak where there are some *local inns*. You can hitch rides from here.

The Afghan Consulate is on the Mall (Shahrah-e-Reza Pahlavi) near the railway station. The Afghan border is officially open, but may as well be closed. Even if you do get admitted, it is unlikely you will be able to travel on from Kandahar to Herat and Iran. It is much more likely that you will have to fly out from Kabul. There are money-changers on both sides of the border, but it is advisable to have enough to see you through to the next town.

QUETTA TO PESHAWAR

Although there are trains north to Fort Sandeman, the route to Peshawar via Bannu is a restricted tribal area. If you want to go into this region you need a permit from the Ministry of Tourism or the Ministry of Home Affairs in Islamabad, but the chances of getting one are slim. Foreigners are not allowed to go past Ziarat either, although some travellers, 'unaware' of the restriction have made it. There are also private bus companies which are unaware of this restriction on foreigners.

Warning Note that in restricted areas there are *no* hotels, but you can stay at police outposts in the more civilised areas. It is extremely dangerous to travel around the wilder areas as witnessed by the circulars and photo displays of missing travellers. See also warning in section on the North West Frontier Province tribal areas.

DERA GHAZI KHAN TO LORALAI

From Multan in the Punjab you can travel south-west to Jacobabad, then north-west to Quetta. If you have a travel permit you can go directly west through Dera Ghazi Khan. From this quite large town in the Punjab it is 270 km to Loralai. The bus leaves at 2 am and the fare is Rs34.

The road is sealed but sections of it are in bad shape due to flash-floods during the monsoon. From flat semi-wasteland the route climbs up a mountain in a series of zig-zags. This mountain is quite unlike any to the north or west in composition or structure. It seems to have surged straight through the earth's crust, its strata perfectly horizontal. It is a continuation of the Sulaiman Ranges which make up the provincial border between the Punjab and Baluchistan.

At the top you pass through Fort Munro, beyond which the land flattens and then gradually slopes down into Baluchistan. Apart from a few patches of green it is generally arid with tiny villages tucked behind ridges that are almost invisible from the road. As you descend you can see the thin black ribbon of the tarred road stretching straight towards another mountain range to the left of which it turns south-west.

As you approach the mountain range

the land becomes alien and mysterious, moaning with a gusty wind that only stops for a short period during winter. Buses are often stopped by the powdery dust that cuts visibility to zero. Beyond this the landscape is less hostile and much greener. You will now see the nomads' tents, which look like huge beetles about to buzz off. Further down the track the tents are replaced by huts made of woven dry, yellow reeds. Two or three pieces of this make a hut, which can be rolled up in a trice and transported by camel.

After this, once again the landscape becomes barren and desolate until out of the sea of sand Loralai emerges. Although it is major town in Baluchistan, Loralai is no bigger than Dera Ismail Khan, having only one bazaar, a few eating places and some *muzzaffar khanas* with rope-bed. Most of the *muzzaffar khanas* are without toilets. Loralai is not geared to tourists at all, but it's a fascinating journey getting there. You can wash the dust off yourself at hammans in the barbershops for a small fee.

LORALAI TO QUETTA VIA ZIARAT
Buses take nine hours to cover the 190 km to Quetta. Minibuses cost a little more but are about two hours faster. While the road is not bituminised, it is not bumpy. This is not a particularly exciting stretch of territory, but it is pleasant enough, crossing gently rolling land which is almost flat until the Chutair Valley. From there it begins to climb gradually up to Ziarat. Although the valleys are wider and the country greener, the area appears to be deserted. It would be quite surprising to see anyone. But once you start climbing up into the mountains you will begin to see signs of settlement. The mountains are covered with junipers that are stunted, gnarled and twisted like desert trees.

The Chutair Valley is very picturesque with huts made out of big stones piled up from the base to form a low wall and branches of trees making the frame for the upper walls and roof. Juniper bark or long grass cover the frame. These huts have no windows and their primitive but attractive design is strikingly like the ancient Viking dwellings in Scandinavia.

Continuing on you reach the surfaced road, then suddenly come across the modern buildings of Ziarat. At 2500 metres, Ziarat is a popular hot season retreat where many *hotels* tend to be expensive and heavily booked during the summer. There is no *Youth Hostel* either so, unless you can afford the expensive *PTDC* complex, your best bets are the *Ziarat Hotel* or the *Grand Hotel* at Rs15 per person. The former has a slight edge over the latter as it's quieter. Ziarat also has good treks including short hikes to Prospect Point about 5½ km away, and Fern George which is 10 km further on.

From here the surfaced road meanders down through a narrow, barren valley to Kach. The unique structure of the terrain here, thrown up in a cataclysmic upheaval eons ago, is of interest to both geologists and lay people. The dry, sandy, barren country is like a vast rock garden. In Kach the bus stops for passengers to get some refreshments and to do their *namast* – prayers. The minibuses zip straight through. The valleys widen as you approach Quetta.

Warning Dacoitry (banditry) is rife along the Quetta – Loralai route, particulary near Loralai. Be careful.

QUETTA TO MAKRAN
The coastal region of Makran in the south of Pakistan is in the process of being developed with US assistance, and is likely to be opened up to tourism in the near future. The land rimmed by the sea is barren and sandy with low, dry, hilly outcrops. Further inland the country rises from 600 metres to around 3000 metres in the north. It is a sparsely populated region, very hot in summer and freezing in winter. Delicious dates grow here.

Since the ports on the Arabian Gulf became duty-free the desert region has become a smuggling area. During the

British era only guns and ammunition were smuggled into the warring tribal areas, but today watches, television sets, radios, tape recorders, Japanese motorcycles, pens, refigerators and innumerable others items are brought through this area into Quetta and all the way up to the North West Frontier Province. Due to the political turbulence in the region the western area of Makran is off-limits to foreigners and is likely to remain so for some time.

South of Quetta is Kalat, 122 km away. The paved road goes through the Lok Pass and continues on to Khuzdar, 144 km further on. From Khuzdar it is 220 km to Bela in the region of Las Bela. The road is paved all the way to Karachi via Sonmiani and is open to general traffic. However, if you have your own transport unless you are travelling in convoy, it is advisable not to go this way as it's too dangerous. It's safe enough to take the bus, but there are *no* tourist hotels yet, only *muzzaffar khanas* or local *travellers' inns*.

At Surab, a tiny village on the Kalat-Khuzdar road, there's a dirt track to Panjgur, which is linked to Taftan by a camel caravan route. Khuzdar and Turbat are connected, and there are rough roads from Bela, Panjgur and the fishing villages to the latter. There is a jeep road from Pasni or Jiwani to Karachi, but it's closed to general traffic.

QUETTA TO LAHORE OR KARACHI

The trains for Lahore or Karachi start out along the same route as far as Sibi and the Jacobabad junction. You have to book aircon first class or first class sleepers two weeks in advance though, so you need time. If you haven't got the time, you'll have to use some ingenuity to make sure you get a seat. Get a concession ticket for the ordinary first class (unreserved coach) and arrive at the station early. Find a porter – they're obvious because they wear red shirts and an oval copper badge – and ask him to get you a seat. Make sure

you show him your ticket so he knows what coach to get you on and stick to him like glue. He will do all the hard work, struggling and jostling through the crowds and for just Rs10 you'll get a seat. Make a note of his number to prevent later arrivals from claiming they have paid someone else for the seat.

At Jacobabad the trains turn north for Lahore via Multan or south to Karachi via Sukkur. From Quetta the train descends down to Sibi – about half-way to Jacobabad – passing a number of minor stations before reaching the Indus Plains. The mountains are forbidding, barren and desolate, almost primaeval in aspects. Except for tiny villages, mostly oases, everything is totally dry. The mountains close in around the rail tracks which slither through to the other side.

Fortresses top the low mountain crests manned by police forces led by the regional tribal leader. They generally wear grey *quamis, shalwar* and *chappals,* topped by an Australian-looking slouch hat with one side of the brim pinned up. As they are native to the region they are a far more effective police force than most others.

After what seems an interminable stretch of barren land, the train finally reaches the green plain, but in summer this is still uncomfortably hot. The train stops for about an hour here – the hottest region on the subcontinent – before going on to Jacobabad.

Archaeology

On the road to Quetta just before Bolan Pass is **Mehr Ghar**, another pre-Indus Valley Civilisation settlement. The neolithic tribes (6000 to 3000 BC) who settled here are considered to be the earliest known in the subcontinent. They apparently had trade links with the Indo-Gangetic people and the Iranian Asiatic civilisation, which indicates that they were a highly evolved and advanced society. They also are believed to have been the first people to domesticate the buffalo.

The site was settled by Hindus later and then by Buddhists. The ruins of a stupa remain but the Hindu temple has now been converted into a mosque.

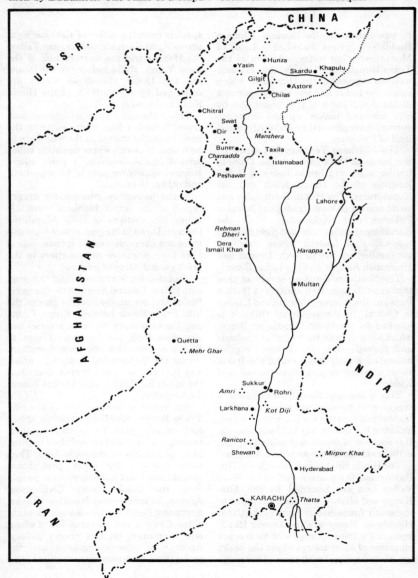

Northern Territory

It was called by the ancient Chinese Buddhist pilgrims, *Polo-Leh* – Land of Mountains – but today is known as the Trans-Himalayas. This is the extreme western segment of the Himalayas which spans the Indus and the Brahmaputra, a distance of 2400 km. It is about 500 by 800 km and makes up the immense corrugated region of the northern frontierland of Pakistan.

The Northern Territory is topped by the hump of the Pamirs on the Chinese border side, and bright below it is the junction of the Hindu Kush and the Karakorams. The Hindu Kush splay out south and south-west straddling Chitral in Pakistan and Afghanistan, while the Karakorams arch south-east right down to the valley of Ladakh where they are surrounded by the Ladakh, Deosai and Haramosh Ranges and the Indus River.

The Northern Territory covers an area that extends from Baltistan up to Darkot Pass and the fringes of Mastuj and Laspur in Chitral. In the region of Gilgit it is blocked by the Great Himalayan Range which slips in from the valley of Kashmir and spreads over the Diamar region, extending a little way beyond the Indus River to terminate just above the valley of Kohistan.

This is the upper northern highland, a craggy, arid, bleak area, where some of the highest peaks in the world are to be found, including K2, second only to Mount Everest. It is also one of the most glaciated regions in the world outside the Arctic and Antarctic.

The Hindu Kush cover the region of Dir, Bajaur and the eastern half of the Swat Valley and are bounded by the Altai Range and offshoots of the Himalayas to the south. Immediately south of the Great Himalayan Range are the Lesser Himalayas or Pir Panjal Range with an average elevation of 4500 metres where the peaks are always capped with snow. This range spreads from the valley of Kashmir right across Azad Kashmir, the Kaghan Valley, the Hazara and the western half of the Swat Valley. Right below the Pir Panjal are the Outer Himalayas which are contained by the foothills of the Hindu Kush to the west.

This is the sub-northern highland, lush green, a timber belt where some of the most beautiful valleys in the world are to be found. It is also where neolithic tribes settled in the foothills, a place where empires sprang up only to be wiped out and others to emerge.

In the incredibly inhospitable craggy region of the upper highland, neolithic tribes left vestiges of their Megalithic Culture. Down in the gentler sub-highland there is a concentration of archaeological sites from primitive rock shelters to the great capital cities of empires.

Neolithic trade routes linked this area with Persia, Central Asia and the Gangetic Plains and eventually became part of the Silk Trade Route between Rome, China and the Gandhara. Its main arteries ran east-west from the Gangetic Plains to Persia and south-north from Gandhara across the 'Suspended Crossing', which was how the ancient Chinese described the upper highland to Kasghar in Chinese Turkestan.

But before it became part of the Silk Trade Route, migratory neolithic tribes had already passed this way on their trading business and carved their impressions of animals on the rocks here. They were followed by other prehistoric, protohistoric and historic people: people from the Indus Valley Civilisation; Aryans; Achaemenians; Bactrian-Greeks; Scythians; Parthians; Sassanians; Hephthalites; Chinese and Tibetans – all of whom left their mark on this craggy gallery. Apart from scenes engraved into the rocks, there are numerous scripts including

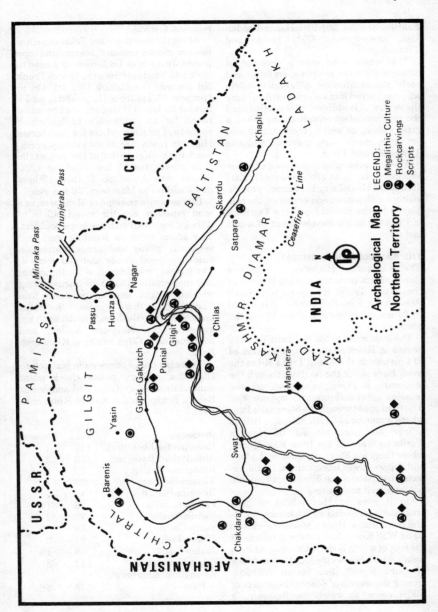

Archaeological Map
Northern Territory

LEGEND:
Megalithic Culture
Rockcarvings
Scripts

Pakrthi, Brahmi, Sogdian, Hanza-Haldei-kish, proto-Sarada, Old Chinese and Tibetan.

The whole area was a crucible of different cultures, religions, art forms and racial stocks from the different invaders who conquered it in succession. It became the centre of Buddhism which influenced the religions of surrounding empires to a great extent, as well as their culture and art style, particularly those of Chinese Turkestan and Tibet.

The archaeological ruins, rock carvings and inscriptions, as explained by Dr Karl Jettmar of Heidelberg University, provide visitors with some perspective on the role played by the glacial Northern Territory of Pakistan in the development of world history.

THE KARAKORAM HIGHWAY

The Karakoram Highway is almost a thousand km from the Hazara District of the Grand Trunk Rd up to Khunjerab Pass on the Sino-Pak border. It is linked by 24 major bridges and about 70 smaller ones.

The main route to the Northern Territory begins in Rawalpindi, at an elevation of 514 metres on the Grand Trunk Rd to the west. Here along the Sagjani, though the landscape is rapidly changing, are the remains caravanserias of a bygone era. The road goes through the Marghalla Pass where a memorial to Nicholson, a British officer, has been erected, on through Taxila to Wah, 43 km from Rawalpindi, where there is a Moghul garden with plane and cypress trees lining canals. It still has water basins and pavilions, but they are not very well maintained.

On it goes to Hasanabdal, a busy crossroads, crowded with bazaars, hotels and restaurants. Here a Moslem shrine to Baba Wali Kandahari crowns a hilltop, at the foot of which is the Sikh shrine of Panj Sahib, which houses the hand impressions of Guru Nanak, founder of Sikhism. During the month of March thousands of Sikhs come to celebrate *Baisakhi*, a religious festival.

Along the way there are fields of yellow flowers, mostly mustard, sesame and rape plants. Just a little bit further on a road to the north heads off from the Grand Trunk Rd towards the Hazara District. On to Haripur, 35 km from Hasanabdal, and a further 22 km to Havelian, a rail terminal noted for an impressive bridge which spans the Dar River, where the Karakoram Highway really begins its journey north-ward. From an elevation of 766 metres the road climbs for 15 km to about 1200 metres into Abbottabad, then slithers down and on to Manshere, 26 km away.

On the northern slope of Manshera, at a road junction, are the moral edicts of Ashoka, inscribed on three large boulders. The edicts refer to avoiding wars and senseless killing and concentrating on kindness, good deeds and self control. The highway meanders down to Batagram and then crawls in tortuous fashion along wooded ridges and spurs down into Thakot. From there it crosses the Indus and heads on to Beshum, a junction 28 km away in the Kohistan Valley, and continues on to Gilgit ending at Khunjerab Pass.

There is a police check point just before Chilas, a military police check point immediately before Gilgit and another at Batura Bridge on the road to Khunjerab Pass.

Distances	km	hours
Rawalpindi-Abbottabad	117	2
Abbottabad-Batagram	103	2½
Batagram-Thakot	28	½
Thakot-Beshum	28	½
Beshum-Pattan	44	1
Pattan-Camila	36	1½
Camila-Sazin	73	2
Sazin-Chilas	68	1½
Chilas-Jaglot	87	2
Jaglot-Gilgit	50	1½
Gilgit-Karimabad	112	3
Karimabad-Khunjerab Pass	209	3½

Total:

Rawalpindi-Khunjerab
Pass   955 km 22 to 26

LOWER NORTHERN TERRITORY

The foothills of the Hindu Kush and the Outer Himalayas rear up from 1000 to 5000 metres above the valley of Peshawar and the Potwar Plateau in the Punjab. The valleys in Malakhand, Swat, Hazara and Azad Kashmir & Jammu are generally broad with gently rolling and undulating landscape, the thickly wooded mountain slopes and ridges terraced for farming.

This luxuriant, heavily forested belt is where the monsoon dumps most of its rain in Pakistan. The climate is alpine, mild and pleasant – neither too hot in summer, nor too cold in winter, except in the higher reaches. Wheat, sugar, tobacco, fruits – apples, pears, peaches, plums and grapes – all grow in abundance. There are numerous wild animals in this region; leopards, black and brown bears, goral or wild mountain goats and markhors. Once there were also rhinos which the Moghuls used to hunt. But it seems they may have been rather too trigger happy as there are none here now. However, there is a great variety of birdlife, which includes the *chikor* and black and grey partridges.

The valleys begin to narrow further up where the mountains crowd in on the rivers. The land becomes steeper and the skyline is serrated with peaks covered with snow, and the mountainsides are split with glaciers. Continuing north the forest belt terminates and the land loses its gentler aspects.

Historically this region is extremely significant for it is where most of the neolithic tribes settled and evolved their cultures, an area conquered by Alexander the Great, where the Mauryan Empire had its beginnings, the great Gandhara Buddhist Culture emerged, where Akbar lost 8000 of his troops and where Winston Churchill failed to shoot a rebel only 20 metres away and had to beat a hasty retreat.

It's a land shared by the Pathans, the Kohistanis and other tribes: the cultural watershed between the south and the north.

AZAD KASHMIR & JAMMU

Azad (meaning free) Kashmir & Jammu is a long, thin slice of the state of Kashmir and Jammu. The border here is defined by a sensitive ceasefire line for this has been the flash-point of India-Pakistan relations ever since Partition.

Three rivers converge here: the Kunhar, Neelum and Jhelum. The scenery is like any part of the Kashmir Valley, mountainous, luxuriant and beautiful. During the monsoon the landscape takes on a rainwashed appearance, with rivers rushing over rocky beds under clear, blue skies.

Azad Kashmir & Jammu is open to tourism from Pirpur and Kotli up to Muzzaffarabad and Khel in the north, but foreigners are not allowed within 16 km of the ceasefire line. They can only go as far as Noseri Bridge on the west banks of the Jhelum, and not beyond to Srinagar. The valleys of Neelum and Leepa, 55 km away, are superb, and are noted – among other things – for their unusual wooden houses, often three-storeys high and gabled like Alpine lodges. Unfortunately, only a small section of these valleys can be explored as they lie within the restricted zone.

MUZZAFFARABAD

This is the principal town in Azad Kashmir & Jammu and was once the administrative centre of the northern area. It is situated on the steep side of a mountain and spreads up the slopes on several levels, even the bazaar straddles three levels. There is one paved street but the town is scattered over the whole valley.

In Muzzaffarabad the Jhelum and Neelum rivers meet, and on the banks of the Neelum is a red fort, with another not far away on the top of a hill. Six km from here is the picturesque Banjora, near the tourist centre of Dhirkote. From Muzzaffarabad the road to Srinagar follows the Jhelum down under the Domel bridge. Just before you reach the Noseri bridge, if you wish, you can continue travelling north by bus via the west bank of the Jhelum River to Keran, Shardi and Khel.

Information

The Tourist Information Centre is in Dhirkote six km from the town centre of Muzzaffarabad.

Places to Stay & Eat

There are medium-class *hotels* around the bus station and main bazaar. *Rainbow Hotel & Restaurant* is reasonably clean and has rooms with fans and attached bathrooms for Rs10 a single and Rs20 a double. Nearby is the *Galani Hotel & Restaurant* which has singles for Rs15 and doubles for Rs30. Or you could try the *rest house* at Rs25 a single or Rs50 a double. Cheap restaurants in the area all have the same menu. There are better restaurants in the hotels. There are also *tourist huts* and a *rest house* in Dhirkote, if it's more convenient for you or you prefer to stay there.

Around Muzzaffarabad
Punch District

To the south of Muzzaffarabad is the Punch District where Kotli and Mirpur are located. The centre of the Punch District is Rawla Kot situated in the heart of the Khunja Valley. There's a nice lake here and there are plenty of buses direct from Muzzaffarabad and also from Pindi. There's not much else around except the Mangla Dam where you can go boating or fishing.

Close to Jhelum and about 160 km from Muzzaffarabad is Khel, which takes about eight to 12 hours by bus. From here you can get a magnificent view of Nanga Parbat. Khel is where trekkers set off east into Kashmir – before Partition – or north

to Skardu over the Deosai Plateau and north-west to Chilas or to Astore and Rama and on to Gilgit. See section on Trekking.

There are a number of *rest houses* around here where you can spend a night or two. Busha Gala and Chuta Gala are particularly scenic hill stations, both of which have *rest houses* for overnight accommodation.

Outside the Punch district you come across the scarred red sandstone region of the Potwar Plateau again. If you're on your way back to Islamabad get off at Rawalkot where you can take a direct bus via Kahuta.

At Jhelum you can go back to Lahore, while at Kharian the landscape changes and takes on the usual flat, fertile luxuriance of the Punjab. Next along the way is Gujrat, 164 km from Rawalpindi, then Gujranwallah, which is 67 km from Lahore.

If you want to include Azad Kashmir & Jammu on tour of the Kaghan Valley you can either start from Jhelum through Kotli or from Rawalpindi via Murree, Ayubia, Nathiagali, Muzzaffarabad, then Ghari Habibullah 24 km away, and from there into the Kaghan Valley.

Chikkar

Forty-eight km east of Muzzaffarabad is Chikkar, an attractive hilly region covered in trees. There are *tourist huts* and a *rest house* here. Fifteen km further on from Chikkar is the village of Noon Baghla, a picturesque spot that is teaming with monkeys. There's a *rest house* here if you want to spend some time exploring the area. From Noon Baghla there is a road that goes to Suddon Gali, another scenic hill station with a *rest house*. You can get direct transport from Muzza to this place.

Nine km north-east of Chikkar is Chinari which has a *rest house*, and on the other side of Chinari is the Leepa Valley. Neelum Valley is further on. You can get a bus to Attahkum, a town with a *rest house*, then on to Danarian, a pleasant place in the hilly region of the Leepa Valley. There are no roads beyond this point, but you can walk further up if you wish. However, nine km before the ceasefire line is a restricted zone, and even the local inhabitants are not allowed in this area.

If you want to, you can get a direct bus from Muzzaffarabad to the Leepa Valley.

Getting Away

There are buses from Jhelum to Muzzaffarabad, a distance of 200 km. Although the road is surfaced it crosses rather rough, mountainous terrain through Kotli and Mirpur and takes eight to 10 hours. From Rawalpindi the 145-km trip takes five to six hours and costs Rs15. The bus passes through Murree, Ayubia and Nathiagali. From Muzzaffarabad there are buses for Khel in the north and to Ghari Habibullah to the west. The 45-minute trip costs Rs3. The bus station is just behind the bazaar and buses depart every hour for Rawalpindi, Kotli, Jhelum, Ghari Habibullah and Khel.

HAZARA & THE KHAGAN VALLEY

Hazara is part of the North West Frontier Province, Pathan country, although geographically it forms part of the sub-northern region of the Malakhand, Swat and Azad Kashmir & Jammu. From the Indus Plains the land rises steeply to this area, then climbs less precipitously northward.

The way into Hazara from Rawalpindi is either via Haripur or Murree, the latter being the more popular with travellers. Although it is in the Punjab, Murree is really part of the sub-northern region. Burbhan, 10 km from Murree, is slightly lower at 1800 metres and has a *Youth Hostel*, but the bus service is irregular. This is a popular hiking place, though accommodation can be a drawback in summer unless you have camping equipment and provisions.

Twenty-nine km away is Ayubia at 2600 metres above sea level. A tiny, summer hill resort, it has a chairlift to a mountain peak. Eight km away, Nathiagali, is another scenic village worth visiting. All these hill resorts have moderately-priced *hotels* but tend to get packed out in summer.

From here you can continue north-east to Muzzaffarabad or north-west to Abbottabad, the principal town of the Hazara, 38 km away. Here the land dips down to 1200 metres, then flattens out before sloping gently downward to the north. The mountains recede along this pleasant route, whether you're heading towards Thakot and Baghram in the west or Ghari Habibullah in the north-east.

If you decide to go north-east you come to Manshera, a city smaller than Abbottabad, but more beautiful in the traditional way. This is the site of Ashoka's rock inscriptions which are just by the roadside at a junction. Approaching Ghari Habibullah, 13 km further east, the mountains start to converge onto the road and the river, which squeezes through Balakot, 14 km away. This is the gateway to the Kaghan Valley and from here on the valleys widen and narrow alternately.

Getting There

Buses for Abbottabad or Manshera are stationed at Pir Wadhai, Rawalpindi. It's a 3½-hour trip to Manshera from Pir Wadhai costing Rs15. If you're heading for Balakot catch a bus from Manshera; it only takes an hour and the fare is Rs7. From Balakot you can go to Naran by bus for Rs20 or Rs 25 by minibus. It takes about five hours. From Balakot there is also a minibus service to Kaghan, which takes 3½ hours and costs Rs15. But it's better to take the direct bus to Naran.

BALAKOT

Though only a transit point situated at around 900 metres, Balakot is very beautiful. The surfaced road slithers out of the village following the Kunhar River through a valley with wide, terraced grain fields.

Information

The Tourist Information Centre is in the Tourist Lodge.

Places to Stay & Eat

The *Youth Hostel* is on the right-hand side before you reach the Tourist Lodge and costs Rs10 per bed. Medium-class *hotels* in the village have a shared bathroom and toilets for Rs15 a single to Rs25 a double. The modern and clean *PTDC Tourist Lodge* costs Rs50 for singles and Rs75 for doubles plus tax. The *local inns* have food from Rs10 and over, while the Tourist Lodge offers a western-style breakfast and other meals from Rs 15.

Getting Away

There are two buses daily to Naran at 6 am and 2 pm. It's a six-hour trip, costing Rs14. There are regular buses on the two-hour run between Balakot and Abbottabad, and the fare is Rs8. There's also a good service to Manshera for Rs8. Minibuses to both Manshera and Abbottabad cost Rs9. Buses to Rawalpindi depart Abbottabad every hour and cost Rs14 for the four-hour trip.

ROUTE TO NARAN

The bus speeds along the flat road for a while, before crawling up the steep mountain slopes. Squat mud and stone huts with flat roofs supported by heavy beams perch on narrow ledges and narrow footpaths zig-zag up the slopes.

In Kawai, 24 km away, a track turns left through a dense pine forest known as **Shogran** – heavenly forest – up to a plateau 2400 high. At the edge of the meadow here are two *rest houses* which have a commanding view of the **Mussa-ka-Mussallah** – praying mat of mosses – and **Makra** and **Malika Parbat**, which at 5290 metres is the highest peak in the Kaghan Valley.

Near Mahandri, 46 km away, the metal road peters out and becomes a dirt track, gravelly and rough in places, and basically just a jeep road used by trucks and buses

to go to Naran. Approaching Kaghan, 14 km away, the valley gets very narrow. Kaghan, after which the whole region is named, is very small with a tiny bazaar lining one side of the main road. Snow begins to appear on the crests of mountains from now on and in several places there are greyish-black glaciers, virtually indistinguishable from the earth, which thaw in the summer heat and rain. They melt from below first, forming caves which eventually collapse. From Naran, where the sides of the mountains crowd in on the river, the road is jeepable only.

NARAN

The Naran Valley is 2400 metres above sea level, less than a km wide and only about five km long. Snow-crested mountains with slopes streaked with white glaciers border the valley. On both sides of the road and the Kunhar, the land is gently terraced, rising to wood slopes. Naran is divided into two areas: the lower region is where all the government administrative offices are located while the bazaars and local hotels, restaurants, shops and the bus and cargo-jeep stations are on the elevated section. Clear blue streams cascade down the mountainside to join the Kunhar River. The valley is quiet, relaxed and has some of the loveliest scenery in Pakistan, but it is also very expensive. Primarily a trekking region, it is comparable with Nepal.

Information

The Tourist Information Centre is at the Tourist Camp site. If you want to hire a jeep, this is the place to make enquiries.

Places to Stay & Eat

The *Youth Hostel* is on the right side, three km before the village and costs Rs10 per bed. The *rest house* has rooms for Rs40 and *local hotels* have them for Rs15 to Rs30. There are also *muzzaffar khanas* which have charpois in the open for Rs5.

The *PTDC Tourist Inn* has single rooms for Rs100, doubles for Rs160 and huts or tents for Rs40 a double. The cabins have 5-star ratings. There is an additional 15% tax. The rest house has a kitchen available for cooking, but there are a few restaurants here with reasonable food for Rs10 and up. The muzzaffar khanas are only Rs5 for a meal. Bring provisions and camping gear if you're going trekking.

Around Naran

Eight km to the east is **Lake Saiful Muluk**, which is about a km long and has midnight blue water afloat with ice during the winter. The lake is said to be inhabited by fairies and legend has it that Prince Saiful Muluk, a poet and philosopher, fell in love with one. It's a scenic spot surrounded by a carpet of flowers in spring and summer. The *rest house* here is very basic and it's preferable to camp if you have the equipment.

The village of Lalazar, 11 km north of the lake and at a slightly higher altitude, offers a magnificent view of Nanga Parbat. The area is covered with pines, hemlocks and spruce trees, and lots of flowers in spring and summer. There's a *rest house* here, and the village is also accessible via Batakundi.

Getting Away

There are two buses daily to Balakot. Departures are at 6 am and 2 pm, the fare is Rs14 and the trip takes six hours. You can hire jeeps from the PTDC Tourist Information Centre for around Rs6 a km, plus Rs75 per day and Rs75 per night charges. The cost of hiring a jeep to Babusar Pass is Rs1200 if returning empty, and Rs 800 there and back if not. It's a seven-hour journey. Jeeps to Saiful Muluk Lake and back will cost Rs150 if returning empty, less if not, for the 45-minute trip. You can also hire a horse for a round-trip to Saiful Muluk Lake for Rs80.

BEYOND NARAN

The Kaghan Valley, though less developed, is similar in topography to the Swat Valley. Both are terminated by the great mountains that form their border with the upper highland. In the Swat Valley there are trails that go over passes either into Dir, Chitral or Gilgit, while in the Kaghan Valley the trail has been turned into a jeepable track over the Babusar Pass into Chilas. On the road to Baghram, 65 km away from Manshera to the west and from Thakot to Beshum in the Swat Valley, the land becomes hilly and is girdled with low, green hills. In the monsoon it is remarkably like some places in East Africa.

BABUSAR PASS

This pass is 4067-metres high and closed for nearly nine months of the year. Officially it's open only from mid-July until the end of August, but it's already trekkable by late June. Late in July a few cargo-jeeps, usually government supply vehicles, and some tourist Land-Rovers cross over the pass into Chilas. Cargo-jeeps are costly – even for a group of four – but the distance is trekkable. The route is gentle and easy-going, but if you're tackling this trek in autumn, you will find that after you pass through Battakundi, most of the hamlets and villages are deserted as the majority of inhabitants have moved down to the plains. You may come across some Gujars in the process of moving their livestock down, but even the Afghan Kirghiz refugees who camp along the trail in summer have left by this time.

From the top of the pass it's a three-hour walk to the village of Babusar, which is also semi-deserted in autumn, but there are always a few people who remain. In the village there is a NAWO (Northern Area Works Organisation) *rest house* which has double rooms for Rs60 or Rs30 per person, and two more comfortable double rooms for Rs90. There is also a *teashop*, which not only sells food but also has a bed for rent at Rs5 a night. The latter is shut in autumn, and although the *rest house* is also closed then, the *chowkidar* will open it up for travellers. From Babusar you have a choice of walking to Chilas 18 km away or hiring a donkey for Rs40 to get you there. You may catch a lift along the way on a tractor loaded with timber. It's a rough ride, but a lot quicker than walking. When you get to Chilas there are three *hotels* in the bazaar area, which have singles for Rs10 and doubles for Rs20. In summer you can get rooftop beds for Rs5. There's also a *rest house* here. See section on Trekking.

If you intend driving you'll have to make the trip in the six weeks or so from mid-July until the end of August. In autumn, when it's extremely beautiful, you can drive up to the top, but the pass itself is closed. However, the *only* vehicle able to negotiate the journey up and over the pass is a medium-sized Land-Rover; it's not wide enough for a larger vehicle and only a four-wheel drive will make it. The way up is narrow with lots of hairpin bends; in places it is so narrow and so steep that jeeps have to back up three or four times to get around. There are two very difficult passages over glaciers where a winch is essential if you get into trouble, so make sure you bring one with you. It is advisable not to attempt this drive on a rainy day, or after it has been raining for a few days, as it gets very slippery and the road slopes down the cliffside due to uncleared, minor landslides.

The alternative to either trekking or driving is to catch a *PIA* flight to Chilas, which has an airport, and take a bus from there to Gilgit. The not-so-pleasant alternative to trekking or flying can mean waiting for days – even up to a week – for cargo-jeeps, tourist vans or Land-Rovers. If you are not able to fly, trek or wait your only option is to retrace your steps to Manshera where you can pick up a bus for Beshum if you wish to travel up to the upper highland.

BESHUM

You can get to Beshum by bus or minibus in three to four hours from Manshera or Abbottabad. The route is scenic all the way up to the bridge where Aornos, believed to be the mountain where Alexander the Great relentlessly pursued native warriors, towers above the Indus. Around here it is lushly green, but not much further on it becomes arid, rocky and almost barren.

Beshum is a little transit village now beginning to assume the features of a modern town and have the trappings of modern civilisation – petrol stations, cafes, restaurants, hotels, barbershops and bazaars. It is the junction for Swat Valley via the scenic Shangla Pass into Khwazakhela; Kaghan Valley via Manshera and Gilgit.

ROUTE TO GILGIT

Out of Beshum the Karakoram Highway stays on the western banks of the Indus, curling and meandering along, then slithering straight up, twisting again then sliding high above Patan. It continues to corkscrew through rocky, narrow junctions of valleys until the sky opens out again. Across a bridge is **Camilla**, a tiny village worth a stopover for lunch or tea. Here the Karakoram Highway follows the eastern banks of the Indus, heads straight up, then twists through a rather barren valley.

Near where the Indus turns eastward is the village of Siazin, not visible from the highway. On both sides of the Indus from here are some extremely important archaeological sites. On the northern banks of the Indus are sites known as **Chilas I**, **Chilas II** and **Shatial Bridge**, which consist of rock carvings of animals and Buddhist stupas, engraved with ancient scripts, beginning with the primitive neolithic art style and the Bronze Age and progressing to the Gandhara period.

Sixteen km east and 10 km below Chilas, is **Huddar-gah**, another site. Numerous petroglyphs cover the cliffs from here up to Jaglot and down to the Alam bridge to the east, and the Kargah Valley in Gilgit to the north. After crossing the bridge in Chilas the Karakoram

Highway shifts back to the west banks of the Indus, leaving it near Alam bridge and continuing north to Hunza.

ROUTE TO SWAT VALLEY

It takes five to six hours by bus over the scenic, 2100-metre high Shangla Pass from Beshum to Khwazakhela. The road is surfaced and starts climbing gradually before coming to a steep section and then again levels out and zig-zags gently upwards. The landscape here is brick-red, patched with green and the mountain slopes are generally terraced. On the way down the scenery is the same until you reach the bottom of the valley where it starts to get dry, becoming green again near Khwazakhela, a busy intersection where the road splits north to Kalam and south towards Mingora.

SWAT VALLEY

Surrounded by towering hills it is a small state of large rocky tracts with only a little level ground here and there. Nature in all her bounty has blessed the Valley of Swat with a charm and verdure that rightly makes it a masterpiece of natural landscape ... (but) undisciplined and wilful life sinks man's morals to such a low depth that many a time his degeneration mars the natural beauty of his homeland as well.

> Miangul Wadud Badshah Sahib, former ruler of Swat

Swat Valley, renowned for its scenic beauty, is also rich in archaeologoical relics. This was the apex of the triangular Gandhara region with its base running from the Peshawar Valley across the Indus to Taxila in the Punjab. Pottery, figurines and other artefacts have been discovered here which predate the Gandhara period and resemble Iranian finds from as far back as the 12th century BC. In 327 BC Alexander the Great invaded this region, defeated the Hindu king here, destroyed guerrilla resistance by attacking the supposedly impregnable fortress at Ora or Aornos, now known as Udegram. Apparently, this was to teach them a lesson and convince other kingdom along the way that capitulation was the best policy, a hint which Chandragupta of Taxila heeded.

Between 324 and 185 BC Buddhism spread widely throughout Swat and reached its peak during the 2nd century AD during the Kushan era. A great number of colleges and monasteries with innumerable stupas were built in the valley and a great quantity of Gandhara sculptural work was produced. It became – like Taxila – a sacred place for pilgrims from China and Tibet, the most famous being Xuan Zhang who, in the 7th century AD recorded 1400 monasteries, with Ming Chili or Mingora having the largest. By this time the area was already in decline and much of it in ruins.

Following the successive invasions by barbarian hordes from the 5th century AD onward it fell into a 'dark age' from which it was never to emerge. Buddhism gave way to Hinduism which in turn fell to the onslaught of Islam in the 10th century and the whole region lapsed into barbarism. Babar unsuccessfully attempted to subjugate it, and the Sikhs who succeeded Babar, only managed to exert a tenuous hold on the land. It was with the British that peace was finally restored. As a reward for his co-operation the Akhund of Swat was given the upper half of the valley, Kohistan, for his administration. It remained an autonomous political agency right through until 28 July 1969.

Lower Swat begins from the district of Buner on the border of Mardan to the south and spreads north to Bahrain. Kohistan starts from the outskirts of Bahrain and continues up and beyond Kalam. The valley has an elevation of 1000 to 5000 metres and is generally scenic, lush green and fertile, stepped with terraces, rivers and snow-clad mountains. The climate here is pleasant, neither too hot in summer, nor too cold in winter.

Archaeological Route

South of Mingora the Karakar Pass, 1400 metres high, has a panoramic view of the Buner Valley where Emperor Akbar lost most of his 8000 troops. He had his revenge when he lured the Swatis down into the plains and routed them, but he didn't follow up his ambition to conquer the Swat region.

Mt Ilam, one of the highest mountains in Swat, is considered to be the seat of tribal deities in prehistoric times. The huge block-shaped rocks are believed to be tribal altars. South of Mt Ilam is Gumbat which has a Buddhist shrine and to the north in Shngardar is a Buddhist stupa. Two km further along is a rock carving of the Buddha.

Another archaeological site is the Gogdara area. There is a cave in this region which has rock carvings – most likely Aryan in origin – of two-wheeled chariots, dogs, horses, ibexes, leopards, oxen and other animals. Higher up are some Buddhist carvings.

Along the Chakdara-Swat Rd are archaeological sites of the Gandhara period. At Haibatgram, eight km from Chakdara, are the ruins of a Buddhist monastery and a stupa. Seven km past Landaki in Nimogran is another Buddhist site and to the north of Birkhot Hill is Bazira, which in ancient times was sacked by Alexander the Great. The fortress at Bazira encloses a large, flat area and locals sell coins, arrowheads and statues to anyone who'll buy them.

Between Mingora and Saidu Sharif is Butkhara, an archaeological site with Buddhist ruins, considered in ancient times to be a shrine. From Mingora there is a side road which follows the Jambil River to the east. This valley is also dotted with Buddhist ruins and rock carvings. Panir is another Buddhist site, but at Butkhara II, Loeban and Matelai, 475

Aryan graves have been discovered. Towards the airport, the town of Aligrama is believed to have been an Aryan settlement around 1000 BC.

Bahrain is the furthest Buddhism penetrated in Swat, but there are very few relics left here now. If you feel like a strenuous climb from Jehanabad Village up to Manglaur you will find a rock carving of a seated Buddha there.

MINGORA & SAIDU SHARIF

Like Islamabad and Rawalpindi, these are twin towns, but on a mini-scale. The more modern, Mingora, is 1030 metres above sea level, and is a largish town, with paved streets, rows of bazaars and shops and facilities such as banks, hotels, restaurants and an airport. Like Quetta it doesn't have any beautiful Moghul architecture, nor any imposing British structures. It is the commercial and businesss centre which extends to Saidu Sharif, the more traditional of the two, which is the administrative and educational centre of Swat. Saidu Sharif is where the Swat Hotel and the palace of the former ruler are. Between Mingora and Saidu Sharif is a **museum**, which has displays of the Gandhara culture. Just before the museum on the left is the road to Butkhara, which was once the site of several prehistoric, protohistoric and historic cultures. Saidu Sharif is a quiet town which is slowly but surely developing.

Information

The Tourist Information Centre is in the Swat Hotel on Saidu Sharif Rd. The post office is on – surprise, surprise – Post Office Rd and the Pakistan National Bank is on the Main Bazaar Rd. The Gemstone Corporation of Pakistan, which deals in emeralds, is three km out of town on the way to Khawakhela. There is a hunting season in this region which extends from mid-October to mid-March.

Things to Buy

The Swat Valley is a great place to buy

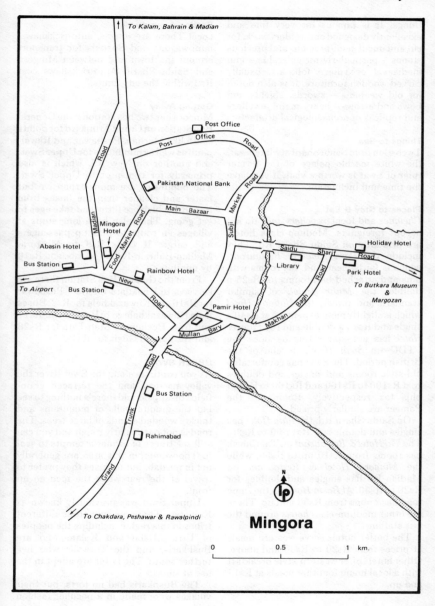

To Kalam, Bahrain & Madian

Post Office

Post Office Road

Market Road

Pakistan National Bank

Main Bazaar

Holiday Hotel

Saidu Sharif Road

Abasin Hotel

Mingora Hotel

Library

Park Hotel

Bus Station

Rainbow Hotel

To Butkara Museum & Margozan

To Airport

Bus Station

New Road

Pamir Hotel

Makhan Bagh Road

Mullan Bary

Road

Bus Station

Trunk Road

Rahimabad

Grand

N

To Chakdara, Peshawar & Rawalpindi

Mingora

0   0.5   1 km.

things. It is famous for very fine and excellently designed embroidery work, for cut and uncut semi-precious and precious stones – particularly for emeralds – and mediaeval or village folk art, usually carved wooden furniture. It is also noted for old weapons – swords, shields and bows and arrows – heavy metal jewellery and replicas of archaeological artefacts.

Things to See

Twelve km from Saidu Sharif at Marghazar, the white marble palace of the former ruler of Swat is worth a visit, if you have the time and inclination.

Places to Stay & Eat

Cheapies and local *travellers' inns* do not accept foreigners. Medium-class hotels are primarily on Saidu Sharif Rd. They include the *Park Hotel & Restaurant*, which is fairly clean and has rooms with fans and attached bathrooms for Rs25 a double; the *Malik Hotel*, of similar standard and prices; the *Holiday Hotel* which is slightly more expensive at Rs40 a single and Rs75 a double and the *Pameer Hotel* has a 3-star rating as does the PTDC-run *Swat Hotel*, a relic of the British period. The Swat has comfortable old-style rooms and singles and doubles cost Rs100 to Rs160 and Rs160 to Rs220 plus tax respectively. Rooms at the Pameer are similarly priced.

On Saidu Sharif Rd, the *Ilam Hotel* has singles and doubles for Rs12.50 to Rs20. The *Taj Hotel & Restaurant* on Taj Chowk has rooms from Rs10 up to Rs50, while the *Mingora Hotel & Restaurant* on Madian Rd has singles and doubles for Rs20 to Rs30. *Al Basin Hotel* on the same road has rooms from Rs50 and up. There are other medium-class *hotels* around the bus stations.

The better hotels serve western meals at prices from Rs20 to Rs30 and above. Other hotels offer western-style breakfast with a local menu for other meals at Rs12 and up.

Getting Around

Local There are tongas, auto-rickshaws, mini-wagons and Suzukis for transport around the town and between Mingora and Saidu Sharif. Auto-rickshaws cost Rs2 within the city limits.

Getting Away

Mingora has two bus stations: the General Bus Station on Grand Trunk Rd for points south like Mardan, Peshawar and Rawalpindi as well as minibuses for Upper Swat; and another on New Rd, which is also primarily for transport to Upper Swat. The minibuses are more expensive but faster and cleaner than the buses from New Rd, which are filthy and take ages to get going. They also have long stops at villages en route to pick up passengers and cargo. It costs Rs8 to Mingora-Madian-Bahrain-Kalam by bus, and Rs10 by minibus.

From the General Bus Station there are services to Chakdara for Rs3, Peshawar for Rs16 and Khwazakhela for Rs2. Buses from Khwazakhela go to Beshum for Rs11 and from Beshum to Manshera for Rs26 and Beshum to Gilgit for Rs48.

UPPER SWAT

As you continue along the Swat River the valley narrows and the terraced grainfields disappear and there's nothing to see but the granite walls of mountains and thickly wooded stands of large trees. The road is not particularly rough and you can still see traces of former attempts to seal it. The women in this area are generally not in purdah, but in buses they prefer to travel at the rear while the men go up front.

Upper Swat was previously known as Kohistan. There are numerous different tribes in this region including the peoples of Utrot, Ushu and Kalam who are Bushkaris, and the Torwalis who live further south. The latter are adept in the use of slings.

The Bushkaris had no forts, but their villages were made in a peculiar fashion for security and defence. Usually built on steep hillsides in succession, one above the other, the buildings had flat rooftops built on the same level as the floor of the one above it, and the whole being interconnected by an outer wall. Inside the villages are a maze of passages, through which runs a stream. All the early houses were made of wood and any built outside the enclosed village were built without parapets – probably for protection.

The Bushkaris and Torwalis hold a similar belief to the ancient Persians and the Minoans of Crete – that is that the world rests on the horns of a cow, which causes earthquakes when it shakes its head from time to time at the sins of the inhabitants. They still believe in fairies who supposedly confer the power of prophecy on certain mortals, a theory which is also upheld in the upper northern highland.

In mediaeval times this region was known as the Land of Fugitives. In spring and early summer, Gujar nomads trudge north, loaded with pots and pans, herds of cattle, sheep, goats, chickens, dogs and horses. Children share the horses with the chickens, while the women tote large baskets on their heads and carry their babies in their arms. They dress in flamboyant, printed fabrics, wear heavy metal jewellery and are of sturdy build and ample proportions.

Along the way, a road forks of west to Kabul, where there is an 18-hole golf course at 870 metres which is open all year round. Further on another road cuts east to Malam Jaba, 2600 metres above sea level. The Austrian government had agreed to assist in setting up a ski-resort here, but the rather grandiose scheme was abandoned recently, and Malam Jaba is now being turned into a hill station for tourists, diplomats and vacationing government officials. Experts considered that it was not only too small for a ski-resort, but that the mountain was not high enough, nor was there enough snow to

make it really viable.

The first town of importance is Khwazakhela, 26 km away, a busy, smallish intersection. If you want to stop off at Khwazakhela for a night, go and see Siraj Ahmad at *Ajar Tajor & Co* about his guest room. Check out the rural folk art of Swat Valley in the shop while you're there. From Khwazakhela there is a road to Beshum, a small village to the east. The main road continues to Madian 26 km away, but before reaching the latter there is another road branching east to Miandam, 10 km off the main road. At 1800 metres, Miandam is another scenic, little village. The *PTDC Motel* here costs Rs100 a single and Rs 160 a double. The only other accommodation is at expensive *first-class hotels* or, if you have the gear, there are a number of places where you can *camp*.

This is considered the most beautiful valley in Swat. There are some superb hikes up the mountains and along the stream here.

MADIAN

The valley becomes slightly claustrophic at Madian, but it's very picturesque. At an elevation of 1320 metres, Madian is a popular town, both because of its beauty and the variety of accommodation available in the valley, along the streams, on slopes and ridges and high up into the mountains. Be careful to boil or purify drinking water from here to Bahrain and Kalam, or you could find yourself in trouble.

Places to Stay & Eat

Summer Hill Hotel is rather rundown, but still reasonably clean and has rooms for Rs10 and Rs15 with share bathrooms, and *Hunza Inn*, on the banks of Swat River, and *Hotel Insof* are similarly priced. *Muambakhan Food Shop & House Rentals* has rooms and huts available at moderate rates and is on the left-hand side going north on the main bazaar street. There are other better *hotels* and *restaurants* with rates from Rs40 and over. If you want to splurge, the *Madian* has rooms which range from Rs100 to Rs250, or else there's the *Nisar Hotel* at Rs50 to Rs180. There are also places on the Bahrain side of the village.

BAHRAIN

Only 10 km away at 1400 metres Bahrain is more developed, but not as attractive. From here the road is rougher and starts to climb steeply: some sections are washed away. The bare mountains close in on the road, which drops away precipitously to the river. This is still an interesting area for explorers, who could stumble on important archaelogical finds. Thirteen km out of Bahrain and about three km before Madian, there's a trail that cuts off to the left then loops north to Jahanabad. High up on a cliff here, is a rock carving of a goddess. It will take you about half an hour to climb up and see it.

Beyond Bahrain is Kohistan where the Pushto tribe gives way to Torwalis and Bushkaris.

Places to Stay & Eat

Medium-class *hotels* here are more expensive than they are in Madian. The *Paris Hotel* on the banks of the Swat River is probably the best cheapie with rooms for Rs15 and Rs25 for singles and doubles with share bathrooms. It's pleasantly quiet with the sound of the river cascading below. The *Darol Hotel* is similarly priced and there are numerous others ranging from Rs40 and over.

KALAM

The road levels off as the valley widens close to Kalam, which is 26 km from Bahrain. Kalam is 2100 metres up and is designed in two sections. The higher one consists of administrative offices and the police station and has more expensive accommodation. It slopes down gradually, terminating in a sharp drop to the main roadway and river.

Upper Swat or Kohistan belongs to the northern region culturally as the architecture of the old mosque and the carvings of wooden pillars, window frames and door jambs indicate. Although there is no road from here to Chitral or Gilgit, the upper northern cultural influence must have filtered in along the foot trails. This region is the boundary marking cultural changes from south to north.

Kalam has a tranquil restful air and a pleasant climate during the day, though nights tend to be cold. On a clear day you can see – not forever – but perfectly the 6257-metre high Mt Falaksher from the upper section of the town. In the north-east of the valley its snow-clad upper slopes and peak rise above dense, lush forests. The river rushes through the town, and right across from it is the old mosque.

Information

The Tourist Information Centre is in the Tourist Lodge.

Places to Stay & Eat

The *Khaled Hotel & Restaurant*, on the main road in front of the bus stop is the cheapest place in town with doubles only and share bathrooms for Rs20. Further up is the *Heaven Breeze Hotel* which has rooms with attached bathrooms for Rs25 a single and Rs40 a double. It's clean, quiet and has good food. The PTDC has a *Tourist Lodge* and several cabins for Rs75 to Rs120 plus tax. Single rooms here cost Rs100 and doubles are Rs160. It has a mega-modern dining hall on the upper slope and a large lawn where *camping* is free. *Falaksher Hotel* and others up here are fairly expensive. Across the river are some nondescript *hotels* which are pricier than the Khaled. Meals available are similar to those in Mingora and other towns down the valley.

BEYOND UPPER SWAT

Beyond Kalam where the Swat River splits, the road also forks, west to Utrot at 2225 metres and east to Ushu. To the north-west in the valley of Utrot is Gabral Valley which is excellent for fishing, while to the north-east is the valley of Ushu, which at 2286 metres also has great fishing streams. On the way up to Ushu there is a magnificent view of Mt Falaksher.

Trekking trails start from here to Dir, Chitral and Gilgit, but they're not recommended by the police and other authorities unless you're accompanied by a guide. See section on Trekking. There are regular bus services to these villages, which usually depart at 2 pm. There are *hotels* here, but many still lack facilities. However, it's quite safe to rough it out here. Unless you're on a guided trek this is a dead end and you have no alternative except to retrace your steps, either to Khwazakhela or Minogora.

Getting Away

From Khwazakhela you can continue on to Gilgit or to the Kaghan Valley via Beshum. The way to Beshum goes over Shangla Pass, where there is a government *rest house*. At Alpurai there are a few *local hotels*.

To Kaghan Valley Buses leave Beshum between 8 am and 4 pm for Abbottabad via Manshera, and from here there are buses, minibuses and mini-wagons for Balakot or Ghari Habibullah, if you're heading for Muzzaffarabad.

To Gilgit Buses for Gilgit leave Beshum at 6 am which means an overnight stay at a *muzzaffar khana* on a charpoi in the open, but your luggage is locked in a storeroom. There is a *rest house* about one km from the village centre, but it's inconvenient if you have to be up early to catch the morning bus. A number of buildings on the main road are being converted into hotels which may be open soon. There are other buses at 10 am and noon, but these come from Abbottabad via Manshera and are likely to be packed out when they arrive here.

To Chitral & Peshawar If you're heading for Peshawar or Chitral via Dir go to Mingora first. There are direct buses to Peshawar from here, but for Dir or Chitral you must get off the Peshawar bus at Chakdara. There are connecting buses for Dir waiting here.

DIR

Bajaur is still tribal and requires a permit to visit the area. It is still reasonably traditional and is extremely interesting. One of the main towns here is Dir, a transit place, which used to be a stopover on the ancient Silk Trade Route that went through Bajaur over Nama Pass into Afghanistan and from there down to Central Asia and China.

In Chakdara, on the way to Dir, there is a fort known as **Churchill's Pique**, just after the bridge. The British dragged their heavy weaponry from here and marched into Chitral to quell the rebellion in 1885. Scattered around the surrounding area are archaeological sites of Aryan settlements along with their graveyards and Buddhist monsteries, stupas and rock carvings. One km after the bridge on the road to Dir is a footpath which runs west for about 1½ km to **Chat Pat**, another Buddhist site. Almost nothing is left here now.

On the north side of Damkat Hill are the ruins of a Buddhist monastery, and at the foot of it are rock carvings of the Gandhara period. Nine km further on there is a track that leads west to Kalash Valley, which has the ruins of yet another Buddhist monastery and what's left of a stupa. At the extreme end is **Kat Kala Pass** which was used by Alexander the Great to enter the region. There's an old Hindu fort here.

Forty km further on is **Timargarha**, the site of more Aryan graves which are elaborately made out of stone slabs. **Ralambat** is another interesting place, once the site of Aryan settlements and later of the Achaemenians, Buddhists and Hindus. Houses excavated here have fire altars.

The paved road – segments of it have been washed away by flash floods – moves up gradually into rolling landscape with encampments of Afghan refugees close to the foothills. It is only as you approach Dir that the mountains begin to tower over the road.

As a transit point, Dir is the administrative centre of the whole valley. It has a number of government buildings, schools and shops. Though still evolving, it has an atmosphere of never having quite made it into a major town. In this region the harvest and fruit season arrives earlier than it does in the upper north. This is timber country and the edges of the road are stacked high with wood. The surfaced road peters out as it begins to climb the dusty, 3075-metre high, Lowari Pass. It's a good idea to have a large scarf handy to wrap around your head and nose to keep the dust out.

Places to Stay & Eat
Dir is a pleasant, scenic spot for an overnight stay. It is also reasonably inexpensive with medium-class *hotels* near and around the bus station. Double rooms are usually Rs15 but you can bargain here. *Al Hayat Hotel*, at the extreme end of the town near the bridge, is a nice place to rest and relax, but rather far away from transport if you're leaving for Swat, Peshawar of Chitral early in the morning. Local food here is similar to Afghan food with *nan* and the usual stewed mutton or beef in a tomato sauce. Meals are always served with tea. You can also buy heaps of different, fresh fruit in the bazaar.

Getting Away
Direct buses from here to Peshawar and Chakdara cost Rs20 and Rs9 respectively. Although from Dir to Chitral is only 115 km, the trip takes 10 to 12 hours. In early June, they cut glaciers in two or three places to open the Lowari Pass. Loaded trucks often get bogged down in the thick, deep, fine dust and the glaciated sections, which are slippery. Landslides can block the roadway and the result is that one, or all, of these obstacles inevitably mean that you arrive in Chitral at twilight time.

In summer the Lowari Pass can look like the freeways to Paris or London at the end of a weekend with long lines of waiting trucks, jeeps and cars jammed to a standstill, particularly if the pass is blocked by a landslide or a truck gets bogged.

Yak

Upper Northern Territory

Where the forest belt ends the topography is radically transformed into granite mountains – bare of any vegetation – and jagged spurs that rise above fine dust and sand.

The landscape appears to be interminably crumpled, pockmarked with vast expanses of rocky deserts at 5500 to 6000 metres in the north, and desert steppes with scrub and tussocks of coarse grass in the middle regions which lie between 4500 and 6000 metres. It is characterised by escarpments, gorges, ravines, moraines and lakes, and criss-crossed by innumerable streams and rivers.

Up here the climate undergoes extremes in temperature, being dry-hot in summer and dry-cold in winter. The heat in the lower, arid regions becomes as intensely hot as quickly as it can become cold when clouds or the mountains shade the sun. In summer the temperature can vary from 35°C at 1500 metres to freezing at higher altitudes. It can also dip precipitously at the slightest rainfall.

Up in the highest reaches of the mountains some of the rarest wildlife in the world exists: the markhor, urial, Marco Polo sheep and snow leopard. In the lower regions at around 2500 to 3000 metres there are prairie-like steppes where yaks are common and the abundant birdlife includes the crested hoopoe, hawks, falcons and eagles. The ground is covered with desert-like plants and there are forests of pines, firs, spruce, Himalayan cedars, willows and poplars.

The whole region is surrounded by great mountain ranges and is right in the vortex of the Hindu Kush in the west and north-west; the Karakorams to the north and north-east which cover 75% of the entire region, and the Great Himalayan Range to the south-east. These mountain ranges form a natural barrier to the summer monsoon causing rains to fall on the plains and the sub-northern area. They also protect the plains from icy, winter winds from Central Asia and Siberia. This is where some of the highest peaks in the world exist along with a few of the largest glaciers outside the polar regions. And running right across the territory, from Tibet through Ladakh, the mighty Indus flows westward, before veering sharply to the southern lowland, down and then out into the Arabian Sea.

The rugged defiles, often bare and narrow, sometimes give way to valleys or settlements of mud-stone huts that somehow exist in regions that seem too barren, bleak and desolate or too isolated and remote for human habitation. With its savage climate and primaeval quality, it must have been too desolate and bleak for human habitation for many centuries. But there is evidence that neolithic tribes concerned with the study of stars and their movement did live here.

Snowbound and sealed for nine months of the year, it was really only accessible in high summer. Astounding though it is, through this extremely inhospitable region routes were cut right down into the gentler lowland of the Indus Plains: routes that became not mere trails for migratory tribes but trade ways, predating the ancient Silk Trade Routes by at least a couple of millennia. It was from them that the Silk Trade Route finally evolved.

The major arterial road began at the foothills of the sub-northern region through Taxila and the Swat Valley, and continued up along the Indus through Gilgit and the valley of Hunza to the 5000-metre high Mintaka Pass into Kasghar and Turkestan. Minor veins branched out in nearly all directions. This important section of the ancient Silk Trade Route, along with the trails from Chilas to Passu and the Mintaka Pass, and those east to Satpara Valley and the Valley of Khapulu, and west through the Valley of Punial and Gukutch and Yasin into Chitral, are all archaelogical routes.

Rock carvings, calligraphy and diverse engraved scripts – in historical sequence – and done in various art forms and styles complement the written history of the different people and their cultures over a span of five millennia or more.

In the upper northern highland the important archaeological sites begin in the region of Chilas which has numerous rock carvings and inscriptions dating back to the Achaemenian period (6th century BC), the Parthians (2nd century BC) and the Gandhara (2nd century AD). There are also some rock carvings dating to the Bronze Age. Here the art styles range from the ithyphallic, bi-triangular animal art form to the sophisticated style of the Gandhara culture. There are also Buddhist stupas and inscriptions of the first half of the first millenium AD.

It is a unique, natural art gallery which serves to throw light on aspects of the lifestyles of many different peoples; prehistoric, protohistoric and historic people. The only other places in any way similar, are the hills of the Bushmen in the Kalahari Desert or the cave-dwelling-artists of Altamira in Spain.

There are some traces of pastoral, migratory Aryans passing this way; and the engraved Old Chinese script in western Turkestan records the passage of the Sakas who, it seems, could have settled in the Trans-Himalayas. It is possible that they became Hindus since Hinduism was replaced by Zoroastrianism, which in turn was replaced by Greek paganism. This is likely to have been spread by the settled communities in the sub-northern region who sought refuge up here. Later still, Buddhism held sway in this region, dominating the culture for a little under two millennia before being supplanted by Islam.

This upper highland emerges in history along with the Patola dynasty (4th to 8th century AD), but it is more than likely that the Patola dynasty was propped up by the Persian Sassanians in order not only to rule Bolor, but also to guard the Tarim Basin, an important crossroads of the ancient Silk Trade Route, through which Buddhism and the Gandhara culture were diffused to influence the religion, art and culture of Turkestan and Tibet.

The population was mostly Caucasian until the Chinese arrived in the middle of the 8th century AD after being booted out by the Tibetans in the 9th century AD, when racial stocks became mixed. When the Patola dynasty of Bolor disappeared it was replaced by the Empire of Dardistan, which also eventually fragmented.

By the 10th century Islam was already established in Chitral and was gradually spreading eastward. In the 16th century it spread from Kashmir and moved westward, and at about the same time, it moved in from Moghulistan in the north. The entire region became Islamic, but it comprised three different Moslem religious sects: the Shi'ites; Maulais or Ismailis; and the Sunnis. With the arrival of Islam mirdom evolved, and the kingdoms which emerged – largely because of religious differences – were always at war with one another until the arrival of the British in the region.

Pax Britannica was established mainly because of Russia's expansion eastward, as it was considered likely that the Russian would carve out a share of the Indian subcontinent. The British consolidated the region, turning the more important mirdoms into political agencies, and establishing administrative centres and military cantonments in the area. They improved the trails and bridged rivers and gorges previously spanned simply by a single-rope bridge. For the first time this region was explored, surveyed and methodically mapped.

It came under the direct administration of Kashmir, with the exception of Chitral which became part of the North West Frontier Province. In 1948 Gilgit and Baltistan kicked out the Kashmiris and joined Pakistan. Geopolitics here have changed, but geographically it is still a strategic and sensitive area as the hump of the Pamirs is also the junction of Russia, China, Afghanistan and Pakistan.

Today this upper highland is developing at a fairly fast pace. The administrative centres of Chitral, Gilgit and Skardu have power supplied by numerous hydro-electric schemes, an improved road network and an air link with the south: most of the infrastructure of modern cities. The Karakoram Highway – it took nearly two decades to build with the assistance of the People's Republic of China, and roughly follows the old Silk Trade arterial route through this region – is the lifeline to the south. But despite all these modern trappings, it is a wild, primitive land, still subject to the whims and vagaries of nature.

Restrictions & Permits

Foreigners can now travel on the Karakoram Highway to Passu and about 200 metres past the Batura Bridge without a permit. But they are restricted to an area no further than 30 km beyond the borders, after that a permit is necessary. Permits aren't necessary for treks in locales below 6000 metres.

Permits to Stay

Expired visas cannot be extended up here. The commissioner and the police superintendent can only give permits to stay in the area for a period of seven days. Note, however, that the Chinese border has been opened to Pakistan travellers and it is possible that an immigration office will be set up shortly.

Immigration and customs headquarters are to be set up in Gilgit shortly.

Banks

The Pakistan National Bank in Skardu and Gilgit deal exclusively with foreign currency and travellers' cheques, but only in pounds sterling or US dollars. Rates offered are usually less than bank rates in the lowland. With the possible exception of banks in Chitral, you would probably lose about 10% in exchange. So be sure to take enough rupees with you to last your visit.

Mail

Postal services are still not reliable, particularly for parcel post. To put it bluntly they're erratic.

Telephone & Telegrams

Domestic and international calls are okay, except that you are likely to end up shouting to be heard. Telegrams arrive, but they're often mislaid or not handed over.

Tourist Season

This extends from spring through summer, particularly for mountaineering, trekking and rafting expeditions. The best time to arrive is between August, September and October. Summer and autumn are the fruit and fishing seasons, **but** swimming in the rivers is forbidden – it's *very* dangerous as the water is running so high and so fast then. Summer fruits include apples, apricots, mulberries, walnuts, peaches and grapes, while in early autumn pears are abundant.

If you like fishing there are plenty of brown, rainbow and golden trout in the rivers, and on average their weight ranges from 1.5 to 2.5 kg.

Wildlife here includes ibexes, markhors, urials, Marco Polo sheep, black and brown Himalayan bears and snow leopards. There's also a myriad of birdlife: mynahs, hoopoe, Indian roller, partridges, wild pigeons, rock birds, finches, Monal or Impeyal pheasant, hawks, falcons and eagles. The valleys of Khunjerab, Naltar, Mizghar and Shigar have been made into wildlife sanctuaries.

Places to Stay & Eat

There are first class, middle level and bottom range hotels and restaurants, as well as travellers' inns. But if you've got camping gear, bring it with you. It's also advisable to bring supplementary food.

Information
There are Tourist Information Centres in every major town, along with hospitals, libraries, fisheries offices, polo grounds, tourist curio shops and bazaars.

Sino-Pakistan Trade
Barter trade, formerly limited to Gilgit and Sinkiang, has been replaced with open trade between China and Pakistan conducted through the Sino-Pak border at Khunjerab Pass.

Khunjerab Pass
The Sino-Pakistan border at Khunjerab Pass is now open to international traffic. So far there has been no infrastructure set up for tourism at Tasgurgh, Kasghar or Urumchi in the Sinkiang Province in the People's Republic of China, but there are hotels and transport is said to be excellent.

For a visa for China apply at the People's Republic of China in Islamabad.

Economy
It's an agrarain society which produces 75% of its food needs and imports the rest. The main source of income is tourism.

Getting There
Air *PIA* has two to three flights daily to all major centres in the Upper Northern Territory.

Flights are dependent on weather conditions: the most certain and regular times being from September into October.

There are no concessions on flights here: fares are already subsidised by the govenment.

Road *NATCO* (Northern Area Transport Co) and other bus lines offers four bus services daily between Islamabad and Gilgit. There are also buses and minibuses from Peshawar to Dir to Chitral.

The Karakoram Highway which links Islamabad with Gilgit is open all year round, however, the Chitral route over the Lowari Pass is only open from early June till mid-October. After this the only way to get to Chitral is by air and flights are often fully booked for two weeks ahead.

The highway is surfaced from Islamabad up to Khunjerab Pass, but the Gilgit-Skardu road is still in the process of being surfaced as is the Dir-Chital route. The latter is also dusty and rough in places. The rest of the roads are bumpy, potholed and 'hairy' in places zig-zagging steeply up the sides of sheer granite walls, across swaying suspension bridges, and suddenly disappearing around acute, narrow corners. Often in spring roads are blocked by landslides which can take a couple of days to clear away.

Night driving on mountain roads is strictly prohibited.

Getting Around
NATCO has buses linking Gilgit, Skardu and Hunza. There are other buses and minibuses, and occasionally, cargo-jeeps to Chitral and other minor towns and villages. There are also ponies and donkeys for hire along with their owners, who act as guides.

Getting Away
There are no exit points out of this area for foreigners. It is a cul-de-sac, which means you have to retrace your steps when you want to leave.

To Afghanistan The borders with Afghanistan are closed and there are police check points along them.

To India There is still no trekking access through the ceasefire line, which is guarded by volunteer UNO observers.

To China The Chinese border was opened in the summer of 1983 to facilitate trade between Gilgit and Sinkiang as well as Pakistani and Chinese traders and tourists. This could be the prelude to it eventually being opened to foreigners.

Things to Do

Mountain Climbing/Trekking/Rafting This is no mere back-to-nature area, but a back-to-the-wilderness region. It's an explorer's, trekker's and rafting enthusiast's playground.

There are a few tour, trekking and mountain climbing agencies in Rawalpindi and some local agencies up north. The PTDC has its head office in Rawalpindi and has branch offices in every major town in the upper highland. Others are the *Karakoram Tours* and *Mrs Waljis Trek-Tour Agency* with offices in Islamabad and Rawalpindi.

Entertainment There are cinemas in Gilgit, Skardu and Chitral which tend to mostly screen local and Indian films, and the occasional western movie. There are polo tournaments in the month of June, August and November, and in Chitral and Gilgit they put on *buzhkasi* tournaments, a game that involves top-speed riding carrying the headless body of a goat from one end of a large playing ground to the other and back again without losing it to opponents or dropping it. This rather gory game was re-introduced by the Kirghiz Afghan refugees. See Facts for the Visitor.

Things to Buy

The local handicraft industry isn't as developed as it is in lowland Pakistan, and consists largely of woollen rugs, long stockings with geometrical designs and woollen Chitrali, Gilgiti or Balti caps. You can also buy various antiques – mostly weapons – including Mongol bows, Russian matchlocks and slim curving swords dating back to Ivan the Terrible. Also available is an assortment of folk jewellery, but they no longer manufacture musical instruments.

Cultural Orientation

You enter an entirely different world here. The population is generally a mixture of Caucasian and Mongoloid racial stocks: heterogeneous in culture, speech and religion, but superficially homogenous in social – this includes a universal belief in fairies and a liking for salted tea – and economic matters.

Traditionally they are endogamous – that is they forbid marriage outside their own group – and as a consequence are inbred.

However, life is not harmonious. Conflict is no longer just religious, but is now beginning to manifest itself in political and cultural rivalry, which flares up – occasionally – in shooting and rock-throwing incidents.

Generally, life in this region is rough and basic, demanding not merely physical fitness, but a 'personal quality' from travellers that enables them to face difficult situations and circumstances.

It is a conservative, tradition-bound society, so the rule 'when in Rome' applies very strictly here.

BALTISTAN

Baltistan, 26,000 square km in area, is right below the serrated, jagged and glaciated ramparts of the Karakorams. Once part of Ladakh, it was known as Tibet-i-Khurd – Little Tibet.

Archaeological exploration has proven that it was encompassed by the Silk Trade Route. Rock carvings have been discovered along the road between Gol and Khapulu and Skardu and Satpara Lake. The trade routes here split in Skardu with one leading to Satpara over the Deosai and Burzil Pass (5000 metres high) into Kashmir and another leading to Gol. At Gol it forks again with one trail leading to Khapulu, the other to Kharmang into Leh.

Between the 9th and 16th centuries it belonged to Tibet, being part of Ladakh until conquered by Moslem Shi'ites from Kashmir, who introduced Islam here. The story goes that one of the more daring rulers pillaged the fringes of Kashmir and married a Moghul princess called Gul Bibi. While her husband was away conquering the northern area, Gul Bibi built a superb garden with an aqueduct. So jealous was her husband of her achievement and so warped his mind that he condemned her to death. But the story does have a happy ending, for ultimately she was reprieved and her skills were eventually acclaimed as engineering feats.

Baltistan consists of five valleys: Shigar; Skardu; Rondu; Khapulu and Kharmang. The most interesting are the valleys of Shigar and Khapulu with Rondu and Kharmang being the most isolated. The whole region is the most important mountaineering and trekking area in the Upper Northern Territory. It is here where K2, the second highest mountain in the world, and Siachen, the largest glacier in this part of the globe, are to be found. It is also the gateway of the mighty Indus River.

Until recently with the exception of Hunza, Baltistan was the most isolated region of the upper highland. There used to be three overland rountes into the region. The first via Muzzaffarabad through Smaro, Khel, the Shuntar Pass (4200 metres), over the Deosai Plateau into Satpara. This route is closed to foreigners. The second route is through the Kaghan Valley over the Babusar Pass (4067 metres) through Astore, the Deosai Plateau and past Katchura Lake. The third route via the Karakoram Highway through Beshum into Skardu is longer. This route is now traversable by truck.

This region would still be cut off were it not for its air link with Rawalpindi. Weather permitting, *PIA* has two, occasionally three, flights daily to Skardu with Fokker 27s. Although flights are uncertain and liable to be cancelled even as they approach Skardu, they still remain the most positive way of getting into Baltistan.

It's a spectacular flight, turning eastward towards Islamabad from Rawalpindi, skirting the Marghalla Hills, then climbing north-east. Below, the black ribbon of tarmac turns grey-white as it zig-zags up into the hills. The little plane gets close to the immense mass of Nanga Parbat (8125

metres) which broods over the surrounding mountains, many of them rising higher than the F-27's flight altitude. Finally in a canyon where the Indus flows westward, it descends into a rather arid, sandy area.

SKARDU

Skardu is the principal town of Baltistan. It is a dry, dusty little place on the banks of the Indus with the **Rock of Skardu**, on which is perched the fort, **Karpochu**, towering above the main street. This is lined with low-roofed structures and wooden box stalls which make up the bazaar area. Princess Gul Bibi's aqueduct is long gone, replaced by a drab-looking concrete structure.

Beyond it, the main road continues. On the left side is the polo ground and right at the foot of the Rock of Skardu, by the banks of the Indus, is a little village. Nearby it is possible to camp. Further down on the the left are the PTDC K2 Motel and a government rest house. Where the road to Satpara veers away to the right are government offices including the Pakistan National Bank, another rest house and the police station. The road continues on to Khapulu and Shigar.

Skardu is 2300 metres above sea level and has a pleasant climate. However, a blustery wind can rise up in spring and summer, which stirs up the dust and blows until evening. These conditions make it quieter, drier and more introverted than it is already. Of the three adminstrative centres in the Upper Northern Territory it is the least developed, but it is now changing at a faster rate than either of the others.

There is a continuous flow of mountaineering and trekking expeditions here from spring through summer until early autumn, but mountaineers and trekkers do not seem to hang around long. Most rush through to the mountains and on return get away quickly.

Information

The Tourist Information Centre is at K2

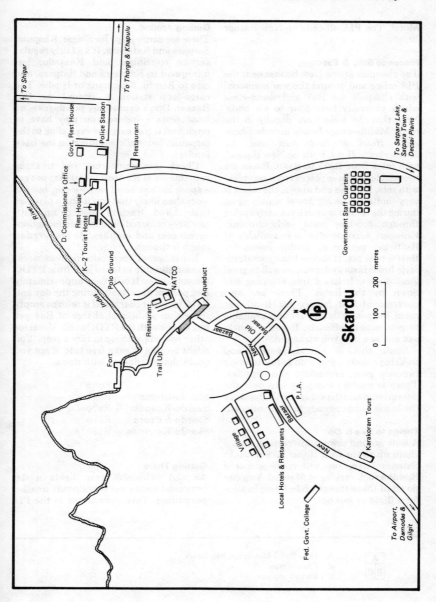

Skardu

Motel. The PIA office is on New Bazaar St.

Places to Stay & Eat

The cheapies are on New Bazaar near the PIA office and around the war memorial with charpois for Rs5 and dorm-class which generally have four to six beds. Note that the toilets are usually in the open. Middle-range hotels include *Shangrilla Hotel & Restaurant* and the *Masherbrum Hotel*, both on New Bazaar, with rates from Rs25 to Rs40. Rates are negotiable but these places come complete with rats. For Rs8 and above, the menu is very limited. The *K2 Motel* is only open during the tourist season from early spring through summer until early autumn. Economy accommodation is available at Rs50 per person or double rooms for Rs100 plus tax. It serves hearty western-style breakfasts and meals as well as good local dishes. It has a free camping site down by the Indus. There are also government *rest houses* for Rs30 per room, but generally they are only available to government officials. If you're stuck, ask and see how you make out.

Since this is mountaineering and trekking country, you'd do better to bring camping gear, provisions and supplies. There is another camping site near the polo ground and the village on the banks of the Indus as has already been mentioned.

Things to See & Do

A walk around town is interesting, as is a climb up to the fort. If you hike down to Satpara Lake, you will come across a Buddha rock carving at Mantlal. You can do all of these things while filling in time for a flight or bus out.

Getting Around

There are cargo-jeeps for Shigar, Khapulu, Satpara and Katchura. It's a fairly regular service to Shigar and Khapulu, but infrequent to Katchura and Satpara, and rare to Rondu, Kharmang or Hushe. The cargo-jeep station is around the Old Bazaar. Don't expect any privileges – no front seats – indeed you may have to crouch on top of cargo or even cling to the tarpaulin bar while standing on the back fender.

Check mountaineering and trekking expeditions at K2 Motel. You may not get a space in their hired cargo-jeeps, but it's more than likely that you'll find a place on their hired tractors loaded up with brightly– coloured camping and mountaineering gear and supplies. Be prepared to rough it though.

If neither of these alternatives work, you may be able to hire a jeep from PTDC for your tour. It will cost approximately Rs6 per km plus Rs50 during the day and Rs75 for night charges. If it returns empty there's an additional charge of Rs4 per km. Check with the PTDC at K2 Motel for other tourists wishing to hire a jeep. You might be able to get a free ride, if not you could share expenses with them.

	Fares
Skardu-Shigar	Rs20
Skardu-Khapulu	Rs20
Skardu-Satpara	Rs10
Skardu-Katchura	Rs20

Getting There

Air *PIA* schedules two flights a day between Skardu and Rawalpindi, weather permitting. Take your ticket to the PIA

A   Lake Saiful Muluk, Kaghan Valley
B   Chitrali man
C   Chitrali woman

Northern Area Office in the PIA building on the Mall in Rawalpindi by 1 pm the day before your scheduled flight. Go back around 4 to 4.30 pm and they will tell you when the plane is leaving – if indeed it is! If your flight is cancelled, ask them to put you up for the night – free – in the PIA hotel. Don't expect anything special – it's the same as any Rs20 a night hotel – but it's free! Also the PIA bus will pick you up and take you out to the airport – free. The fare costs Rs165 including tax, but because flights are so heavily booked and because they are cancelled so frequently due to the weather, the Fokker is often replaced by Pakistani Air Force aircraft. This means the flights are crowded with service personnel and the chances of getting a good seat for the view are nil. If you want to see Nanga Parbat and are lucky enough to have a choice in seating, try and get right up front or down the back of the aircraft. If you sit in the middle your vision can be obscured by the engine of the Fokker Friendship. There are no longer any flights between Skardu and Gilgit. The return trip from Skardu to Islamabad is usually very heavily booked. Westerners should go to the Tourist Information Office at K2 Tourist Motel and ask for a priority booking.

There are mini-buses for around Rs7 to 10 or a bus for Rs3 from the airport to the township of Skardu, a distance of about 16 km. The airport itself is tiny and has few amenities – no toilet, washroom, cafe, nothing.

Road NATCO and Masherbrum Tours have two buses daily, departing for Gilgit at 6 am and 7 am. Concessions are given to four students for each trip – local or foreigners – which amount to about 50% discount of the normal fare. The bus station is near the Shangrilla Hotel on New Bazaar.

It is an eight to 10-hour trip barring landslides en route. The road is now sealed to beyond the airport. The bus route does not go through Katchura anymore. About three km before Katchura the bus crosses a bridge over the Indus and then follows the right bank. The other road goes to Shigar Valley.

On the way to Gilgit the bus stops for lunch, usually shortly after Damodas. Be sure to fill up your water bottle with lemon tea here as this is the only stop in a long journey. Try to get a front window seat, both for comfort – it's much less bumpy – and the scenery.

KATCHURA LAKE

This is a village 30 km from Skardu on the way to Gilgit. It is now by-passed by buses heading for Gilgit as the road has been moved to the right bank of the Indus following the construction of the new bridge three km from the village.

There is a luxurious 5-star hotel here called the Shangrilla Tourist Resort, considered by the proprietor, a retired brigadier, to be heaven on earth. That aside, it's worth a visit just to see the set-up. It consists of a complex of cottages, four-room lodges, camping ground, shops and a restaurant with local and western cuisine. It also has a library, fish hatchery and a mini-zoo. If you like aircraft, you can stay in the old Dakota which crash-landed at Kachura Lake decades ago, and is now converted into a tourist cottage. Motel rates are Rs100 a single, and Rs180 to Rs250 a double; the four-room cottages cost Rs600 to Rs900 and it's Rs50 to camp. There are half rates for children and free transport from the Skardu airport and back. If you're interested check for an advance booking at Shangrilla Reception Centre, (tel 6 6936), 14/N Murree Rd, Rawalpindi.

Things to Do & See

It's an ideal place for relaxing, particularly if you're keen on fishing. You can also go swimming, take a short trek or walkabout or a tour by jeep of some of the valleys in Baltistan.

SHIGAR

Shigar is 30 km north of Skardu. Five km out of town on the road to Khapulu there is a turn-off to a sandy wasteland, which leads down to a bridge and up into Shigartang – the desert plain of Shigar. The road is dusty, desolate and rough, and jeep passengers hanging from the rear often have to jump off to lighten the load for the steep climb up.

Shigar is a pleasant little village with a nice climate. Set in a lush, green valley 2300 metres above sea level, the atmosphere of cascading rivers dominates the atmosphere. One of my strongest images of this place is students sitting in the grounds of the modern school, singing sad songs about faraway places and inspiring mountains. On the left-hand side of the road is a traditional **Tibetan mosque**, topped with a star-shaped tower. Near here are two or three wooden box stalls which comprise the bazaar, and right beside the Shigar Nallah (stream) is the *Karakoram Hotel & Restaurant*.

Up a rocky plateau are the ruins of a castle, now a crumbled pile of rocks. And across a little wooden bridge is the *teshildah* or administrative heart of the valley. Of a quaintly Ladakhi design as are the houses clustered behind it, the architecture in old Shigar is distinctly Central Asian in style. Around the fringes are modern buildings like the rest house, the hospital, government staff quarters and a hydro-electric plant.

It's pleasant and relaxing here with only the sound of the cascading stream and singing birds, like the mynahs and the *hazardastan*, a lovely yellow bird streaked with brown, usually called *mayon* in Chitral. The *rest house* is clean and furnished but has limited food – bring some with you if possible. There is also a lawn here where camping is possible. A nice way to spend some time is to walk around the environs, but there's nothing much to do here.

This is the gateway to Dassu 80 km away and to the trekking route to Concordia via the Baltoro Glacier. Out of Shigar a trail forks off the route to Dassu down to a bridge where it continues to the other side of the valley. There are a few interesting villages on this side of the valley. Many children from around here – particularly infants – are dressed in traditional attire and headwear. It is also the setting off point for Khapulu.

KHAPULU

Situated 102 km to the east and at 2600, this valley is considered to be the most stunning in Baltistan, and is regarded by the natives as the Garden of Eden. The desert plains along the River Shyok are reddish in colour. In 1892 the Earl of Dunmore, a British explorer, who spent a year crossing the Karakorams wrote that the Shyok Valley 'was more beautiful than anything I have ever seen in my life ... magnificent and on an enormous scale, larger than anything even in the Rocky Mountains of America.'

Cargo-jeep transport is frequent, twice daily at 7 am and 2 pm, but quite often loaded to capacity. The route to Khapulu is similar to the journey to Shigar, and while rough and bumpy, the discomfort is offset by stunning scenery. It can be roughly divided into three sections. The first wanders through archaeological petroglyphs, then through a narrow valley which broadens further up the Shyok Valley and on past the Humayun Bridge.

This section is crossed by numerous irrigation canals.

Khapulu is the principal town of the Shyok Valley with villages built along gentle slopes shaped like an amphitheatre. It has a small bazaar, and perched on elevated land overlooking the valley near the polo ground, is the palace of the erstwhile ruler. Villages near Khapulu are **Shaling** and **Chakchang**. The people here belong to the Nurbuksh Sufi faith and their mosque is of a particularly interesting design and well worth a look.

The people, language, culture and architecture in this fascinating valley are distinctly Tibetan. Part of its fascination lies in its summer festivals when the tradition of presenting offerings to the fairies, though not as popular as it once was, still exists. They also perform two special dances at these festivals: one a flower dance called *mindak*; the other a sword dance known as *stamno*. Another magical element of Khapulu and its people is their use of the serpentine stone as an antidote to snake bites. They crush it into powder, apply it to the wound and it works.

There is a furnished *rest house* here which has tolerable food, but *Shyok Inn*, once an alternative accommodation spot, has now been turned into a clinic by an elderly Austrian couple from spring until early autumn. *Camping* is possible near the rest house, and if you don't have camping gear and are finding accommodation a problem see Alam Dar, nephew of the former rajah. He might be able to arrange something for you.

SATPARA LAKE
Eight km from Skardu and 2400 metres above sea level, this lake is half-way to the town of Satpara. It is quite possible to trek there and back in a day. The only building apart from a watchman's hut is a forlorn-looking *PTDC Tourist Motel*. There is a small island in the middle of the lake, which is topped by a low, mud-stone hut. The road continues to the town of Satpara

– further south is Deosai Plateau.

GILGIT-HUNZA
Like Baltistan, the entire Gilgit-Hunza area is in the shadow of the ramparts of the Karakorams. Sandwiched between Chitral and Baltistan, it is 26,500 square km and spreads up to the Hindu Raj Range and the Khunjerab Pass in the north, to the fringes of Mastuj and Laspur in the west, down to Darel and Tanger in the south and the Nagar Valley and the Rakaposhi and Bagroth Range in the east.

It has a number of high mountain peaks which include Mt Distaghilsar (7895 metres), the Momhilsar (7342 metres), Rakaposhi (7788 metres) and the Haramosh (7479 metres). It also has huge glaciers, such as the Hispar and Batura. Both the mountain peaks and the glaciers are in the western region of the Karakorams in Shimshal, Hunza and Nagar.

Further west, below the Hindu Raj Range, is the Iskhoman Valley, and beyond is the Yasin Valley. All these valleys in the north, from Shimshal to the Khunjerab and Mizghar, and from the valley of Nagar across Passu, down to Chalt, and right up to Iskhoman and Yasin comprise what is known as the Hunza region. With the exception of a few Wakhi-speaking villages, all these valleys are inhabited by the Burushuski – speaking people, who are Ismailis, followers of the Agha Khan.

South of Chalt from Bagroth Valley, right through the Punial-Gakutch river valleys to Darel and Tanger in the south, and beyond Shandur Pass is the Gilgit region. The people in these valleys speak Shina and are generally Shi'ites.

This entire area used to be known as Bolor during the Patola dynasty which collapsed when the Chinese arrived in the 8th century AD. With the advent of the Tibetans in the 9th century AD, it was referred to as Dardistan which declined and fragmented into several mini-republics, which in turned evolved into mini-kingdoms. With the arrival of Islam in the

10th century they developed into mirdoms, which appear to have been constantly at war with one another. At this time it became customary for women to work the fields while the men stood guard or fought battles. Despite being devout Moslems, they were fairy-worshippers until two decades ago.

The opening of the Karakoram Highway – which roughly follows the old Silk Trade Route through this region, branching east towards Leh and west through Punial and Yasin into the Oxus to Samarkhand – wiped out traditional customs, the social caste system and ways of celebrating festivals and beliefs. As a result it is now an ambivalent society caught between two worlds: the conflict of traditional Islamic culture and progressive revolutionary trends.

GILGIT

The 240 km between Skardu and Gilgit are in the process of being surfaced, but it is rugged going most of the way. Once you reach Alam Bridge, the road joins the sealed Karakoram Highway.

Apart from the final mountainous stretch from Jaglot, the highway wanders north through rolling green landscape into Gilgit, which is right in the centre of the upper highland. Gilgit is larger and more developed than Skardu, and has all the usual trappings of an administrative town: government offices, rest houses, banks, hotels, a polo ground, bazaars, tourist shops, teashops and a couple of cinemas.

Originally the capital of Bolor and the centre of the Patola dynasty (4th to 8th century AD) and of Dardistan (9th to 10th century AD), it was a transit trading centre of the ancient Silk Trade Route. It was still a slave-trading area until the arrival of the Sikhs and the British in the middle of the 19th century, and was Buddhist until around the 17th century when it was invaded by the Shi'ite Moslems from Baltistan.

Historically it is an important archaeological site and part of its history is recorded in the Gilgit Manuscript discovered in the area above Nowpur near the Kargah Valley. This was written during the Patola dynasty period in Sanskrit-Persian script and inscribed on birch bark. On a rocky cliff in the Kargah Valley is a carving of the Buddha executed during the Tibetan period, and further up the valley is a cave inscribed with rock carvings. In the village of Danyor is a house which has a boulder covered in inscriptions – some dating back to the 7th century – recording the line of the Buddhist rules of Bolor.

Gilgit is a reasonably quiet, pleasant town through which the river of the same name flows. Spanned by one of the longest suspension bridges in Asia, the Gilgit River heads south, joining the Hunza River and finally the mighty Indus. The people living here now are predominantly Ismailis from Hunza and a large group of Sunnis, a situation which makes for social conflict at times.

Of all the administrative centres in the Northern Mountain Zone of Pakistan today, this town is the most important geographically, being right in the centre of the highland. It is a major junction for the Gilgit-Sinkiang barter trade.

Refugees

There used to be many Afghan Kirghiz refugees living here, but almost all have emigrated to Turkey over the past couple of years. A few remain however, and more trickle through here in summer when the high passes are open. But they generally move down to the refugee camps on the plains of the North West Frontier Province to register for assistance. Migration tapers off in autumn.

Information

The Tourist Information Centre is at the PTDC-run Chinar Inn, within walking distance of the airport. You can cash travellers' cheques at the Pakistan National Bank, and for books on the northern area and handicrafts, check Dad

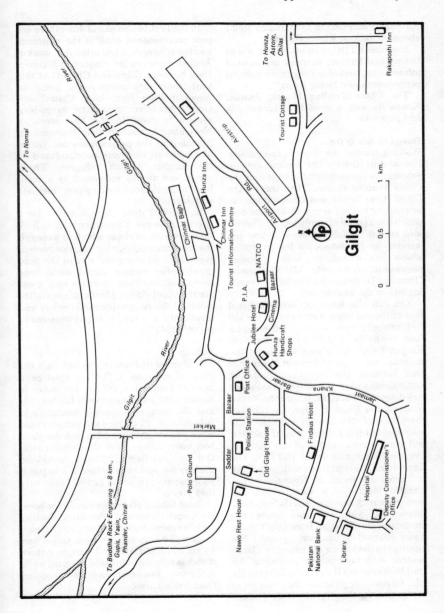

To Nomal

Gilgit River

To Buddha Rock Engraving — 8 km., Gupis, Yasin, Phander, Chitral

Airstrip

Chinnar Bagh

Hunza Inn

Chinnar Inn

Airport Rd

To Hunza, Astore, Chilas

Rakaposhi Inn

Tourist Cottage

Tourist Information Centre

NATCO

P.I.A.

Cinema

Bazaar

Jubilee Hotel

Hunza Handicraft Shops

Market

Post Office

Bazaar

Bazaar

Jamaat Khana

Police Station

Saddar

Old Gilgit House

Firdaus Hotel

Polo Ground

Nawo Rest House

Hospital

Deputy Commissioner's Office

Pakistan National Bank

Library

Gilgit

N

0   0.5   1 km.

Ali Shah's and Gulam Mohammed Beg's shops on Jamaat Khana Bazaar.

See the PTDC tourist officer about fishing and hunting licences and related information, and also for gen on cultural programmes and hiring jeeps.

The China Trading House, Jamaat Khana Bazaar, is good for Chinese silk and porcelain.

Things to See & Do

Walking around the town is fascinating. For a start there's the bazaar area to explore, or the handicraft shops and the China Trading House. Then there's the Gilgit River banks and **Chinar Bagh**, an interesting but not very well-kept garden, which has a patch of sandy beach. There's also an old British **cemetery** or you can wander up to **Rakaposhi Inn** in Jutial, which has a balcony with splendid, panoramic views over Mt Rakaposhi, Diran and Deobani – particularly interesting late in the afternoon.

You can also go on an **archaeological tour** of the old town centre site of the old fort, though nothing much is left except a lone tower in a military cantonment. Kargah Valley has a rock carving of the **Buddha**, and in the vicinity of Nowpur is Giri Yashani, the site of a Buddhist settlement where the **Gilgit Manuscript** was discovered in 1931. It is on the Punial road via the Rajah Bazaar. On the way there's a trail off to the left just before the suspension bridge, turn down it and you will see the rock carving of the Buddha, over nine metres up on the cliff face. The figure itself is about three metres tall and is framed in a pentacle. Near the hydro-electric plants is a **cave** which has numerous rock carvings. On the way back follow the water channel along the mountainside. The trail from Gilgit to the water channel begins just opposite the airstrip. In the village of Danyor is a large **boulder** with inscriptions recording the Buddhist rulers of Bolor in the 7th century AD. To get there go across the suspension bridge and via the Afghan refugee camp.

In the first two weeks of June there are **polo tournaments**, both in the mornings and the afternoons; and in the first week of August there is a polo match in Shadnur Pass between Gilgit and Chitral. At this time there are cargo-jeeps going to Shadnur Pass from both Chitral and Gilgit. At other times the cargo-jeep service is rare. In the first week of November is another polo tournament. Included in the programmes are games like *buzhkazi* that were re-introduced by the Kirghiz Afghan refugees. These games are usually enlivened by a small band of musicians playing pipes, trumpets and drums.

In the old days there used to be a specific **polo day**, a day when women took their revenge on those who had wronged the community. Sitting on low-roofed, stone huts all along the way to the polo ground, the women would wield long sticks and flay their enemies with great accuracy and vigour. Most often the latter included the village ruler and traders and merchants, who tended to pay ransoms to get off lightly.

Fishing

The Bureau of Fisheries is just past the PNB. If you want to fish you must get a licence from this office. Be sure to mention the exact number of fishing rods and the number of people intending to fish. Also check if there are certain times when you are not allowed to go fishing and how many fish you are allowed to catch. Over-zealous fishing officials could ruin the day for you even before it's begun if your papers are not in order. Make sure they are.

Good fishing grounds close to the town are **Kargah Nallah** and **Gilgit River**. Further away **Bashiret Nallah** is also popular with anglers. Twenty-two km from Gupis and 44 km south of Darel and Tanger, **Batesh Nallah** is renowned for golden trout, while to the west, **Phander Lake** is also a popular trout fishing area.

Hunting

Hunting is banned here.

Places to Stay – Bottom End

Accommodation can be a problem during summer, so if you've got camping equipment, make sure you bring it with you. Otherwise try the *Jubilee Hotel* on Cinema Bazaar, which has double rooms only for Rs25. Western-style breakfasts and local meals are available. Down an alley off Jamaat Khana Bazaar, the *Firdaus Hotel* has doubles for Rs10 and charpois in the garden for Rs5. Only local food here. There's a new hotel on Airport Rd which has singles for Rs20, doubles for Rs30 and rooms with three beds in them for Rs45. The *Vershinghum Hotel* on Cinema Bazaar has singles for Rs20 and doubles for Rs40. Western-style breakfasts are available here and you can get local meals for Rs15 and over. The *Tourist Cottage* in Jutial, has singles and doubles for Rs12.50 and Rs25, and dorm accommodation with share bathrooms for four for Rs40. You get western-style breakfasts and the best dinners in town here. It is very popular and is generally packed with local people and tourists in summer. Meals cost Rs12.50 and up.

Middle

The *Hunza Inn*, near Chinar Bagh, has singles and doubles for Rs25 or above, and also offers western and native dishes. The *Park Hotel* on Cinema Bazaar, has singles and doubles for Rs50 and Rs75, with western-style breakfasts and local menus.

Top End

Rakaposhi Inn, 2½ km away from the town centre, is the poshest PIA-run hotel in town. It has rooms for Rs300 and over plus tax, but the rates come down in the off-season by about 25%. It has western meals and local dishes, and the best yoghurt in town. The *Chinar Inn*, which is run by the PTDC, has rooms from RS100 and up plus tax. You can get western or local

meals here from Rs35 and above. The *rest house* is used mainly for officials.

Places to Eat

There are a number of local restaurants which serve good meals for Rs5 along Cinema Bazaar. There's also an excellent bakery in the same street. Fruit and nuts are available in shops along Saddar Bazaar and soft drinks can be bought in local kiosks and teashops. Also on Saddar Bazaar right opposite the mosque is the *Kasghar Restaurant*, which offers Chinese or Kasghari meals at very reasonable prices.

But as already mentioned the *Tourist Cottage* is the place for dinner. They serve a mixture of Chinese, Pakistani and western food, which includes a thick noodle soup called *daudo* by the locals, rice, chapattis, salad, french fries, sliced roast mutton, and beef, chicken or mutton curry. On meatless days – usually Wednesdays – meat dishes are replaced by *dahl* followed by custard pudding with apricots and nuts, or sometimes apples. All this is washed down with Chinese jasmine green tea or coffee. The menu may vary from time to time, but it's always good value.

Breakfast is served any time, but dinner is put out on a long table between 7.30 and 8.30 pm. In summer the tables are out on the lawn and you may be lucky enough to see an aurora in the sky to the north. Manifested by a white light rising over the mountains and eclipsing the stars, it is considered to be electrified gaseous matter in space, and looks rather like a fluorescent light. The Tourist Cottage has a relaxed, social atmosphere and should not be missed.

Liquor Alcohol is not available here. If you have your own supply, drink it in your hotel room. The thing to drink here is *Hunza Water*, and it comes in two varieties – grape and mulberry. The former is a cloudy-green colour and sweet, the latter reddish in colour and tasting rather like dry wine. Make discreet enquiries if you want to try some. Islam is intolerant in this regard. However, there are some kindred spirits out there. A bottle is worth Rs60.

Getting Around

Local There are mini-wagons plying between Jutial – the Tourist Cottage – and the centre of town for Rs1.50. If they have to diverge from the usual route – to go to the airport or the commissioner's office for instance – the fare varies between Rs5 and Rs10.

Gilgit is a starting out point for mountaineering expeditions, trekking parties and tourism. It has mini-wagons, vans, buses and cargo-jeeps going in all directions.

NATCO has buses and cargo-jeeps for most places in the area. It also has jeeps for hire. Rates are negotiable but are based on Rs6 per km, Rs4 per km if returning empty, plus Rs50 a day or Rs75 for night charges. There is room for eight passengers in each jeep.

The PTDC Tourist Information Centre at Chinar Inn also has jeeps for hire at the same rates. They are new and comfortable, but only have space for six passengers. Rates are not negotiable, but you can be assured of excellent service.

There are other private jeeps for hire, but they are not as reliable as NATCO or the PTDC. Suzuki wagons are also for hire and the usual agreement is Rs3 per km or Rs30 per hour. You are obliged to pay whichever works out as the higher rate. But you can hire them on a flat rate basis over certain routes.

Bus On Cinema Bazaar, *Masherbrum Tours* has buses which go from Gilgit to Skardu daily. Concessions are available to four students each trip.

Generally the vans, minibuses and buses are stationed on Jamaat Khana Bazaar and the Cinema Bazaar. They usually do the round of bazaars for passengers and cargo, then return to their usual station before finally departing.

Getting Away

Air Gilgit is linked by air with Rawalpindi. Try and get a seat on the right-hand side up the front of the plane or down the back as the flight path is quite spectacular, following the Indus River up the Kaghan Valley and over Babusar Pass. If you get a seat in the belly of the Fokker, you view is obscured by the engine. Down below, the mountainous landscape appears lush green, with beautiful, clear lakes, and on the right is the panorama of Nanga Parbat. Gradually the country becomes more arid and barren.

The *PIA* office, on Cinema Bazaar, schedules two F-27 flights daily between Gilgit and Rawalpindi depending on weather conditions. Departure times are usually around 10.30 am, 1 pm and occasionally, 3 pm. The fare is Rs160 plus an airport tax of Rs5.

Road Gilgit and Rawalpindi are also linked by the all-weather Karakoram Highway. Foreigners do not require a permit to travel on the highway nowadays, but they do have to register at two police check-points along the way. It takes about 14 hours by car, between 15 and 16 hours by minibus and 16 to 18 hours by bus. However, that's an optimistic estimate, as it can take up to 24 hours.

Suzuki wagons going to Chilas are stationed near the Firdaus Hotel in an alley off Jamaat Bazaar. They take you right into the centre of Chilas and the fare is Rs20. *NATCO* and *Kohistan* buses charge the same price and drop you off on the Karakoram Highway some three km from Chilas.

Bus The *NATCO* office is also on Cinema Bazaar and has two bus services daily to Rawalpindi. The earlier one leaves at 11 am and arrives in Rawalpindi between 2 and 3 am. More convenient is the 8 pm bus which pulls into Rawalpindi some time between 11 am and 12 noon. It costs Rs75 and there is a 50% concession available to four students on each trip.

There are other buses that depart daily for Rawalpindi from Cinema Bazaar.

North

To Passu A *NATCO* bus departs every alternate day to Passu for Rs26. Student concessions are available. Occasionally there are also minibuses and vans that go to Passu, but don't rely on them.

To Hunza The service to Hunza is regular. Buses, minibuses, vans and mini-wagons are frequent. Bus fares cost Rs12, everything else is Rs14. For the best view make sure you sit on the left-hand side. If you sit on the right all you'll see is the side of the mountain range along which the road is built – and this only changes towards the end of the trip.

To Nagar Cargo-jeep service to Nagar is irregular and costs Rs16. Take the bus for Hunza and get off at the junction if you intend trekking.

To Chalt Transport here is also irregular. The fare is Rs15. Take the Hunza bus and get off at Chalt.

To Naltar Cargo-jeep service here is irregular and costs Rs15. As an alternative you can take the bus to Hunza or Passu and get off at Rahimabad, then cross the river and go to Nomal and trek from there.

East

To Skardu There is a regular bus service to Skardu for Rs60. Student concessions are available.

To Bagroth The cargo-jeep service here is irregular and costs Rs25.

To Astore Frequent cargo-jeep service for Rs50 and an additional Rs25 for the return trip.

South

To Jaglot There is regular transport here for Rs6.

To Chilas Regular bus service for Rs8.

To Darel & Tanger Cargo-jeep service only from Chilas.

To Rawalpindi Regular bus service via Beshum for Rs75.

North-West

To Imit (Iskhoman) Irregular cargo-jeep service to this town for Rs30.

West

To Punial, Gukutch, Gupis, Phander & Yasin Almost regular cargo jeep service to all these places. Fares in same order are Rs15, Rs20, Rs30, Rs55 and Rs40.

To Teru Very irregular cargo-jeep service here for Rs60.

To Chitral The cargo-jeep service along this route is very rare. On the Teru-Chitral route cargo-jeeps are also rare. The Shandur Pass on the Chitral road is only open from early May until mid-November.

At the time of the polo match between Gilgit and Chitral during the first week of August, cargo-jeeps are regular, but once that is over, it is difficult to get there again. In early autumn you may be able to get a ride on the cargo-jeeps that take Chinese goods to Chitral from Gilgit.

ROUTES TO HUNZA

The old route starts across the suspension bridge, follows the right bank of the river to the village of Danyor, and from there heads into Nomal, a transit village to the Naltar Valley 27 km away. It continues to Chalt, 51 km from Gilgit, taking the left bank of the Hunza River upstream. The road is bumpy and broken up here. If you're trekking to Hunza, Chalt is a good overnight stop. Continue from here on to Maun on the Karakoram Highway.

Seven km east of here, the highway, acknowledged to have the best surface in Pakistan, veers north and climbs gently up past mountains that have been blasted with explosives. The Chinese influence is obvious along this stretch of road, and is particularly noticeable in the bridges which are made with railings and posts, and decorated with stone-lions' heads. About 1000 members of the Sino-Pakistan labour force are believed to have lost their lives in the construction of this road and there are numerous memorials – distinctly Chinese in character – com-

Old Fort Tower, Hunza

memorating the deaths.

You are now going through a section of the 'Suspended Crossing' of the old Silk Road. At the village of Jeethal, 16 km from Gilgit, you will come across cliff faces that are decorated with carvings of animals. Along a tributary of the Hunza River, some way up, are large flat rocks which depict ibexes, markhors, horsemen and other hunting scenes. Forty-eight km further on at Sonikot, there is a boulder with two stupas carved on it.

Two km out of Hunza is what is called the **Sacred Rock of Hunza**, a rocky ridge of barren mountain between the Hunza and Hispar rivers, which, according to Dr Karl Jettmar, appears to have been a frontier post. Basically a rocky gallery divided into four sections, it contains a multitude of engraved scripts – mostly in Kharosthi and Brahmi – and carvings of animals, warriors on horseback. There are more petroglyphs all the way to Gulmit, Passu, through the Kilik and Mintaka passes and into western Turkestan.

Here, despite its name, the all-weather highway and its 70 bridges are subject to landslides, avalanches and blockages from shifting glaciers, which can take days – sometimes weeks – to clear or cut detours around. It may even be necessary to blast the glacier off the road. However, the road is not particularly steep and it is scenic all the way, passing through tiny hamlets and offering glimpses of the majestic Mt Rakaposhi from half-way up.

At Hindi it rejoins the old Hunza route, passes through Hunza, and continues north through the villages of Gulmit and Passu, where a dirt track veers east to Shimshal Village. Beyond Khudabad, at Bely, another dirt track splits off the highway, north-west to Peshit and Irshad Uwin Pass. And another one leads to the village of Mizghar, Kalamdarchi Post and Murkushi and the 4700-metre Mintaka. This is the old way along the ancient Silk Trade Route, which continues on to Kasghar. From here the Karakoram Highway wends its way to Khunjerab Pass where the barter trade with China is conducted. The Chinese bring in matches, porcelain, jasmine tea, razor blades, silk, and ready-made clothes in exchange for woollen blankets, dried fruits, medicinal herbs and other woollen garments.

The Khunjerab Plateau is mainly sandy wasteland, broken with chasms. It is about 175 km from Karimabad, the junction for camel caravans, heading to Leh from Central Asia. It was here that the Khanjuts, the brigands of Hunza, used to collect taxes or, quite often, simply attacked and plundered the camel caravans. The word *Khunjerab* means Valley of Blood in Kirghiz.

Fairy Worship

Past Aliabad on the way to Ganesh, there is a trail off to the left leading up to Hyderabad, a small village perched high on a ledge. This region of the Ultar Range was once a ruby-mining area, and like almost every hamlet and village in the Hunza Valley, a centre for fairy worship. Hyderabad has a sacrificial altar known locally as a *haligan* where ibexes were offered to the fairy goddess or godmother in ritual ceremonies. The people from these parts believed that fairies were a ghoulish lot who thrived on viscera and warm blood.

There are a number of other villages around here including Nominabad just up from Ganesh, Ganesh itself and Altit that have similar altars. By the glacier in Passu, right at the entrance of an amphitheatre-like valley there is another *haligan*, and on the trail to Shimshal Valley, half-way to the village, yet another. Many have specific names which may possibly refer to their own particular fairy goddess. For example the altar in Altit is known as *Ahaz Ziarat*; the one in Ganesh as *Bulchi Toko*.

Although traditional fairy worship is disappearing slowly, there are still festivals throughout the year where the walls, posts and pillars of houses and huts are painted with ibexes, markhors and Marco Polo sheep, and the altars bedecked with pennants and flags, as some kind of appeasement to the fairies in the valleys.

PASSU

If you're heading north, it is best to go straight to Passu and from there slowly down to Hunza, visiting places on the way. It's 125 km from Gilgit to Passu, and a further 35 km from Hunza. The bus passes through Passu over Batura Bridge, and 200 metres beyond the bridge is a police check-point. Foreigners are not allowed beyond this point. Passu is about five km further back, but it is better to get off here and walk back, rather than get off before.

The village of Passu is half a km before the *Batura Inn*, where you can stay for Rs25 a single with heating or Rs 40 a double. Dinner is available at the inn for Rs20. Passu was previously the site of the base camp of the Sino-Pakistan road construction team, and has an unused airstrip, a cinema and some recreation halls. There are two shops here which are only open for a few hours in the morning, another building which used to be a dining hall and the Batura Inn.

The trip is worth it for the scenery, but try and avoid going there in autumn or spring as there are seasonal duststorms and it's cold and windy. The **Batura Glacier**, the largest and longest glacier in the region – about 56 km – is directly below the Batura Peaks (7785 metres). It seems rather unprepossessing from the road, just a mass of earth strewn with boulders, and no ice visible unless you climb to its top. To really get a good look at it, you have to walk up to Passu, turn right before the bridge over a stony area. After walking a further 50 metres or so, you will arrive at a trail up the face of a cliff, which leads directly to the **Passu Glacier**. Almost 1½ hours later, you will come to a bowl-shaped valley between the Passu and Batura glaciers. Another hour brings you to the edge of the valley and a panoramic view of the Batura Glacier. You can get to the **base camp** of Batura Peaks from here. The latter are considered by some experts and *afficionados* as the loveliest mountains in the world.

There are *shepherds' huts* up there and the people are friendly. Back-tracking takes two hours, or you can go to the edge of the Batura Glacier and then follow it down to the highway. This is a difficult route, but if you time it right, you will be rewarded by a dazzling sunset right across the serrated horizon.

If you're interested in archaeology try searching for petroglyphs along the highway. This is a starting point for trekking through the valleys of Batura and Shimshal.

Places to Stay

Batura Inn has four doubles with two attached bathrooms for Rs25. Breakfast at Rs10 consists of two fried eggs, two parathas and tea. Lunch and dinner cost Rs30 and consist of potatoes, chapattis, eggs/chicken and tea. Dahl is available on request. That's the complete menu.

GULMIT

The *NATCO* bus that goes up to Passu departs early the next morning for Gilgit, and will drop you off anywhere between Passu and Hunza. However, if you miss the bus, it's quite a pleasant three-hour walk to Gulmit, which is 10 km away in a broad valley with gently sloping hills. Twenty-seven km further on is **Karimabad**, which has several options for accommodation – see below.

Burit Lake, five km away, is said to be good for trout-fishing. The trail goes via the hamlet of **Husseini**. On the way to Hunza you have the option of waiting for the *NATCO* bus or you can try hitching. There is a good chance that you will get a lift on a tractor or even a jeep all the way down to Hunza.

HUNZA

Buried in a gigantic mountain range, Hunza has been one of the most cut-off regions in this part of the world. It only became known to the rest of the world in the 1880s, and ever since has been described as a lost paradise, the Shangri-la of the Karakorams. Little is known of the region's history.

Due to the harsh environment and the severity of their lifestyle, people here practised a form of natural birth control, which involved the women leaving the husband's bed and no intercourse until each baby was completely weaned. The groom's mother would accompany the newlyweds on their honeymoon as guide and teacher, for they considered marriage too important to be left to chance. The women here wear round caps, seven to 10 cm high, embroidered with bright floral or geometrical designs, usually with red or maroon as the predominant colour. They are similar to those worn by the women in Phander and Laspur in Chitral, Like the Chinese they beat drums during a lunar eclipse to drive away the dragon, which they believe is devouring the moon.

This is a region of rubies and garnets. Early in December of 1891, following the successful assault on the fort at Nilt, Colonel Algernon Durand, the commanding officer, was wounded. When the bullet was finally extracted, it turned out be a garnet enclosed in lead. 'There were sacks full of similar bullets within the fort,' wrote an Englishman in the expedition. Sir Francis Younghusband, who arrived in 1887, was the first European to visit Hunza. He came to negotiate the end of brigandage in Baltistan with the mir.

Most of the people from this region are Ismailis and until the 1950s, continued to practise their own culture and hold their own traditional festivals. These festivals were similar to those of the Kalash Kafirs, consisting of a kind of *mardi gras*, involving much feasting, drinking and dancing, dressed in very brightly coloured clothes. In spring they would hold a festival known as *Thomothaleno*, a night procession, lit by flaming torches and celebrating the death of an evil-doer.

Once again the completion and opening of the Karakoram Highway marked the end of these customs, and eventually brought about the complete merging of the valley with the rest of Parkistan. The death of the last mir shortly after the opening of the highway also signified the end of mirdom.

KARIMABAD

The Hunza Valley begins in Chalt where the Hunza River turns sharply south. It is rather narrow and featureless here until the village of Hindi, where the valley begins to open up. Approaching Aliabad at 2300 metres you pass the showroom of the Gemstone Corporation of Pakistan, the PTDC Tourist Camp, the police station, the hospital and the primary school, just off the highway on a slope. Aliabad has a few *hotels* and a tiny bazaar with tourist shops and general stores.

Eight km away is Karimabad. The road, lined with poplar trees, passes grainfields and the **Chumar (Iron) Fort** – though there's nothing much left of it now – climbs gently up to Ganesh, skirts the village reputed to be the oldest settlement in Hunza, then climbs a steep slope to Karimabad. If you wish to stay overnight at Ganesh, try the *Yagbar Inn*, which has singles with heating for Rs10, and also provides dinner – rather a spartan meal – for Rs20.

In this region the vertical area is made up of tiers of flat, narrow ledges on a sheltered corner of the Ultar Massif. Here villages are stacked one above the other, with mud-stone huts packed tightly together against the granite flanks of the Ultar. The administrative centre of Karimabad is quite small, comprising the new house of the family of the former mir of Hunza, the bazaars, government school, rest houses, offices and hotels. A trail leads up to another village called Baltit where the old **fort** perched on an upper ledge looms like a sentinel over the

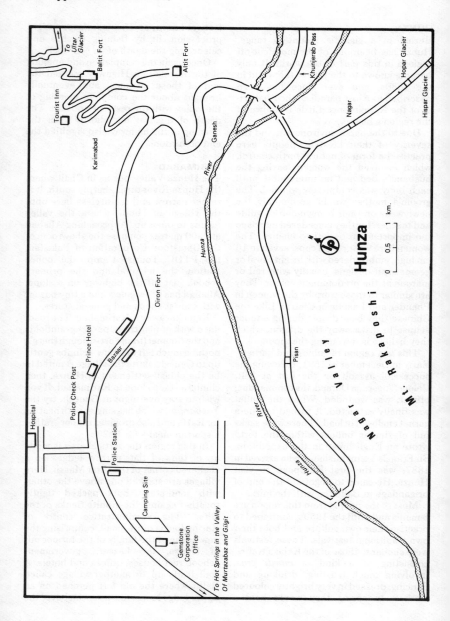

whole valley.

The fort, designed along Tibetan lines, was remodelled in the middle of the 19th century and looks more like a castle than a fort. Originally the first floor was used as a storage room and grain depot, with a jail and kitchen above it, and the upper floor was the mir's official room. From here the balcony offers a commanding view of the whole picturesque valley, which is dominated by the Rakaposhi. The smoke-darkened interior is lit by only a few, small windows and to get there you must climb equally smoke-blackened ladders. The wooden window frames, doors and posts are carved ornately.

It is built of heavy wooden beams, covered with twigs and branches and covered with a mixture of sand and mud. A Tibetan-style star-shaped tower surmounts the building. Only a few decades ago Huk Gukkur, a *bitan* or local seer, was jeered at for predicting that the castle would be empty one day. Today, it is just that: an ill-kept and poorly managed museum with a collection of old swords and scimitars, old Chinese porcelain, photos of the mir and of some English noblemen. It exudes a feeling of mediaeval gloom.

Behind the castle is the trail up to the **Ultar Glacier**, leading to a *shepherd's hut* where camping is possible. The trail continues to the Ultar base camp.

Below Baltit is a watercourse which leads to Altit, where another smaller **fort** is located. This was built in 1503 and the architecture is Kashmiri in design. The track down to it involves a number of hairpin turns, and crosses a suspension bridge to the polo ground. The *chowkidar* is invariably in the fruit orchard, but if you can't find him, ask any of the women or children to take you up to the fort. For a fee of Rs5 they will unlock it for you so you can have a look-around. It consists of a number of small rooms and towers, and like the other fort, has carved window and door frames and posts. It is topped by a wooden goat or ibex. The whole region is spectacularly steep and cramped, with very little space to move about, except up or down. Beyond Altit is Amotabad, a six-km or two-hour walk along cliff ledges high above the Hunza River. There are great views of the peaks and the valley below from here.

Things to See & Do

Walking around the area is fascinating, and a trip to both forts is a must. There are also numerous curio shops that are worth checking out. For a panoramic view of the whole valley go up to the shepherd's hut, or climb to the Ultar base camp. The **Ultar Glacier** is just up the slope. **Warning** Don't attempt to trek up to Ultar Glacier in autumn and early spring. It's far too dangerous; too rough and too windy.

If you are interested in archaeology the 'Sacred Rock of Hunza' is just three km down from Ganesh. The petroglyphs here are mostly rock carvings of animals, hunting scenes, warriors on horseback and ancient scripts.

Places to Stay & Eat

The government *rest house* here is for official use only. There are, however, several medium-class hotels including the *Tourist Inn*; *Hunza Hotel* and *Babar Hotel*, all of the same standard and rates, and with the same menu. Rooms cost from Rs20 to Rs45, and meals start at Rs10. During the season from May to September a room that costs Rs20 any other time will sky-rocket to Rs75. The Hunza is clean, quiet, and has friendly staff, reasonable food and good views of the valley. On the other hand the Babar has heating in autumn and early spring, and also provides tents and dorm accommodation for Rs5. There's also the *Diran Hotel* with singles for Rs20 and doubles for Rs40 or five people can share a room for Rs70. You can rent a tent here for Rs15 per head. The *Park Hotel* is as small as the Diran with similar rates. Another option is the *New Tourist Inn*, which is a price-notch higher. A tourist camp is being set up by Ghulam Mohammed Beg.

NAGAR VALLEY

Nagar is 19 km from Ganesh, and about 26 km from Aliabad. Heading off from Ganesh the route crosses the Karakoram Highway bridge, then leaves the highway and goes up a rather steep slope. It's a jeepable track which meanders up to the village of Nagar and ends there. There is a footpath which climbs up a steeper slope and runs along the edge of a high escarpment before dropping sheer down to thawing glaciers. It rejoins the jeep track further up.

The valley is strange, almost unearthly, barren and desertlike. It's scarred with moraines, gorges and ravines, and surrounded by snowcapped peaks. Although the valley is at the foot of Rakaposhi, the surrounding foothills cut off the view.

This is a starting out point for mountaineering and trekking expeditions. From Nagar a trail leads out to Hispar, a tiny village 18 km away. Here it splits up with one trail leading north to the base camps of Mt Distaghilsar and Momhislar, and the other continuing straight up to Hispar Pass, over the Hispar Glacier to Arondu or Astore. Another trail from Nagar goes south-east to Hopar or Hoparkhund, 14 km away.

Nagar was formerly a minor mirdom. The mir's palace is just off the trail to Hopar. The only accommodation here is an unfurnished *rest house* with no beds or toilet. There is also a general store but more often than not it's closed.

CHALT

Chalt is roughly 50 km from Gilgit, 24 km from Nomal and about 62 km from Karimabad. Another starting point for trekkers; there are trails to Baltar Glacier, Diantar Pass via Bar and Naltar via the Chaprot River Valley. It has an old *rest house* with a guest book which dates back to the 1930s – well worth reading.

NOMAL

Twenty-seven km away from Gilgit on the west banks of the Hunza River opposite Rahimabad, Nomal is a tranist point to Naltar. There is a little *inn* here for overnighting. You can cross the river by raft for Rs1.50.

NALTAR

This is an alpine valley, 14 km from Nomal. It's set in a forest, has crystal clear lakes, and is encircled by snowcapped peaks. Naltar also has a ski resort, a *rest house* – you have to book ahead for this in Gilgit – and a few shops, but once again, they're often closed. There's also a local *hotel* here with a few beds and tolerable food. However, the latter is closed from late autumn until mid-February.

This is the starting point for treks up the Diantar Pass into Chalt or to Iskhoman via Naltar Pass and Pakhora.

BAGROTH VALLEY

In this valley and the adjoining one, Haramosh, there are numerous ruins of altars comprising stone pillars set up like *menhirs*, which were supposed to house the protecting spirit of the village, usually an ancestor of one of the local people. This is an indication that the people from these valleys practised a mixture of fairy and ancestor worship. The latter was probably introduced by the Chinese in the 8th century AD. Despite the fact that Islam was – still is – acknowledged as *the* religion of Pakistan, until two decades ago various forms of syncretic faiths were practised openly. Today, you would be lucky to find any villagers willing to admit to such forms of worship or even to talk about them, but if you're interested in religions, you can take a look at some of these stone altars on a ridge near the village of Datuche in Bagroth Valley.

There are no regular cargo-jeeps to this valley, 40 km east of Gilgit. The road is partly sealed and runs along a picturesque, narrow valley, terminating before the Bagroth Range. Get off the jeep at a footbridge and climb up a steep path to the first village, about three km off the road.

The houses here have no windows – not even for ventilation – and use round poles with steps cut in them for ladders. The huge box on top of these strange houses is used to store meat after cattle have been slaughtered during their winter festivals.

A jeepable road leads from this village to the government *rest house* about two km from the glacier. **Deobani** is visible from here but the **Chogolungma Glacier** is a disappointment, being dark grey, almost black in colour, and thawing in summer. Although it is 2500 metres high, it does not get much snow in winter.

ROUTES SOUTH

The Karakoram Highway follows the Gilgit River south, then the Indus passing Jaglot, the transit village to Bunji, Astore and Skardu. Off the highway a trail leads down to a bridge for Bunji and Astore, and two km before Jaglot, the Alam Bridge. From here it branches off to Skardu. A bit further down is the Rakhiot Bridge, which is the setting off point for Fairytale Meadow or the base camp of Nanga Parbat.

Just before Chilas is another starting point to the base camp of Nanga Parbat on the Diamar side. The highway passes Chilas, which is off the road and a transit point for Darel and Tanger, then goes through a route covered with petroglyphs, past Siazin, a police check-post, and another before Camilla. It continues to Patan and finally reaches Beshum.

DIAMAR

This is the last region in the Northern Territory to be defined by the ancient name of Dardistan, an empire which emerged on the disappearance of Bolor. Historically Dardistan covered the whole of Gilgit as far as Chitral to the west, with the exception of Baltistan which was then under the Tibetans, east to the edge of Kashmir, and south as far as Chilas.

Situated immediately south of Baltistan and south-east of Gilgit, this is where the western bastion of the Great Himalayan Range slips in from the valley of Kashmir, extending some way beyond the Indus to Darel and Tanger and finishing just in front of the ramparts of the Hindu Kush. The area is dominated by Nanga Parbat, known locally as *Diamar* – Naked Mountain – which is now the accepted name for Dardistan.

Nanga Parbat soars to 8125 metres and is the eighth highest mountain in the world. The only peak within a hundred km radius, it stands out like 'some huge marble cathedral ... above all meaner buildings – a sight never to be forgotten. It is the culminating point of the Kashmir Ranges, linked with the central chain of the Himalayas as it turns southward running parallel with the Indus,' wrote Arthur Neve, an English explorer and travel guide writer.

It has been dubbed a killer mountain by climbers and has taken a toll of more than 50 of those attempting to conquer it, beginning with A. F. Mummery, who led the first British expedition here in 1897. After this disastrous attempt, Norman Collie, his companion, was to write:

The sunshine and beauty were gone; savage, cruel and inhospitable ... The dominant sensation in this strange land is that of fear and abhorrence; and what makes it all the more appauling is that this thing before one is there in all nakedness; it has no reserve. There is nothing hidden. Its rugged insolence, its brutal savagery, and utter disregard of all the puny effort of man, crushes out of the mind any idea that this spot belongs to an ordinary world.

Dardistan or Diamar is also known as the Land of Fairies and Nanga Parbat is believed, by the local people, to be the home of the Queen of Fairies. According to legend, she lives in a castle made of solid, crystal clear, ice, and is guarded by gigantic frogs and snow snakes over a hundred km long. Women from the surrounding valleys were so frightened of attracting the envy and jealousy of the fairies, they refused to wear brightly-coloured clothes. Today, like the women in Hunza and Laspur, they wear black or white headgear to indicate whether they are married or single — black means they are married, white, unmarried.

Summer nights are clear and starry up here. But in mid-July the monsoon affects the area causing occasion snowfalls. During winter the temperature can plummet to −40° or −50°.

CHILAS

Chilas is the adminstrative centre of Diamar, 122 km south of Gilgit where the Indus veers westward, and slightly beyond Siazin turns sharply south to the lowland of the Punjab.

Chilas is a large, sprawling town where the momentum of development seems to have lost force. There is no real town centre, the *rest house*, police station and commissioner's office being km apart. In the old days the Sunnis used to murder Shi'ites travelling south. Today, conflict has diminished, but has never disappeared.

The Indus which runs east to west delineates the border between the subnorthern and upper northern region. Petroglyphs along this route appear far more numerous than any other archaeological site in the area. You will come across them just below Chilas at the confluence of the Butogah and Thakgah rivers, on the south of the river, between Chilas, Shatial and Thor on the north bank, at Soniwal, Huddur and at the village of Thalpan.

Chilas is a transit point for trekkers going over the **Babusar Pass** into Kaghan, to the **base camp** of Nanga Parbat on the Diamar side, to the **archaeological sites**, and to the valleys of Darel and Tanger.

DAREL & TANGER

Near Shatial, a trail leads down to the banks of the Indus. It crosses over a bridge and continues to the valleys of Darel and Tanger, which are immediately north of Chilas.

The inhabitants speak Shina and have much in common with the Kohistanis, and like the Pathans, they are armed to the teeth. In summer they have a peculiar custom of segregating men and women, probably a primitive method of birth control. Most marriages tend to occur in winter. They live in houses fortified with tall towers like those in Waziristan.

Both valleys are fertile and relatively rich, but a lot of their wealth is wasted on litigation due to continual feuding. In the past, like Kohistan, this was rebel territory where strangers would not dare to venture without being accompanied by a powerful police contingent.

Spring is brief, and by the middle of June the harvest is over. The main crops are wheat, barley and millet and there are also abundant fruit orchards.

Archaeology

Fogit-i-Run is the site of an early Buddhist settlement, and further on, at Ghor, there is a **sculpture** of the horse-god Talban, worth looking out for. From Ghor to Seo along the banks of the Indus are numerous ancient rock carvings and scripts.

The trails in Darel and Tanger, which once went right up to Gupis, Ghizer and north Badakshan, are dotted with archaeological sites.

The Departments of Agriculture and Forestry have government offices here, and there is a *rest house*. This is also a trekking region so make sure you have camping gear and provisions.

ASTORE

Astore is 115 km south-east of Gilgit, perched on a green, wooded ridge at about 2800 metres. It has precipitous cliffs which drop sheer down into the Astore Nallah. It's a small place with the usual government offices, banks, schools and basic local travellers' inns

There are no tourist facilities here so far, although it is a transit point for trekkers to Rama, Rumpur, Muzzaraffarabad, the Deosai Plateau, Chilas and Gilgit.

Trekking permits are not required for Rama or Rumpur, but they are for Muzzaffarabad and the Deosai Plateau. See section on Trekking.

Note that travellers have to register at the police checkpoint here.

There are lots of different kinds of fresh fruit available including a local taste treat called *chilgoza*, strawberries and raspberries. There is also a wide variety of wildlife and birdlife around. Among them are the ibex, music deer, snow leopard and peacocks.

Getting There

Of the four districts of the upper northern highland, the area of Diamar is the least developed, its administrative centre, Chilas, being a long way west of Astore, another main centre, also at the foot of the north-eastern flanks of Nanga Parbat. Eight km from here is Rama, a small scenic village.

There is no direct transport from Chilas to Astore, but there is a direct cargo-jeep service from Gilgit and Jaglot. About four km before you get to Jaglot heading from Gilgit is the Alam Bridge. The route continues from here to Skardu and about two km further on a trail leads to a bridge over the Gilgit River. Continue on through Bunji for Astore.

Having passed the bridge, the trail climbs up to a flat, desolate sandy plain, strewn with detritus, beyond which is Bunji. After Bunji, it crosses Saitan Nallah, continuing into the mountains, and along the Haramosh and Deosai Ranges, following the Astore Nallah upstream. This flows south-west to join the Indus. The valley is long, narrow, arid, and featureless in sections, broken occasionally by patches of green where villages and human settlements have cropped up.

There are several small villages with hotel signboards and *rest houses* along the way. From here on you will come across postmen called 'runners'. Their job is to carry the mail five km on foot – although often they hitch rides on jeeps – then pass it on to a colleague in a kind of postal relay system, introduced by the British. This idiosyncratic system continues despite the introduction of a modern postal system throughout the rest of the region.

Approaching Astore the bare granite walls become sparsely wooded with junipers and alpine scrub, and the sky begins to open up. The junipers eventually give way to pine trees.

RAMA

To get to Rama from Astore you go via a road by the school building and then through a scenic valley eight km on. It zig-zags up steeply taking a jeep 35 minutes to cover the distance, and hikers almost two hours. To hire a jeep from Astore costs around Rs200.

The country, at 3200 metres, is lush green and wooded with many fine grazing meadows. The *rest house* is three km from the village and is basically used by government officers only. It is also the only building in the area.

You will come across numerous shepherds with flocks of sheep and occasionally cattle, but at this height you will not be able to see Nanga Parbat, unless you climb another 200 metres up to the lake. From here you can catch a glimpse of Chongra Peak. There are two lakes close to the glaciers, and beyond it another, larger one.

After crossing a bridge, you will find a shepherds' village on the right side, and Sango Sar Lake, which is fed by the glaciers and has good trout fishing.

The area is dotted with snow-covered glaciers, and sections of it are filled with moraines and scarred with ravines. In summer it is still cold and often drizzling with fine rain. In winter the shepherds leave their villages and move further down, as the land becomes blanketed in metres of snow.

GILGIT TO CHITRAL

The road from Gilgit to Chitral was once a vital section of the Silk Trade Route, with minor trails branching off to the north for the Darkot and Boroghil passes. It then continued towards Bukhara and Samarkhand. Today, just a few km from the Kargah Valley in the Punial River Valley is **Buber**, site of a number of rock carvings and engraved scripts. At Gakutch there is a trail which forks off towards Imit in the Iskhoman Valley. Along this route is **Hatun**, another archaeological, petroglyph site.

Between the valleys of Vershinghoom and Yasin is **Gupis** where there are stone formations of the megalithic culture, which have continued to baffle archaeologists over the years. You can't miss them as they are about 10 metres in diameter and about 1¼ metres high.

The 400-km road to Chitral is only just jeepable. It goes north-west then dips down slightly to Teru, 190 km away, the last fair-sized village before the border of Chitral. On this route from Gilgit you pass Punial, 34 km away; Singal, 54 km; Gakutch, 72 km; Gupis, 109 km; Phander, 168 km; all of which have *rest houses* and are good trout fishing spots. At Gupis a road branches off to Yasin across the Punial River, proceeds to a tiny village called Tari-i-Taus and beyond is Dash-i-Taus – the Desert of Peacocks. From here the route splits into several tracks, one continues to Ishkoman, Naltar and Hunza, while another leads to the 4500-metre Thui Pass, 19 km away, another to the Darkot Pass, 22 km away and 4690 metres above sea level.

Unless you take it easy, stopping at villages and doing some fishing, this is a long trip. Getting a ride is tricky as cargo-jeeps using the route usually start full and do not have room for more passengers at intermediate villages. If you do fluke it, an additional Rs10 will get you a front seat and cover luggage charges. Most travellers try to make it to Yasin, then cross the passes into Chitral.

From Rajah Bazaar in Gilgit the road becomes unsurfaced and the country is lined with stone walls and large fruit trees. Only eight km further on is a shaky suspension bridge where you have to get off the cargo-jeep and walk across. The country road continues beyond Buber to Punial where a policeman will enter your name and passport details in a register. At Singal you make a tea stop and again register with the police.

Beyond this village the road becomes more dramatic, climbing up steep mountainsides and running parallel to the river far below. Here you will see several hanging bridges – usually made of a single strand of wire-rope – which are used by locals to haul themselves across while seated on loops. You will pass a more modern bridge at Sher Quila where the road begins to climb in earnest.

Across the Punial River, a trail leads to the Valley of Iskhoman from Gakutch. In the village of Rosan, before Gupis, are the petrified remains of a pair of dragons on the upper strata of a cliff face. Legend has it that they so angered a saintly old man when they began devouring children that he put a curse on them and turned them into stone.

Just before Gupis and the confluence of the slick grey Punial with the clear blue water of the Yasin River, is a bridge which leads to a track on the other side that goes through barren, rocky country into Yasin.

YASIN VALLEY

It is not more than 134 km away but it takes almost seven hours by cargo-jeep. A tiny village 2500 metres above sea level, it hasn't a single shop but it does have a well-furnished *rest house* where you can get food, and a police station, previously the fort-castle of the former ruler of the region, down on the banks of the Yasin River. A new police building has been erected recently, and it's probable the fort-castle will be turned into a tourist hotel.

Tart-i-Taus, another tiny village further north, has a small bazaar and a post office. Past this village is Dash-i-Taus, which is close to Darkot where the English explorer, Captain George Hayward, his interpreter and five porters were all murdered on 17 July 1870. Years later Frederic Drew, author of *Jammu & Kashmir*, took his remains and buried him in the British cemetery in Gilgit.

Higher up the route splits into several tracks: one continues to Iskhoman, Naltar and Hunza; another leads to the 4500-metre high Thui Ann Pass, 19 km away; and a third veers towards Darkot Pass, 4690 metres above sea level, and into the Chitral Valley. In late spring or early summer both Thui Ann and Darkot are still impassable and are often still slushy with melting snow in late summer. Only at the end of summer and early autumn do they become passable.

If you are unable to get through, your only alternative is to backtrack to Gupis, which has a *rest house*. But you may be able to get a jeep to Phander on the same day. Cargo-jeeps leave Yasin at 7 am and arrive 45 minutes later in Gupis.

PHANDER

Phander is a pleasant little village known as Tiny Kashmir, and less than 40 km from Gupis. From Gupis – a long, spread out village – the road starts to get rough, but once you leave Shashi it's really rugged, even for jeeps.

The *rest house* on the hill above the lake is reserved for officials only, but more often than not, it is closed altogether, and rarely accepts foreigners. Get off the jeep about four km before the main village. There are some small *hotels* with basic facilities here where you can put up for the night or for a few days. The cargo-jeep service usually finishes at this point, but occasionally continues to Teru.

Across the bridge a trail leads to a broad opening to the north, which eventually turns westward towards the 5009-metre high Chumarkhan Pass and the Zagar Pass, just a little north of Shandur Pass, which is 3730 metres high. See section on Trekking.

TERU

Teru is almost 32 km from Phander and it takes almost two hours by cargo-jeep to get there. A little less than half-way is Ghizer, a tiny village where the trekking route to Kalam in the Swat Valley begins. See section on Trekking.

Teru is 3100 metres above sea level and is bitterly cold at night. There are two small shops which are hardly ever open for business and a *rest house*, which also appears to be closed most of the time.

Perched on a slope north-west of the rest house is the *Agha Khan Primary School*. The school master here will give you a bed if you're having difficulty finding accommodation. If you're not organised for trekking, for a small fee or present, he can also arrange a horse and guide for you at less than the usual rate of Rs100.

SHANDUR PASS

Shandur Pass is about 24 km from here, and it's another 16 km down to Laspur. One of the most scenic routes in the region, it dips gradually down to a small hamlet six km away. The latter is the last settlement before Laspur. It's a fairly broad valley, with flat meadows, hedged on both sides by brown and gun-metal blue, snow-flecked granite mountain slopes. There is no danger here from possible avalanches.

You will hardly see a soul along this road, except, occasionally, a few men working on the jeep track, or perhaps some nomads camped along the wayside. You may also come across a few local trekkers in woollen caps, urging their pack donkeys to go faster or occasionally men on foot or horseback coming from Laspur. Other than that, no-one.

The mountain streams are clear, cool and safe for drinking. There are horses grazing along the river banks and higher up you will see herds of black, woolly yaks. The route swerves away from the valley and follows another river upstream to the pass. The pass is very narrow and has sheer granite walls that are usually topped by clouds.

The pass opens up as you turn into a broad valley. Soon you will reach a small lake, which is riddled with mosquitoes – not a good spot to camp. Here, too, the weather is changeable, often drizzly, but beyond this point the sky is blue and often there's a pale, watery sun. Not much further on you will come across another, bigger lake, and in the distance you can see a silvery-grey mountain. About here the land begins to open up and is either rich red or chocolate brown in colour, but barren. The route meanders around the lake to the great rocky flanks of mountains where the road is surfaced. It leads straight on to Chitral.

On the way down to Laspur the trail drops abruptly into an arid, dusty, gravelly region, slopes steeply for about five km, then levels off. In the distance on the rim of a ridge is a patch of green, surrounded by huge bare mountains. This is Laspur. The trail continues to be rough, rocky and precipitously steep as it zig-zags down.

CHITRAL VALLEY

Chitral, about 11,500 square km in area, is 80 km at its widest, 50 km at its narrowest and 400 km long south-west to north-east. It's shaped rather like a crooked little finger and has an altitude ranging from 1000 to 4000 metres. Right in the Hindu Kush, it borders Nuristan in the west and Badakshan in the north in Afghanistan.

The extreme south, lush green with gently rounded slopes, is cloaked in pines and firs, has fertile terraced valleys, and a climate similar to Kashmir. Heading north the landscape gradually changes, becoming less lush, more arid. Higher up it is barren, craggy, desolate and inhospitable, and the temperature never gets hot but can dip precipitously to below freezing in winter.

Here the Panjkur Plateau joins the Kasghar Valley in Mastuj and beyond Boroghil Pass is the Yarkhund Valley where the Yarkhund River flows south to join the Mastuj. Below Mastuj Valley is the Kho Valley and further west is the Tirich Mir Valley which runs northward for about 96 km, gradually looping north-eastward to join the Turikho Valley, then flows south to meet the Kasghar Bala. The Turikho Valley, which runs from the south-west to the north-east and parallel to the Yarkhund River, is a fertile area covered with cedar trees.

It is here that the sheer cliff faces of the valleys meet and you will see foot bridges made of plaited osier. The Kasghar River which rises to seven metres in summer is the natural borderline between the Valley of Chitral and Yasin. Seven km below this junction are the valleys of Chi Trai and the Ludkho Valley. The Kasghar Valley is interesting but it is a restricted area. There are forts here with ramparts over

Young Chitrali Girl

nine metres above ground level and towers that rise 4½ metres above the parapets.

The region is dominated by the majestic Tirich Mir, which at 7750 metres is the highest mountain in the Hindu Kush. Like Nanga Parbat it has several peaks. It is also believed, by the local inhabitants, to be the home of the fairies. The guards of this fairy palace are visualised as giant frogs known as *bugzai* rather than snow snakes which are supposed to guard the fairy domain of Nanga Parbat. If you are not frightened away by the giant frogs, then Tirich Mir apparently has other, more malicious and more whimsical guards. These are fairies who tempt any unfortunate and thirsty adventurers who do manage to get there with bowls of milk or blood. Legend has it that those who accept this hospitality never return home.

Like Baltistan, Gilgit and Hunza this was a region traversed by the ancient Silk Trade Route from Dir and Gilgit in the east to Ferghana and Bukhara. The village of Barenis has rock carvings, engraved proto-Sanskirt script and evidence of primitive settlements, probably Aryan, dating back to the 4th century AD. There are also Buddhist settlements and rock carvings here.

Buddhism existed in Chitral until the 9th century AD during the time of Jaipal, King of Kabul and Chitral. Afghanistan – in the Hindu Kush – was part of the Moghul Empire until it lost power in the latter part of the 18th century. The British tried to annex it, unsuccessfully, and subsequently the Durand Line was cut across the Hindu Kush to separate Chitral from Afghanistan, which eventually came under the administration of the North West Frontier Province.

Recorded history begins here with Yue-Chi tribes, who were Hephthalites or White Huns who invaded Kattor and Gebrek, now known as Kafiristan and the Peshawar Valley. Having conquered these regions, they established the Kingdom of Little Yue-Chi, and in the 5th century AD they conquered Balkh and Gandhara and occupied Chitral, which later fell to the Uzbekhs. In the middle of the 8th century AD the Chinese came, and in the same century it was invaded by the Moslems. But the southern areas of Lotkah, Chitral and Drosh did not adopt Islam until about two centuries later, with Kafiristan – Land of Non-believers – remaining outside its fold to this day. Islam wiped out all the colourful traditional customs and festivals of the Chitralis.

In the 1880s this region came under the suzerainty of the Maharaja of Kashmir, and fell into British hands, becoming an autonomous political agency of the North West Frontier Province. In 1885, stirred up by the Pathans in the south, the Chitralis rebelled and beseiged the British forts, but were reconquered by Sir George Robertson.

It retained its autonomous political agency status until 1966 and eventually in 1970 became a district of the Malakhand Division of the North West Frontier Province. In April 1972 the mirdom of Chitral was completely abolished.

LASPUR

From Shandur Pass the first town in Chitral is Laspur. As you enter the village the trail appears to turn away, but then crosses a dry riverbed and makes a U-turn back into it. The streets here are narrow and gravelly, and the village is hardly visible for trees.

Laspur is situated at an altitude of 2600 metres and is so small it doesn't have a single shop – not even a teashop – or inn. The *rest house* is closed, but camping on the lawn is possible. Villagers will offer their huts to travellers for nothing, but food is hard to come by.

This is the setting off point for trekking routes to Mastuj, Madaghlast, Kalam and Teru.

Early the day after arriving hike up to Harchin, 11 km away. Cargo-jeeps are rare along this route – particularly from spring to early summer – but the road is easy going and follows the Sorlaspur River upstream. Harchin is a fair-sized village, with a few government buildings, *local inns* and teashops. From here there is a regular cargo-jeep service to Mastuj.

MASTUJ

Sixteen km away, Mastuj is a hikeable distance through a remarkably narrow, arid, barren valley. This is where the Mastuj and Yarkhund rivers meet. Approaching the village the trail crosses numerous irrigation channels. At 2400 metres, Mastuj has a small bazaar and a teashop which also serves as a *travellers' inn*. There is a *Tourist Cottage* here, but it's expensive and it's preferable to *camp* if you are equipped.

At the foot of a mountain not far from the village, is the **fort-palace** where the retired ruler of the region still lives. On the side that opens out onto a lawn is a *guest room*, in disrepair, but still furnished. There is a guest book at this place, which dates back to the 1930s with comments like: 'Had a super-duper time', from an Australian geological party in 1951, or more recently, 'This place seems to be the end of the world – traversed frightening road to come to a warm reception'.

In the spring of 1895 this fort was one of those defended by two British officers, Lieutenant Moberly and Captain Brethertton, until relieved by the force of Colonel Kelly who came all the way from Gilgit.

Mastuj is also a setting off point for trekking routes up to Darkot, Thui Ann and Chumarkhan passes into Yasin, Laspur and Chitral. There is more variety in food here, but it is advisable to bring camping gear and supplementary provisions all the same.

CHITRAL

This is a mini-version of Gilgit with the same physical surroundings, bazaars, polo ground, government offices, banks, hotels and restaurants along a single main street, Shahi Bazaar.

It used to be an important stopping point on the ancient Silk Trade Route, and like Gilgit was a slave-trading centre. One of the local legends reveals that a female slave owned by a Chinese was raped by a Chitrali, bringing about the destruction and depopulation of the valley and consequently turning it into a tributary of China.

The **mosque** on the banks of the Mastuj River has been recently constructed in a Moghul style, but the adjacent **Chitral fort** which is Central Asian in design, is literally falling apart with age. It's been converted to a police station but looks more like a museum with the muzzles of 1860s cannons jutting out from the corner of an outer hall.

Like Gilgit, the town bustles through spring, summer and early autumn, but by mid-October, when the Lowari Pass gets snowbound, it's completely cut off from the rest of the world; even though it is connected by air link to Peshawar, 200 km away, this service is severely affected by weather. A long tunnel has been designed to pass through the mountains, but it appears that construction work is being held up due to financial difficulty.

Information

The Tourist Information Centre is at the PTDC Tourist Lodge. Foreigners have to register with the police superintendent immediately on arrival.

You also need a permit for the places you wish to visit, which you can get from the deputy commissioner's office. If you want to do any fishing, you must get yourself a licence which will cost Rs16.

The post office, banks and police station are all along an alley leading to the river. The *PIA* is in the next alley.

Things to See & Do

Walk along the river bank where the old fort and the mosques are located to the polo ground. Also check out the bazaar while you're here, it's colourful and fun.

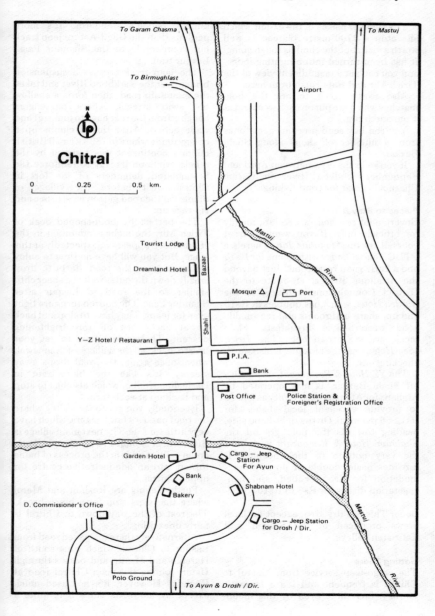

Chitral

0   0.25   0.5 km.

To Garam Chasma
To Mastuj
To Birmughlast
Airport
Tourist Lodge
Dreamland Hotel
Mosque
Port
Mastuj River
Y–Z Hotel / Restaurant
P.I.A.
Bank
Post Office
Police Station &
Foreigner's Registration Office
Garden Hotel
Cargo – Jeep Station
For Ayun
Bank
Bakery
Shabnam Hotel
D. Commissioner's Office
Cargo – Jeep Station
for Drosh / Dir.
Mastui
Polo Ground
To Ayun & Drosh / Dir.
Bazaar
Shahi

The **summer palace** of the ex-mir which sits atop a 2700-metre plateau is well worth a visit, but the climb is tough going. It has been turned into a hunting lodge, and you can get a magnificent view of the Tirich Mir and Raja Kush from here.

Also worth going to are the polo matches which are put on each weekend at 4 pm and 5 pm.

You can buy semi-precious gemstones from a number of shops along Shahi Bazaar.

If you're in the area between April and September, Ludkho River in Garam Chasma is great for trout fishing.

Places to Stay & Eat

Government *rest houses* here are mainly for officials only. If you want to treat yourself try the *Mountain Inn*. There's a PTDC *Tourist Lodge* with rooms for Rs75 and a fairly good restaurant. Just beyond the Attalique Bridge, en route to the District Commissioner's office, is the *Garden Hotel*, which has doubles at Rs15 and up, share bathrooms and reasonably good western-style breakfasts. Main meals are vegetarian only. The *Tirich View Hotel*, near the mosque, is also worth checking out.

The *YZ Hotel & Restaurant*, on an alley off Shahi Bazaar, is now operated by Afghans for Afghans only. A pity as it used to provide excellent local dishes for Rs12.50 per meal. On the right-hand side, heading towards the polo ground the *Shabnam Hotel & Restaurant* is right at the very bottom of the cheapies. It provides basic, double or dorm accommodation for Rs5 per bed, and non-vegetarian dishes for Rs6 to Rs10.

Liquor This is a dry area, except for local brews produced in the Shugur and Kafiristan valleys.

Getting There

The cargo-jeep service from Mastuj to Chitral is frequent and it's a fantastic journey: incredible even by this moun-tainous region's standards. It's more perilous than the Gilgit-Astore jeep track but comparable to the Shandur Pass-Laspur trail.

The jeep track crosses a suspension bridge over the Yarkhund River and takes the mountain road, then fords a shallow but swift stream, where passengers hanging from the rear have to jump off and wade across. After this it climbs up a craggy defile where in 1895 a small British military contingent was trapped by the rebels, while on its way to reinforce the beleaguered defenders of the fort in Chitral. Just before the village of Shanewal the road gets even steeper and zig-zags up.

The perfect pyramid-shaped peak of Tirich Mir, the highest mountain in the Hindu Kush appears unexpectedly at this stage. But you will have no time to enjoy the scenery as the road starts to drop crazily down the outer wall of a sheer cliff, similar to the road to Laspur after Shandur Pass. The hairpin turns are tight even for jeeps. They have to stop and back up at each turn on this frightening descent. There's just time to get your breath back at the village of Shanewal, when, once again, the road drops away steeply. It's like the blue train in Darjeeling (India), which also has to stop and back up at each turn.

Eventually you get to the valley where the road passes a few bazaars, which have very little for sale. The next main village is Buni, which is built in a fairly wide, long, green valley and is in the process of being turned into an adminstrative centre for upper Chitral.

Further along are Reshun and Maroi where the jeeps stop for a lunch break. The rest of the way down to Chitral is fairly unexciting.

Alternatively there is a paved road from Laspur to Chitral, which runs south of Harchin and Mastuj and passes through Ustur, joining the main Chitral road at Koghozi. However, it's not used much except by motorists since it is quite a distance to Ustur. It forks near Ustur to Madaghlast, Kalas and Drosh, by-passing Chitral and continuing to Lowari Pass.

Getting There

Air *PIA* has two F-27 flights daily to Peshawar, which cost Rs150 plus an airport embarkation fee of Rs5. Flights are subject to weather conditions.

Road Cargo-jeeps to Dir cost Rs75 for front seats and Rs60 for back seats. Lowari Pass opens in early June and closes around mid-October. Fares to other places are: Ayun, Rs10; Birer, Rs15; Bumburet, Rs15; Garam Chasma, Rs12; Mastuj, Rs35.

The Shandur Pass is open from early May until mid-November. Cargo-jeep pick up stations are at Shah Bazaar for Garam Chasma, Mastuj and other northern villages, or just past the Attalique Bridge on the left for Ayun, Birer, Bumburet, Drosh, Ashret and Dir.

The PTDC has jeeps for hire at the usual government rates. They also arrange and organise treks. Private agencies are a little cheaper but not as reliable or responsible. Jeep-hire to the Birer or Bumburet area costs Rs500 to Rs750 a day.

GARAM CHASMA

North-west of Chitral, 45 km and 1½ hours by jeep, is the natural hot spring resort of Garam Chasma. It's a delightful, restful little village at an elevation of 1900 metres. Until half-way up, the road is surfaced and truckable, but from then on it's narrow and dusty.

It passes Shugur where *Hunza Water* is still distilled, then crosses a suspension bridge. On the right as you approach the village, almost hidden by trees, is an old **fort**, which once used to guard the route into Afghanistan.

The village itself has a tiny bazaar, some *local hotels, restaurants* and *teashops*. It is a hilly region with a number of mud-stone

bathing huts through which the spring water courses. The low-roofed mud huts line the river and it will cost you Rs5 to bathe. There's a superb teashop here with tables and benches overlooking the river.

The way to the Afghan border goes through a lush, open field, which is a good site for camping. The *rest house* is often closed and the cheapies are mainly dorm-style for Rs5 per bed. There's very little choice in food.

Note that there are police check-points along the border here.

BIRMUGHLAST

Fourteen km west of Chitral at an elevation of 2700 metres is Birmughlast. It's a steep four-hour climb up to the little old fort, which is looked after by an old man and his grand-daughter, who live in a mud-stone hut nearby. They will offer visitors here tea, curd and bread.

Most people leave the trek up until late in the afternoon when it's cooler and then camp overnight. The view is magnificent, particularly on a bright, moonlit night. It's cold here though, so you need a good sleeping bag and some extra food. Trek back early next morning.

KALASH VALLEYS

South-west of Chitral, 35 km away, are the deep, mysterious valleys of the Kalash people, where the Kafirs, or 'unbelievers' have carried on their traditional culture, religion and way of life for 2000 years without change.

Particulary striking are the Kalash women in their coarse, black cotton ankle length clothes and headwear decorated with cowrie shell, beads, buttons or tiny bells hanging from the end of a tale piece. Tending their little herds and flocks of sheep, goats and cows, they not only look mysterious, but also have a timeless quality about them.

The people in these valleys are often called the Children of Nature. They lead simple lives, surviving on subsistence farming, small flocks of sheep, and a few goats and cattle. They also have fruit orchards. They live in windowless, mud-stone huts and use neither soap nor money.

They celebrate their religious festivals in January and May with group dancing, feasting and drinking, and are regarded by many as pagans. Some of their gods are similar to those of the Romans and Greeks, though they strongly believe in ancestor worship, which the practise by worshipping wooden effigies. Their rect-angular coffins are made of thick hard wood, the lids seldom being nailed down, but more often held down by large rocks. The coffins are generally laid out in the open at the foot of nearby mountains.

One theory of their origin is that they are descendants of the Greek troops of Alexander the Great, who settled in these valleys with their Persian wives, after wearying of the long military campaign which began in Egypt and continued all the way across Persia to the Indus. This is highly controversial however, and there is no bona fide proof of it. What is likely, is that they were settled in the lowlands for a long time and, following the death of Ashoka, were driven further and further up with successive waves of invasions. The whole style and dress of the women is similar to the Gandhara bas reliefs you can see in the Museum of Peshawar and this would seem to indicate that is where their origins lie.

Kafiristan consists of three isolated villages within a radius of 18 km. **Bumburet**, the largest is about five km long and about half a km at its widest. It is approximately 35 km from Chitral and accessible by jeep. Bumburet is sand-wiched between **Rumbur**, 11 km away and the second largest village , and **Birer** the smallest, which is five km to the south-east behind a massif. Birer is also accessible by jeep from Chitral.

The village of Bumburet has quaint water-run mills, a trout hatchery, and is more developed than the other two. It also has several *medium-class hotels* and *cheapies* with basic facilities and food. Superficially, it seems less mysterious than the other two, both of which are very remote and isolated in narrow hilly valleys. The mud-stone huts of Rumbur and Birer are either built on steep ledges in tight clusters or are perched on hilltops and narrow ridges with sheer cliff faces.

From Bumburet there is an occasional cargo-jeep that goes to Rumbur. But if you don't want to hang around waiting for public transport, it's within walking distance. At Rumbur there is a two-room *hotel* with six beds for Rs5 per per person. The food is limited, but it is an interesting valley to explore. You can walk from Bumburet to Birer via the massif, but it's a steep climb, followed by a precipitous path down. There's a small *hotel* here with just three rope-beds for Rs5 per person. Once again, food is very limited.

CHITRAL TO DIR

From Chitral you can take the one-hour flight to Peshawar, go overland to Gilgit via Shandur Pass, or take the 115-km route over the Lowari Pass to Dir.

Cargo-jeeps take eight to 10 hours to get there, depending the condition of the road. In spring and summer through to early autumn the truck shuttle between Chitral and Peshawar is continuous. Travellers in Dir can hitch rides there and back without any worry during these months. You'll find the truck station on Shahi Bazaar.

From Chitral the metal road passes the villages of Gaihret, Drosh, Mirkani and Ashret. From here on the road is unsurfaced and it gets pretty dusty as it zig-zags up to Lowari Pass. Be sure to take a couple of scarves to cover your face and hair to keep out the fine dust.

On the other side of Lowari Pass the road is surfaced again.

Trekking

Introduction

The Northern Territory of Pakistan is cragsman's country with many opportunities for mountaineering and trekking. Since it's covered with fast-flowing, turbulent rivers, including the Indus, it also offers numerous different kinds of rafting and white watering. Skiing is another outdoor activity which can be pursued here. What is more, it's an anthropologist's and archaeologist's paradise.

Recently, the western extremity of the Himalayas has become a playground for mountaineers, trekkers, rafting and skiing enthusiasts. It's larger, craggier, more barren and more glaciated than the eastern Himalayas. Awesome in its ruggedness, unsympathetic and daunting in aspects, appallingly arid, desolate and bleak, neither the terrain, nor the culture of this region are easy to grapple with. Trekking routes often seem much more straightforward than they are, their dangers underestimated, and the culture, in the process of being transformed, can too easily be taken for granted.

It is a land of uncertainties, where schedules cannot be strictly adhered to; a region where women turn their backs and refuse to talk to male strangers for fear of being killed by their own kin. It presents enormously varied experiences, some anticipated, others surprising. But any undertaking – either physical or intellectual – needs forethought and organisation, and physical fitness and mental toughness, if you are to conquer the challenges of this rough region.

The Mountains

The Upper Northern Highland with the great mountain ranges of the Hindu Kush, the Karakorams, the Great Himalayan Range, and further south the Lesser and Outer Ranges, contains more than 120 peaks with an average height of 6550 metres. Some of these are still unclimbed and unnamed.

Many of the highest peaks – among them, some of the highest in the world like K2, Nanga Parbat and Hidden Peak – are barely visible. Even when you're right underneath them, the high foothills in deep valleys obstruct the view, whereas the magnificent Annapurna Range in Nepal is wholly visible in all its grandeur from that exotic city, Pokhara. Rakaposhi and neighbouring Diran Deobani are occasionally visible from the Karakoram Highway, as is Nanga Parbat which can also be seen from the air, from Fairytale Meadow and from the Rupal Valley on the Diamar side, and Tirich Mir, which is visible from Chitral. But by and large, most are remote and hidden by surrounding mountains. For example, it is a two-week trek to Concordia, the inner sanctum of the Himalayas to see K2.

K2, or *Chogori*, as it is known to the natives, is hemmed in by the Gasherbrum, Masherbrum and Kangri Peaks, which have an average height of almost 8000 metres. Hidden Peak was only discovered in 1934, which was why it got its name. These mountains are more difficult to scale technically and more dangerous than any other mountains in the world, not only because of their physical structure, but also because of the unpredictability of the weather patterns in the region.

Before being conquered, they invariably took their toll in human lives. At the end of the 19th century, Italian and American mountaineeering expeditions attempting to scale K2 and Broad Peak were both defeated by weather conditions, which confined assault parties to their tents, causing illness. One person in each party died as a result. Successful though they had been previously, Eric Shipton, one of the great mountaineers, and Hermann Buhl, Austrian conqueror of Nanga Parbat in 1954, were killed in this glacial region.

Masherbrum, immediately to the south, is called 'Doomsday' or 'Judgement Peak', because it is a killer mountain. This description was also coined for Nanga Parbat originally, when A. F. Mummery and two Sherpas perished on the first British mountaineering expedition there in 1897.

More recently, in the summer of 1982, a Swiss mountaineering party failed to scale Kangri Peak because they found the peak had iced over and it was technically impossible. They hammered away at the ice covering for two hundred metres, only to give up when they discovered they could not break the solid ice which capped the summit.

Most of the great peaks are in the Karakorams in the Aghil Range east of the Muztagh in Baltistan. K2, Gasherbrum, Masherbrum and the Kangri Group are all concentrated within an area of 24 square km. To the west, in the valleys of Hunza, Nagar and Gilgit are Distaghilsar, Malangute and the Batura peaks, which are regarded as being among the most beautiful mountains in the world. To the south are the Rakaposhi, Diran and Haramosh, and in Diamar, south-east of Gilgit, is the last western segment of the Great Himalayan Range where Nanga Parbat, majestic in its solitude, reigns over minor peaks. In Chitral, the Tirich Mir is the highest mountain in the Hindu Kush.

The Valleys

The valleys at the feet of these great mountains are deep and narrow, and do not seem to run in any specific direction, but all over the place. Often their junctions are not only forbidding but confusing. They are anywhere between 16 km and 48 km long, covered in rocks and cascading rivers, and occasionally scarred with ravines, gorges, moraines and glaciers. They usually open out into a sandy wasteland with long, craggy, arid escarpments, or flat plains strewn with detritus; sometimes into fan-shaped meadows with ridges that are lushly cultivated. Finding the way into some of these valleys is not only circuitous and tortuous, but also involves climbing high passes.

Only a few valleys, like Chitral and Gilgit, are below the usual 2500-metre elevation. Most are between 2500 and 3500 metres, which means attaining extraordinary heights quickly, and tends to make climbers and trekkers forget the necessary acclimatisation period before moving on to higher altitudes. Changes in the ecological level are significant up here, particularly over passes.

The craggy, barren and arid nature of the valleys seems interminable at times, stark and unrelieved. Sir Francis Younghusband, who explored this region extensively in the latter part of the 19th century, used to run uphill to see the snow-covered ranges to refresh himself after the desolate march through these featureless valleys.

The western segment of the Himalayas is corrugated not in a spectacular manner like Nepal, but in a regular fashion where the great peaks tower above surroundings at an average height of 6500 metres.

The Rivers

Eric Shipton wrote that to describe this region was to indulge in superlatives, for everywhere you look are the highest, longest and largest mountains, glaciers and rivers in the world.

The Indus, known as the 'Father of Rivers' or the 'Lion River', has its source in Lake Manasarowar at the foot of Mt Kailash in Tibet. It begins its 3300-km odyssey roaring out of Tibet, crossing Kashmir and Ladakh in a north-west direction, and closely skirting the border of China. Looping west, the Indus forces its way through constricting granite walls, and rushes turbulently onwards. By the time it enters Baltistan it has already gone 800 km, descended around 3500 metres and still has a 1500-km journey ahead, through deep gorges and some of the bleakest, most barren and most scenic areas in the world. When it gets to the Upper Highland of Pakistan it veers off at a sharp 90° angle and then plunges 1500 metres into the lowland of the Punjab, crossing through Sind and finally sweeping into the Arabian Sea.

On the way through Baltistan it is joined by the Shyok River, and further west by the Hunza, Gilgit and Astore rivers. Turning to the south, it is joined by other tributaries like the Swat and Kabul rivers.

There are other rivers in the region: the Ishkoman and the Harambul in the Valley of Hunza; the Yarkhund, Sorlaspur and Mastuj rivers in Chitral; and the Punial, Hunza and Gilgit rivers in the Valley of Gilgit. Because they are mountain rivers they are all turbulent and fast flowing, particularly in summer. But for sheer adventure, none beat the Father of Rivers.

The Glaciers

Of the entire Himalayas, the Trans-Himalayas of the Northern Mountain region of Pakistan has the most glaciers. The Karakorams consist of 25% glaciers, while in Baltistan, there are some of the largest and longest glaciers outside the Arctic and Antarctica.

The Siachen, near the border of Ladakh, is about 74 km long and the largest glacier in this part of the world. Others include the Baltoro, Biafo, Hispar and the Batura, all roughly 58 km or so long. They run parallel to the Karakorams and arch up from the Valley of Ladakh, north-westward over Baltistan to the Hunza Valley.

Many of the glaciers are thawing slowly and, as a result, are shifting and sliding into the valleys. Some are inert masses of ice and rocks sculpted by wind, sun and rain into weird, often beautiful, shapes, which vanish suddenly leaving only moraines in their wake. In this region it is possible to travel over a hundred km without ever setting foot on earth, particularly along the Biafo-Hispar segment, which runs from Ashkole to the Valley of Nagar, a distance of 240 km. It takes approximately 10 days to a fortnight to do this trek.

Apart from the Batura, which is just off the Karakoram Highway, the rest of the gigantic glaciers are remote and difficult to reach.

Warning

Note that unless you're oriented to travelling on glaciers, it can be extremely dangerous, particularly in summer when they are liable to develop fissures and collapse into yawning crevasses. When they do collapse, the explosion reverberates around the valleys. Unless you know what you're doing, this region can not only be daunting, but terrifying.

The Seasons

Spring arrives in mid-February, and the weather begins to get warmer. By March it is pleasant, the valleys are turning green and it's time for festivals. The April downpours are renowned, and often whole mountainsides are dumped down on the road, blocking them for days. In May, snow and glaciers begin to thaw, and streams and rivers start to swell, the villages and towns stir into life, and mountaineers, trekkers and tourists trickle in.

June marks the beginning of summer and temperatures soar to over 38°C in the lower valleys, but it is still pleasant in the higher reaches. This is the season for polo and tourism. The rivers become fast-flowing torrents and the shepherds move upland with their stock. By mid-July the monsoons are inundating the plains, though they don't have any effect on the high country. The temperature starts to drop by mid-August, and the high mountain passes are clear of ice and snow.

In September, autumn moves in and tourists start to move out, just when the climate is becoming pleasant and the valleys beautiful, the rivers and sky clear and the stars sharp, dense and dazzling. There's a nippy crispness in the air by October, and the trees turn amber, through russet to brown. By November the valleys are cold and stark and the tourists have disappeared.

In December it starts snowing and winter sets in. It's quiet and cold and the temperature sinks to as low as −20°C. Daylight only lasts for between four and six hours and the valleys are dark and desolate.

Facts for Trekkers

Maps
The first thing you will discover is that there are no good maps available on the Northern Territory in Pakistan. However, the Pakistan Survey Maps, available near the post office in Murree, are better than none at all. Others are available from bookshops in Japan, Germany, France, UK, USA, Spain, Italy, Austria *et al* with specialised sections on mountaineering and trekking.

Books
Apart from *Pakistan – a travel survival kit*, there are several guide books on Pakistan, but most of the books on the Northern Territory are written by British explorers and are 'historical'. The most recent books on this region cover the geology, anthropology and archaeology of the area. The only available mountain guide book is the *Tourist Guide to Kashmir-Skardo Etc.* by Major Arthur Neve, published in the early 1900s. The Ministry of Tourism and the PTDC are currently working together on publishing a trekking and mountaineering guide, which could be helpful to both individual and group trekkers.

Trekking Agencies
There are a few trekking and mountaineering agencies in Rawalpindi, and a few local operators in the Northern Territory. *The Pakistan Tourism Development Corporation* (PTDC), *Karakoram Tours* and *Mrs Waljis Tour-Trek Agency*, all have offices in Islamabad and Rawalpindi. The former is a quasi-government corporation; the latter two are operated by private companies.

They all assist in clearing trekking parties through immigration and customs, preparing advance hotel bookings, fixing formalities with the Ministry of Tourism, booking flights to central points, arranging alternative transport and providing camping gear if required. They also arrange for the storage of equipment, for supplies to be sent on ahead of the party, work out an approximate cost of the tour or trek on enquiry, and even provide medical kits and trekking equipment if necessary. They handle large parties of up to 50 and over, and treks that last a month or more.

Enquiries on trekking or mountaineering can be made from any travel agency, but the PTDC has offices in some overseas countries, and failing that, the Pakistan embassies and consulates provide literature which sets out the terms and conditions for obtaining permission to trek or climb a mountain in Pakistan. Also included is detailed information on fees, insurance, cancellation charges, porterage, equipment, clothing, supplies and foreign exchange rates.

Useful Addresses
Islamabad & Rawalpindi
Pakistan Tours Ltd,
Flashman's Hotel,
The Mall,
Rawalpindi.

Travel Waljis Ltd (Licenced),
Box 1088 Waljis Building,
10-Khayaban Suharwardy,
Islamabad.

Koh-E-Noor Treks (Licenced),
6-6/1-1 T &T Centre,
Aabpara Centre,
Islamabad.

Karakoram Travels (Unlicenced),
Rawal Hotel,
Shahrah-E-Pelvhi,
Rawalpindi.

Karakoram Tours (Unlicenced),
F-7/2, Street 19,
1-Baltoro House,
Islamabad.

Sitara Travel Consultants (Licenced),
Box 63,
25-26 Shalimar Plaza,
Rawalpindi.

Chogori Adventures Ltd,
Box 1345,
Islamabad. Tel 2 3795

Gilgit
Ghulam Mohammed,
Hunza Baig,
Jamaat Bazaar.

Ibrahim Baig,
Karimabad,
Hunza.

Nasir Sabir,
Tourist Cottage,
Jutial.

Other
If you want to trek in both open and regulated zones, and intend applying for a permit before you head off to Pakistan, don't forget that it takes three months minimum for it to be processed. However, if you are in Pakistan already, you will have to wait at least a month for your permit to come through, unless you are a member of a small group, in which case it may only take four or five days. For detailed information on terms and conditions of trekking, get hold of the brochure published by the Ministry of Culture & Tourism, Islamabad, Pakistan.

Mountaineering
Mountaineering clubs wishing to scale any of the peaks in the Northern Territory have to meet special requirements and conditions. Applications must be made at least a year in advance between 1 January and 31 October, and it's done on a 'first come, first served' basis. All applications to climb K2 must be made two years in advance of the intended date of the expedition through any Pakistan Embassy or Consul's Office.

Equipment & Supplies
Non-consumables can be imported free of duty on condition they are to taken out of the country when you leave. Consumables – including liquor – are allowed in free of duty as long as they are to be consumed. Anything left has to be taken out with you or burned. You are not allowed to sell non-consumables or give them away, except to institutions with government approval.

Remember, walkie-talkies and radio-transmitter sets for communication between party and district headquarters are indispensable for large parties attempting to scale major peaks.

Royalties
These vary according to the heights of the peaks. For a mountain of 6000 metres or under it costs US$700; anything over

6000 metres costs twice that; and for K2 the maximum is US$3000.

Should a foreign mountaineering club join up with a Pakistani one, the royalties are halved. Concessions are made to small parties attempting the smaller peaks.

Foreign mountaineering expeditions must be accompanied by at least one English-speaking member to obviate communication difficulties. There must also be at least one doctor in a large expedition, or a medical assistant if it's a small party.

Liaison Officer
A liaison officer is usually detailed with large trekking or mountaineering, rafting, skiing, or even filming expeditions over hazardous or strenuous and restricted regions. Like high altitude mountain guides and high altitude porters, they have to be provided with insurance, equipment and supplies.

Rafting & Skiing
The same restrictions and permit requirements apply to rafting and skiing expeditions. There are no agencies in Pakistan that handle rafting or skiing parties. You should either join an agency overseas – there are a number in the USA – particularly in California – and in the UK – or, if you're in Pakistan, approach the PTDC for assistance.

Rafting or skiing equipment is not locally available here and has to be imported. Once again the same customs rules and regulations apply to rafting and skiing expeditions.

A liaison officer is also detailed by the Ministry of Tourism to rafting and skiing parties, but it's highly unlikely that the liaison officer will make it through the whole trip, particularly skiing parties.

Filming & Photographic Expeditions
Aerial photography is allowed only if the pilot or liaison officer is informed beforehand. Photography and filming of military sites and local women is strictly prohibited.

In the Northern Territory the customs rules and regulations also apply to photographic or filming expeditions. But there is no restriction or permit requirement in the rest of Pakistan.

A liaison officer is usually assigned to filming parties, but seldom to photographic expeditions except in restricted regions.

Mountain Guides
The Northern Territory has some of the finest high altitude mountain guides in the world. Considered the equal of the Sherpas of Nepal are the Balti mountain guides, and more particularly, those from Hunza. A particularly skilled guide is Nasir Sabir, who accompanied the successful Waseda Mountain Expedition to K2 in the summer of 1980, and in the summer of 1982 topped both Broad Peak and Gasherbrum with Reinhold Messner.

Porters
At low altitudes the porters' maximum load is 25 kg over a distance of either 10 km or a day, which must include rests of about five to 10 minutes' duration. If a night camp is struck before the traditional 10 km to 13 km has been covered, the shortfall has to be made up the next day.

High altitude porters must be provided with insurance against accidents, camping gear – tents, sleeping bags, boots, food – and medicine.

Maximum Load
5000 – 6000 metres altitude	25 kg
6000 – 7000 metres altitude	17 kg
7000 – 8000 metres altitude	14 kg
Above 8000 metres	12 kg

This load has to be carried up at each level (advance base camp) and back to base camp or lower level base camp on each trip. Porters have to sign an undertaking of good behaviour, particularly for mountaineering expeditions as they can ruin an expedition by refusing to move on unless paid more, and negotiation could go on *ad infinitum*.

For your own benefit check the references of any prospective porter/guide. It is advisable to choose one who comes with good credentials and recommendations. It is often better to hire porters for short distances only – i.e. to the next village only – as there will be local porters waiting there who know the area well. Of course, this is only possible if you are trekking by stages over a long route from valley to valley.

If a porter has served you well, be sure to recommend him in the notebook he keeps for such commendations.

Tour & Trekking Agencies Service Fees

US$300 for two to four people
US$400 for five to 10 people
US$500 for 11 to 15 people
US600 for more than 15 people
These rates are liable to change. The anticipated rise in service fees in the next couple of years is between 25 to 50% – may be as high as 100%.

Porter Rates through Agencies

US$25 for guides per day plus food
US$20 for porters at high altitudes per day plus food
US$15 for low altitude porters per day plus food
US$20 for cooks per day plus food

Porters Hired in Villages

US$15 for guide
US$8 for low altitude porters
US$10 for high altitude porters
US$6 if returning without a load

Note that in Chitral porterage and guide rates are much lower than they are in Gilgit and Baltistan.

Jeep Hire through Agencies

US$1.50 per km
US$5 per day
US$7.50 per night
US$1 per km if empty on a return trip

Established Government Rates

US$0.50 per km
US$5 per day
US$7 per night
US$0.40 per km if empty on return trip

Trekker's Requirements

Personal Quality Up in the Himalayas, which begin where the Alps end, physical fitness is not enough. Stan Armington notes in *Exploring Nepal*, a more-or-less hassle-free country for tourists, that both trekkers and travellers 'must have the ability to adapt to unusual situations, to accept confusion and lack of certainty'. This advice is applicable to the whole of Pakistan, but particularly to the Northern Territory, where in addition a trekker must have almost infinite understanding and be able to stay cool and positive.

Insurance Trekking and mountaineering insurance is obtainable in Pakistan, but it is preferable to get it in your own country from your trekking or mountaineering agent. The policy for illness, accidents and luggage, must cover trekking and mountaineering emergency services such as helicopter evacuation and hospitalisation. If there is an accident up here, a helicopter rescue is more-or-less inevitable, particularly in remote areas. This is a clause which is indispensable in the insurance policies of individuals, group trekkers and mountaineers, and rafting and skiing enthusiasts.

Insurance for the liaison officer, mountain guides and porters is obtainable from local insurance companies in Islamabad.

Visa Usually a one-month visa is enough, but if you're likely to go trekking for over a month, it is advisable to get a three-month visa.

Also it's a good idea to take into account possible delays of up to two weeks because of unpredictable weather conditions. Flights could be cancelled or the Karakoram Highway blocked.

Ways of Trekking In contrast to Nepal, Kashmir and Ladakh, the craggy, barren, glacial trekking region of the Northern Territory is sparsely populated.

Villages, hamlets and shepherds huts are few and far between. Moreover, they are not tourist-oriented. With the exception of a handful of local people who would offer overnight accommodation and food to trekkers, the Moslem society is closed to outsiders.

What Stan Armington describes as the 'living-off-the-land' approach to trekking in the Eastern Himalayas is simply not possible here. The one exception is if you're trekking along the main jeep tracks which have local travellers' inns or government rest houses. Out in the true trekking regions, you are virtually walking on untrodden ground along tracks which have only been used by villagers themselves. Trekkers must bring food supplies with them, which means careful forward planning is vital. You must take into consideration the availability of food, distances from village to village and trekking time.

What to Take
Camping Gear Thorough preparation in organising a trip and knowing what to bring can mean the difference between an enjoyable and a miserable trek.

Comfortable boots and thick woollen socks plus cotton inner socks are essential. Trekking trousers must be made of strong material and not too tight. Longjohns, preferably woollen, a crew-neck or polo-neck woollen pullover (sweater), light woollen jumper and windbreaker, and woollen shirts and cotton underwear are musts. Warm gloves and a raincoat make the difference between relative comfort and sheer misery.

Your tent must be light, have a flysheet, and preferably be waterproof. A water-proof, down-sleeping bag with an inner cotton sheet and ground pad with waterproof groundsheet are also essential.

Food must be similar to mountaineers': dehydrated, sealed packed food and the usual essentials. In summer fruit is available and you can also get milk, curd, cheese and, occasionally, eggs from shepherds. Bring some fishing rods and obtain a fishing licence as the rivers are full of trout.

The kind of rucksack you take depends on what is most comfortable for you. Generally packs with frames are too large and cumbersome, but some individuals prefer them. Whatever you choose, make sure it's big enough to contain all the essentials. You should also make sure you pack everything in 'solid', so that you don't have clothes, food and equipment moving around. Rucksacks must be made of strong material for rough travelling.

Odds & Sods Useful items include a torch, candles, matches or lighters, spoon and fork, Swiss Army knife, needle and thread, leather sewing awl with extra strong thread for running repairs on packs and boots, a tube of glue or adhesive tape for other repair work and a nylon cord for laundry and other uses.

Health Staying in good physical shape is of primary importance to any traveller, particularly when roughing it, trekking, mountaineering, rafting, skiing, fishing or filming in this rugged terrain.

One simple way of maintaining your health is to be very careful about the water you drink. Well-known Netherlands mountaineer and trekker, Egbert Bardoel, suggests the following precautions in order of preference: boiling water for five minutes; filtering which involves taking a mini-filter with you; or purifying with tablets – there are a number of brands you can choose from, most of which taste terrible and only last six hours, but do not have any negative side effects. It is also advisable to add lemon juice if you have any available. Iodising is the worst method as it affects the digestive system negatively, strains the liver and cannot be taken continuously.

Bardoel believes garlic is the best natural antibiotic for all-round good health measures. It fortifies the digestive system, increases resistance to diseases – especially stomach problems, dysentery etc. – cleanses the blood, protects the liver, wards off colds and has no negative side effects. He recommends a minimum of three cloves or pills a day, and double that if you are having trouble. The cloves have to be cut in tiny pieces or chewed, and if you're concerned about being given a wide berth by the rest of the party, keep your breath fresh with celery.

Common Diseases Apart from travel fatigue and sore feet, influenza and intestinal infections, particularly giardiasis, are the most common afflictions for trekkers and mountaineers.

Be sure you have the following in your medical kit: iodine for cuts and bruises or contusions; Tetracycline Hydrochloride, 250 mg capsules are excellent antibiotics for influenza, bronchial or respiratory infections and abdominal ailments; Fasigyn for gut problems or giardiasis; Flagyl for amoebic dysentery; Lomotil for diarrhoea; Strepto-magma and dehydration salt for diarrhoea and other gut problems; antihistamines for high altitude respiratory congestion and APC tablets for headaches, muscle pains and fever. Terramycin is a good cream for skin infections and wounds; Multifungin footpowder; Moleskin or Telpa Pads for blisters and Dextrose tablets for exhaustion or travel fatigue.

To counteract scabies Benzyl Benzoate is good; and take some insect repellent for bedbugs, mosquitoes, sandflies and fleas. Ophthalmic ointment for sore eyes; skin cream to prevent lips and skin from cracking or flaking; gauze; cotton; bandaids; and some rolls of adhesive and elastic bandages for sprains.

Physical Aids A good pair of sunglasses to protect your eyes from the glare of sandy wasteland or snow; a hat, preferably made of cloth, scarves which are large enough to cover your head and nose against duststorms or cold winds, are all essentials.

Vitamins B and C are also indispensable. If possible, carry your special medicines in your pocket or keep them in a handy side-pocket of your rucksack, so that you can get at them quickly if necessary.

Checkups Be sure to have a medical checkup before heading off into the mountainous wilderness of Pakistan. As a special precaution it may be a good idea to have an injection of Gamma 16 (immune serum globulin 16.5%), a prophylactic against diseases and infections for a period of 20 days.

For the inexperienced, getting fit is also necessary. Choose a rugged place and go for regular five km hikes several weeks before you go. Make sure this includes rock climbing.

General Advice

Dr Karl M. Herrligkoffer, successful expedition leader to Nanga Parbat and Broad Peak in 1953-54, and again of Nanga Parbat from the Rupal side in 1982, believes the same advice applies to mountaineers, trekkers and skiers in high altitudes.

Altitude sickness begins at the level of 3300 metres and is caused by lack of oxygen, and thus of pressure, at higher levels. The body has certain faculties that adapt to any changed environmental conditions. Dr Herrligkoffer writes that the body 'reacts as it would to any physical exertion: The heart beats faster and the blood circulates more quickly. Lack of oxygen makes the body lethargic and the climber's will-power and orientation decreases. The comparatively small physical exertion involved in pitching a tent or preparing food loom large and call for a tremendous effort.

The degree of acclimatisation varies widely with the constitution of the individual. It may also be affected by the enormous fluctuation in the outside temperatures and the damaging influences of the sun radiation.

At higher altitudes there is a loss in carbon dioxide. The carbon dioxide acts as the normal regulator of the breathing function by stimulating a rhythmical activation of the breathing muscles without the conscious intervention of the brain. A diminished carbon dioxide content of the body may cause a disturbance in the breathing function in the following manner: after a long pause respiration starts with very shallow breaths, which gradually increase into a very deep and panting breathing movement known as *Cheyne-Stokes* breathing.

On the physical side, the disturbance of proper brain-functioning may cause severe headaches, vertigo, sickness and vomiting. The subjective mental phenomena may be equally marked: the climber suffers from feelings of great lassitude and general lack of will-power. Lapses of consciousness may occur, and the faculty of reasoning is affected . . . The normal activities of consciousness are considerably restricted and a diminution of the rational critical powers may lead to a serious underestimation of objective dangers . . . '

At 7000 metres acclimatisation becomes impossible and at 7600 metres you reach what is known as the 'death zone' and, 'a climber may have a race with death to conquer the peak'.

Trekkers must not on any occasion try to climb over 3000 metres in one day. If you ignore this advice, you risk having altitude sickness compounded with pneumonia. Note that treks in this area start at an elevation of around 2300 metres to 2600 metres and can easily ascend 750 metres or more in a few hours. So watch your breathing and mental condition. Slow down when you start getting a tight chest or a headache.

Too much alcohol before climbing is verboten. This is a region which teaches you to accept your limitations and not to over-extend yourself. Moreover this mountainous wilderness cannot be hurried through, or out of, or up. Above 3650 metres you need two days of acclimatisation before going any further. If you haven't spent enough time in acclimatising yourself, you will soon begin to feel the symptoms of altitude sickness.

The safest method of approach is to climb an average of 300 to 400 metres only each day.

The first symptoms of altitude sickness are persistent headache, nausea, loss of appetite, sleeplessness, shortness of breath, fatigue and increased output of urine. As soon as you become aware of these symptoms, descend at once to rest before ascending again at a slower pace.

More severe symptoms include an abrupt decrease in urinary output, gross fatigue, severe headaches, breathlessness, coughing blood or foaming saliva. This indicates pulmonary oedema or waterlogged lungs.

Other possible symptoms are extreme weariness, vomiting, staggering walk, irrational behaviour, drowsiness or unconsciousness. This indicates cerebral oedema or water-logged brain.

In either of these cases, *you must descend at once*. With the former you might recover and be able to continue the trek, but with the latter the trek must be abandoned altogether.

This warning cannot be stressed often enough or strongly enough: 'Don't go too fast, too high'.

In the summer of 1982 a Japanese doctor died on Ultar Peak of altitude sickness compounded by pneumonia. A Swiss doctor who fell to his death from Nanga Parbat was suffering altitude sickness, but insisted on following the rest of the team up. Many accidents that occur are due to negligence in getting acclimatised.

Trekking Zones

The Northern Territory has always been a sensitive region because of its geopolitical importance. By and large, trekking and mountaineering expeditions, and this includes rafting and skiing parties as well, are not allowed outside the boundaries of the 15-km ceasefire line in Azad Kashmir & Jammu, and are restricted to staying within about 30 km of the Chinese and Afghanistan borders.

Circumstances and conditions along borders are subject to change, so suss out the latest information before you set out. At present trekking regions are divided into three zones – free, open and restricted. The free zone covers unrestricted areas with general elevation, not exceeding 6000 metres and permits and guides are not necessary. The treks are generally easy ones of two days and up to a week, and are considered simply as walkabouts. The open zone covers unrestricted areas but the altitude is higher than 6000 metres, and treks go over a period of two weeks to more than a month. They rate from moderate to strenuous, a high altitude guide is necessary, and often a permit. The restricted zone covers areas in prohibited border regions above 6000 metres, where trekking is very strenuous and covers a period of over a month. Usual prerequisites are a permit, porters and high-mountain guides. Often a liaison officer is detailed to the expedition or party by the Ministry of Culture & Tourism.

This region has become increasingly sensitive since the Russian invasion of Afghanistan. Some trekking areas have been deleted from the official list approved by the Ministry of Culture & Tourism. These are strictly off-limits to foreigners – indefinitely, probably until the situation is resolved – until the Russians get out of Afghanistan.

Heading Off

Before setting off into the unknown of open or regulated zones, trekking or mountaineering expeditions have to register with the Foreigner's Registration Office at Rawalpindi or Islamabad and at the Police Station in the administrative town of the region where they are going to trek. They must also notify the same offices when they are intending to depart.

The Northern Territory is a particularly special trekking mountainous wilderness, not merely because of its cragginess, vastness, ruggedness and weather conditions, but also because of the special cultural, social and geopolitical milieus. Attention is drawn to these facts, not only for reasons of safety, but also for increasing the pleasure of trekking up here.

Essentially this is a peaceful place, but it is in the process of undergoing enormous changes – always unsettling – initiated partly through the influx of tourists in recent years. This has been further complicated by the situation in Afghanistan, which has led to many refugees from the Wakhan region entering Pakistan, and is made all the more complex by international pressure on Russia to get out of Afghanistan. Added to all this is the pressure being put on Pakistan by the US to eradicate the cultivation of poppies and plug one of the main narcotics sources.

Like most mountainous trekking regions in the world – Latin America, Africa, Nepal, Ladakh and Kashmir – a few trekkers have disappeared mysteriously up in this region. People trekking on their own or in small parties should be particularly aware of this danger. Always doublecheck with the police, tourist officers or mountain people themselves about which areas are risky and whether or not you need a guide.

Try to see the headman or the teacher in villages along the way to let them know you are in the area and ask permission

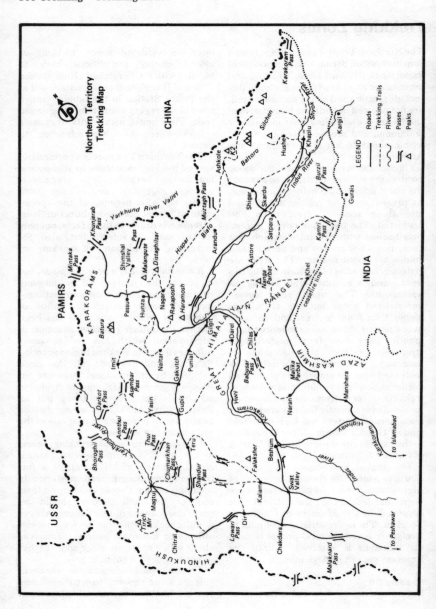

Northern Territory
Trekking Map

CHINA

INDIA

PAMIRS

KARAKORAMS

GREAT HIMALAYAN RANGE

AZAD KASHMIR

USSR

HINDUKUSH

LEGEND

Roads
Trekking Trails
Rivers
Passes
Peaks △

Karakoram Pass

Shyok

Khel

Khaplu

Kargil

Silchen

Hushe

Baltoro

K2

Ashkole

Shigar

Skardu

Arandu

Hispar

Biafo

Muztagh Pass

Yarkhund River Valley

Khunjerab Pass

Mintaka Pass

Shimshal Valley

Malangute △

Distaghisar △

Batura

Passu

Hunza

Nagar

Rakaposhi △

Haramosh △

Imit

Naltar

Gakutch

Gilgit

Punial

Darel

Chilas

Gupis

Yasin

Asambar Pass

Darkot Pass

Bhoroghil Pass

Yarkhund R.

Thui Pass

Anthui Pass

Chugnarkhan Pass

Teru

Shandur Pass

Falaksher △

Beshum

Kalam

Swat Valley

Magtul

Trich Mir △

Chitral

Lowari Pass

Dir

Chakdara

Malaknard Pass

to Peshawar

Naran

Manshera

Karakoram Highway

Indus River

to Islamabad

Babusar Pass

Malika Parbat △

Nanga Parbat △

Astore

Satpara

Kamri Pass

Burzil Pass

Gurais

ceasefire line

Indus River

before camping. Once permission has been granted you are automatically under the protection of the whole village. They will also be able to give you some good tips on dangers, weather, food etc. If you take some small gifts with you and hand them out as you go, it always makes for better relationships. If you're not camping near a hamlet or village make sure you choose a site that is not in danger from landslides or flash floods.

Up here the Islamic culture takes on a special character. Local women should never be photographed or even approached, and if they turn away do not try to follow them. Apart from being frightened of foreigners, they also dread being caught talking with strangers by male members of their family or clan. This is not true of the Kalash Valleys of Birer, Bumburet or Rumbur in Chitral.

Try to avoid any discussion on sensitive political matters, or religious tenets. Communal clashes occur here from time to time. The mountain people are friendly, hospitable and trustworthy, but there are rules to be observed on a trekking trail. Always greet them first and take time to shake hands with everyone in their party. Never approach them with suspicion, be friendly and smile. While this approach may not work all the time, it does on the majority of occasions.

Most successful mountaineering or trekking expeditions get on well with their mountain guides and liaison officers, so energy should be put into establishing a rapport and mutual trust and confidence from the outset.

If possible bring a gas stove and some portable gas with you, as, generally, the country up in this region is arid, rocky and barren, plants and trees are precious and wood in short supply. Also make sure you leave your **camp** sites clean when you go.

Both the inexperienced and the uninitiated in trekking ventures involving rock climbing would be unwise not to start on easier routes first. It's quite possible for middle-aged, and fit elderly people, to go on trekking expeditions in this region, but take it slowly at first. Do not cover any more than 10 km a day, rest often and increase the distance covered gradually day by day.

People trekking should walk together, keeping each other in view. Do not allow anyone to lag behind, and if you're with a guide, never get ahead of him. Those left behind can become confused, lose their way or, at the very least, are quite likely to injure themselves in their hurry to catch up.

In a glaciated region guides are indispensable because it is so dangerous, particularly if you're unfamiliar with such phenomena as fissures, cracks and crevasses. Never disobey the guide in glacial, mountain regions. Most of the porters are veterans of trekking expeditions, and know exactly what to do. What's more, they will do almost everything but trek for you, from choosing the best and safest camping sites and finding water and obtaining food, to carrying the equipment. The majority are frightened of receiving poor references, so they work very hard. Do not abuse them because of this.

Good preparation and good luck!

SUB-NORTHERN TREKS
AZAD KASHMIR & JAMMU

The distance between Muzzaffarabad and Khel is accessible by road, but beyond Khel it is a restricted area.

Khel-Chilas Trek

This takes six to 10 days and you need a permit, guide and porters. Setting off point: Muzzaffarabad. It is a restricted zone; strenuous trek at an elevation of 6000 metres. Best time to do it is from July until September.

From Khel to Moti it's 24 km; turn northwest to Domel; 2-1/2 hours' easy travelling with huts along the way. The trail forks at a stream, one path leading to

Astore, the other to Chilas.

It is 16 km from Moti to Kalan ascending gradually to a pass, 4000 metres high.

Between Kalan and Paloi there is a steep climb of 32 km. The route goes north then west; then north again for 1½ hours, ascends a pass at 4900 metres; then turns west into a valley, descending to 3300 metres. After walking another four hours you will reach a lake. Once you've passed the lake there is a 2½ hour' descent through cultivated land, then through pine forests. Paloi is situated at an elevation of 3150 metres.

There are 16 km between Paloi and Buner which takes about 4½ hours to cover. After 2½ hours you will reach the village of Kilbai, which is surrounded by walnut trees. The trail splits at Kilbai with one path leading to Bunar and the other over Mazeno Pass to Tarshing. The trail to Bunar follows the right bank of the river and leads into the village at 1850 metres above sea level after a two-hour' trek. There's a good view of Nanga Parbat from here.

From Bunar Village to Bunar Parao it is 19 km or five hours; gradual descent to a plateau, then down and across the river. Follow the trail along the Indus to Chilas, elevation is 1650 metres. The left bank of the Indus is sandy and stony.

From Bunar Parao to Chilas it's 27 km or 5½ hours.

(From Major Arthur Neve, *A Tourist Guide to Kashmir & Skardo Etc.*)

There are other routes from Muzzaffarabad to Chilas but the usual tourist trekking route is via Naran in the Kaghan Valley.

KAGHAN VALLEY
Naran-Saiful Muluk-Lalazar Trek
This takes two to four days and you don't need a permit or guide. Setting off point: Naran. Free zone. Easy trekking. Elevation 2500 to 2800 metres. Time from spring through summer and early autumn.

The distance from Naran to Saiful Muluk Lake is eight km, and involves an ascent of 2800 metres. This section is steep, scenic and bracing. There's a *rest house* and a *teashop* which has basic food. Accommodation costs Rs5.

From the lake, the trek can be continued to Lalazar Village, 11 km away and at the same altitude. The country along this part of the trek is shaded by trees and forests and carpeted with flowers in spring and summer. If you have time spend a couple of days in the village; it's a beautiful spot.

From Lalazar trek to Batakundi where the jeep track continues north to Babusar Pass into Chilas. Sixteen km to the south is Naran.

Naran-Babusar-Chilas
This takes five to six days and you don't need a permit or guide. Setting off point: Naran. Free zone. Moderate. Elevation 4080 metres. (From Naran to Chilas the track is jeepable. You can take a jeep as far as Besal all year round, but only from mid-June to early October to the pass.)

From Naran to Batakundi is 16 km; 2700 metres. Batakundi is a tiny village with an equally tiny bazaar, which sells almost everything you would require. There are several *inns* in the village where you can stay overnight.

There are eight km between Batakundi and Buruwai, 2900 metres. Food is obtainable in Buruwai and there's also a *rest house*.

The distance between Buruwai and Besal is 34 km involving a descent down an escarpment with a 300-metre drop for four km; local *inns* with reasonable food. Half-way along is a trail leading to the scenic, wooded **Luluzar Lake** to the northwest.

Besal to Gittidas, 12 km. The trail up to this hamlet is glaciated, rough and steep, but the people are friendly. Basic food is available and there are several *inns* here.

There's a climb of 6½ km between Gittidas and Babusar Pass, 4067 metres; panoramic view of surroundings, particularly enchanting on a full moon.

From the pass to Babusar Village, where you can get a cargo jeep to Chilas, it's 15 km.

SWAT VALLEY
Kalam-Laspur

This takes seven days. A permit is not usually required – police warning here – but porters/guide necessary. Setting off point: Kalam. Restricted zone. Strenuous. Elevation 3600 metres. Time from mid-July until September.

There are eight km between Kalam and Ushu, 2286-metre elevation. The trail passes through Baloga Meadow and attractive birch forests on the way to Matiltan where there is a basic *rest house*.

From Matiltan the route, which is considered to be one of the most beautiful in Pakistan, leads to the foot of Falaksher via Lake Mahodand, 15 km. Don't attempt this trek on your own; it's far too dangerous, you must take a porter. The trek continues to the campsite of Kruederi and from there up to Kachikhani Pass – 3600 metres – and down to the Metha Uth campsite. There are no no clearly defined paths to Metha Uth – just snowfields and glaciers – nor is there any sign of human habitation.

From here you head towards the edge of the Valley of Shandur. From the *camp* at Shandur Valley to the next *camp* at the foot of Kha is 10 hours and then another

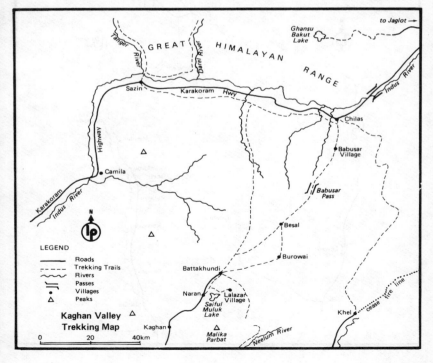

Kaghan Valley Trekking Map

six to eight hours to the *campsite* at Laspur. The next day set off on the 10-km trek – three hours – to Harchin where there's a cargo jeep service to Mastuj and another from there to Chitral.

From Laspur you can continue trekking to Koghozi, a three to four-day trek where jeeps are available for Chitral. If you are on an extensive trek continue to Shah Jinali in the Yarkhund Valley, then round via the Turikho Valley to Chitral – see Chitral Valley trek.

You can also trek into Yasin or to Shandur Pass from Mastuj – see Chitral-Yasin trek.

Kalam – Ghizer

This takes seven days, police warning here and porters and guide are necessary. Setting off point: Kalam. Restricted zone.

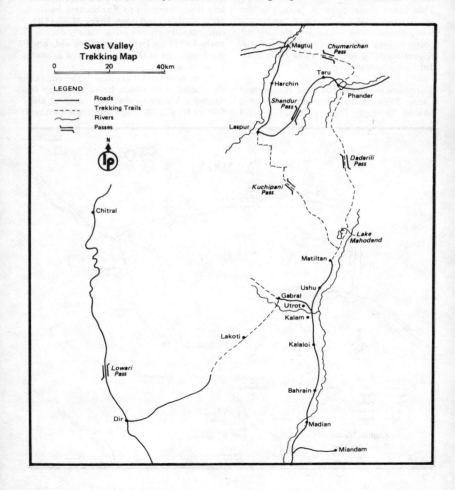

Swat Valley Trekking Map

0   20   40km

LEGEND
Roads
Trekking Trails
Rivers
Passes

N

Magtuj
Chumarichan Pass
Teru
Harchin
Shandur Pass
Phander
Laspur
Dadarili Pass
Kuchipani Pass
Lake Mahodand
Matiltan
Chitral
Ushu
Gabral
Utrot
Kalam
Lakoti
Kalaloi
Lowari Pass
Bahrain
Dir
Madian
Miandam

Strenuous. Elevation 4600 metres. Time from mid-July until September.

In the same valley following the same route, but on the fourth day of the trek just after Kachikhani Pass, 3600 metres, the trail forks, and one branch leads north-west to Laspur, the other goes east over Dardarili Pass, 4600 metres. The route is rough and hard-going over snowfields and glaciers, before ascending to Dardarili Pass. From the pass it descends into Ghizer Valley. From Ghizer Village it's about 30 km to Phander where jeeps are available for Gilgit.

If you are on an extensive trek you can trek from Ghizer Valley through Shiasi – five km from Phander – to Yasin where jeeps are available for Gilgit – see Gilgit Valley treks.

Kalam-Utrot-Dir

This takes three days and no permit is necessary, but police warning here. Porters and guide are optional for large groups. Setting off point: Kalam. Restricted zone. Fairly strenuous. Elevation 2225 to 4500 metres. Time from June until September.

It's five km by bus from Kalam to Utrot, which is situated 2225 metres above sea level north-west of Kalam. There is a *rest house* in Utrot. Further west is the Valley of Gabral where the trout fishing is excellent.

From Utrot it's a one-day trek to Lamoti – the first phase is up a steep, snowy pass, and after this it's possible to glissade for one km. The next section is through a scenic, wooded area. The people in this region live in caves and the majority of men carry guns, so be prepared. This is how two Lonely Planet correspondents from Switzerland described their experience: 'Troglodytes up there . . . bathing in the river . . . bearded fellow menacingly pointed gun at me. Got up to give him money . . . shook his head . . . said he needed medicine!'

It takes another day to get from Lamoti to Thal. You must register with the police in Thal. Camping is strictly prohibited, but you can sleep at the police station. Get the bus from Thal to Dir the following morning.

UPPER NORTHERN TREKS

DIAMAR
Chilas-Babusar-Naran

This takes five to six days and you don't need a permit or a porter or guide. Setting off point: Chilas. Free zone. Moderate. Elevation 2900 to 4067 metres. Time from mid-June to early October.

From Chilas to the village of Babusar it's 18 km or from six to eight hours of steep climbing. There is a cargo jeep service between Chilas and Babusar for Rs18. It's four hours of steep climbing from the village to the top of Babusar Pass – 4067 metres – and another three to four hours to Gittidas. The huts in this region have their walls and floors thickly padded with dried grass, which make them very cosy. Food is limited to corn or barley chapattis, lassi or curd and tea. The people in this village are friendly and hospitable. They will not accept money, but appreciate small presents of sugar, knives, needles and thread, medicine etc.

From here you can do a short side trip to Luluzar Lake, a 2-1/2 hour walk. There are no villages along the way, but there are camping spots and occasionally you will come across Afghan refugees camping near the lake. They offer food and tea in exchange for presents, particularly medicines.

From Luluzar Lake it takes half an hour to get to Besal which has a *teashop* that supplies basic food. You can sleep on their padded floor for Rs4 a night. Cargo jeeps occasionally go as far as Besal nowadays to bring supplies from Naran. A jeep to Naran will cost you around Rs30.

Note that the trek from Babusar Village through Gittidas to Besal is pretty steep and rough for 12 hours, but the scenery en route is magnificent.

From Besal to Buruwai is seven hours. There is a *rest house* at Burawai which has two double rooms, but no bedding, for Rs20 a bed or Rs40 a room. There are also *teashops* here with beds and bedding for only Rs4. Food is basic but good, and there are two small shops where you can buy basic essentials. There is a cargo jeep service from Buruwai to Naran for Rs20 per head.

It takes 3½ hours to get from Buruwai to Batakundi where there are *teashops* which not only provide food but also offer accommodation for Rs4. You can get a cargo jeep from Batakundi to Naran for Rs10. If you want to trek, it will take four to five hours.

Chilas-Nanga Parbat-Diamar Base Camp

This is a four-day trek. There is a police warning here and you need a permit and a porter. Setting off point: Chilas. Restricted zone. Elevation 3800 to 5500 metres. Strenuous. Time from June until early October. Warning: Never camp in the vicinity of Chilas or nearby surroundings. No trekking alone here. This is a restricted area where a permit is required for safety reasons. The local men, like the Pathans and those in Darel, Tanger and Kohistan are always armed.

The trek starts near Chilas, just off the Karakoram Highway in the Indus Valley. The trail to the *base camp* on this side crosses glaciers and is rough, arid, rugged and steep. It takes two days to climb up and two days to get down. See Tarshing-Chilas trek below.

Rakhiot Bridge-Fairytale Meadow

This takes four to five days, no permit is necessary, and a porter or guide is optional. Setting off point: Gilgit. Fairly moderate. Open zone. Elevation 5500 metres. Time from early spring to early October. Warning: No trekking alone here.

Get off at Rakhiot Bridge on the Karakoram Highway. The bridge is 2½ hours from Talichi. The Indus Valley in this region is situated at 1000 metres, and is sandy, barren and desolate. The sheer walls of the valley increase the intense heat during summer.

The trek from Rakhiot Bridge to Thatto Village takes six hours; *camp* here. The trail goes via Rakhiot Valley over Buldar Ridge, 2950 metres high, with arid precipitous cliffs. It passes through terraced fields and several primitive hamlets. Around here you will come across local women – adorned with heavy, brass jewellery – herding goats. The path then zig-zags up to Thatto.

From Thatto to Fairytale Meadow it's a three to four-hour' walk. Vegetation starts at 3200 metres. The area is thickly wooded with birch trees, firs and dwarf pines that spread up to the snowline at 3600 metres. The trail through the woods spirals steeply up to Fairytale Meadow. There's a good view of the north-west section of Nanga Parbat from here. Two days backtracking.

Further up at 4500 metres is the interim base camp. It takes another day to get up here and back to Fairytale Meadow, but the view of **Silver Pinnacle** to the right of Diamar Gap and the 5900-metre high **Ganalo Peak** is spell-binding.

Harchu-Rama-Astore

This takes three days. You do not need a permit and a porter is optional. Setting off point: Gilgit. Free zone. Fairly moderate. Elevation 2800 to 3800 metres. Time from June until September.

Harchu, 16 km before Astore, is on the main jeep track. From here to Rama it takes two days and you cross over two mountains. It's an attractive route and you can spend the night in a *shepherd's hut*. You can also buy milk, curd and local cheese along the way.

From Rama to Astore it's eight km, or two hours.

(From Abdul Karim, Tourist Cottage, Jutial, Gilgit.)

Astore-Katchura

This takes four days, and you don't need a permit, but a porter or guide is necessary. Setting off point: Astore. Open zone. Fairly strenuous. Elevation 2800 to 5000 metres. Time from June until September.

Follow the Astore Nallah from Astore down to Bullen Ga Village, then cross the river to Finna, a little hamlet. From Finna the trail leads into a valley, and up over mountains into Katchura. It's scenic along the way. See Skardu-Astore trek.

(From Khaled Aziz, Geologist Gemstone Corporation, Dassu.)

Astore-Rumpur-Rupal

This takes five days. You must register at the police check point, and a porter or guide is optional. Setting off point: Astore. Open zone. Moderate. Elevation 2800 to 3800 metres. Time from June till September.

The distance between Astore and Rumpur is 19 km at 3000 metres and involves a steep climb for six to seven hours. Rumpur is the gateway to the Rupal side of Nanga Parbat. There are ponies and

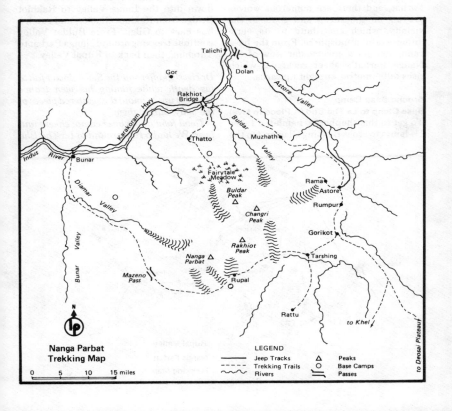

Nanga Parbat Trekking Map

0   5   10   15 miles

LEGEND

— Jeep Tracks   △ Peaks
- - - Trekking Trails   ○ Base Camps
〰 Rivers   Passes

guides available in Rumpur from Rs100 to Rs150. The trail from Rumpur is easy-going for a while, but becomes rough and difficult, going up and down hills and across streams. It passes Chorit where one branch forks off to Rattu in the east, the other leads to Tarshing, a beautiful village at the foot of some glaciers, and then continues to Lower Rupal, 10 km or 2½ hours' walk away. It takes half an hour from Lower to Upper Rupal. There's a good view of Nanga Parbat's Rakhiot Peak from Upper Rupal. The trek from here to the **base camp** at the foot of Nanga Parbat takes two hours. There's fresh spring water nearby.

Rupal is on the south side of Nanga Parbat, and there are numerous wolves preying on the sheep and goats in the vicinity, which contribute to its eerie 'other-world' atmosphere. From the base camp you get a spectacular view of the Nanga Parbat's sheer rockface, which rises 5000 metres straight upwards.

Around Base Camp
Base Camp to La Tho Bho (A Place to Live)
To get to this shepherds' hamlet, it takes 1½ hours to cross Bashing Glacier. On the right is a lake, and one km further up is a larger lake, which has clearer water, but it's full of frogs. At the end of another glacier are some beautiful stones – probably semi-precious. Ponies are available in Rupal for this trip.

From La Tho Bho a trail leads to Shakeri Pass, at 5000 metres.

Around Nanga Parbat
Dr Herrligkoffer says it is possible to walk around the great mountain in two weeks via Shakeri Pass, but extremely difficult via Mazeno Pass, at 6000 metres, Diamar Glacier, Patro Glacier, Rakhoit and Buldar Valley.

If you wish to cut the trek down, walk down into the Indus Valley to Rakhiot Bridge from Rakhiot Glacier, and catch a bus back to Gilgit. From Buldar Valley continue trekking around Nanga Parbat to Tarshing, then back to Rupal Valley.

Dr Herrligkoffer saw the Swiss doctor fall to his death while filming his own team's progress up . . . found the scattered pieces of the body, buried them.

Good food at the base camp: cheese and beer. We had a ride around to La Tho Bho

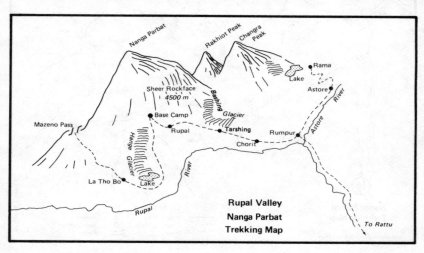

Rupal Valley
Nanga Parbat
Trekking Map

and back. When we left we were stacked up with German tinned foodstuff.

(Rein Hillhorst, Mountaineer, Amsterdam)

Other Treks

The following treks are from Major Arthur Neve's *Tourist Guide to Kashmir-Skardo, Etc.*, published in the early 1900s, and updated with material collated from travelling officials and scientists, particularly on the Astore-Deosai route.

Tarshing-Chilas

This takes seven days and you need a permit, porter and a guide. Setting off point: Astore. Open zone. Strenuous. Elevation 6000 metres. Time from mid-June until September.

It's 22 km from Tarshing to Kaonagod along the Rupal Nallah; and 15 km from Kaonagod to Zambazi; over Mazeno Pass at 6000 metres; then 16 km to the Bunar Valley before descending to the Indus Valley. The trail up and down is rugged and tough, but the scenery is spectacular.

The route from this part of the Indus Valley to Chilas is easy.

Astore-Rattu

This is a four day trek – two days up and two days down – and you need a permit and a guide, a porter is optional. Setting off point: Astore. Restricted zone. Moderate. Elevation 2800 to 3200 metres. Time from June until September.

From Astore to Rattu it's 34 km. There is a fine view of Nanga Parbat past Mons and Chagam, after crossing Rupal Nallah, which has huge granite boulders and moraines. The latter indicate that glaciers once filled the ravine, which turns right towards Nanga Parbat. The chocolate-coloured river is spanned by a wooden bridge. Not much further on the trail splits, with one branch leading to Astore, the other to Chorit and Tarshing.

The tiny hamlet of Fopun, and its entire population of a hundred, was completely wiped out by an avalanche in the spring of 1983.

Astore-Arondu

This takes six days and you don't need a permit, but a porter and guide are essential. Setting off point: Astore. Open zone. Strenuous. Elevation 5600 metres. Time from June until September.

It's 23 km from Astore to Thingeh; and another 15 km from Thingeh to the *campsite*. Leave the main *nallah* (river) after 12 km, and go north. The campsite is situated at 4000 metres and the ascent is steep. It's 18 km from one camp to the next. There's a steep climb to 5600 metres. Traverse the glacier, then descend to some stone shelters along a rough route through snow and rocks. Then there's a long trek of 29 km through several villages to the camp at Mendi, followed by a steep descent to the Indus River. From here it is two km into Arondu.

Reverse Trail via alternative Route Mendi to Balamik, 19 km; a fairly easy trek or six to eight hours by pony. From Balamik to Baltal it's a 10-hour trek which passes through a village about two hours below the camp. Between Baltal and Thingeh it's an easy eight-hour ascent to the pass, apart from the last stretch into Thingeh, which is hard-going. From Thingeh to Astore it's 23 km.

Astore-Deosai

This takes seven to 10 days and you need a permit, porter and a guide. Setting off point: Astore. Restricted zone. Strenuous. Elevation approximately 5000 metres. Time from June until September.

From Astore to Gorikot it's 10 km heading south-east; steep trail up to 2000 metres. At Gorikot, there's a steel-cable suspension bridge about 65 metres long. The trail goes up to a 4456-metre high pass, descends to villages along a stream; and cuts through a luxuriant valley speckled with goats and cattle before arriving in Gudhai, 26 km away. From Gudhai the route goes through hamlets so tiny they mostly comprise wooden huts. There are numerous scenic spots along the way. Fom here to Bubin it takes nine hours along grassy, wooded country and across streams. Then it's another 10 hours to the *campsite* by the side of a ravine.

Bubin-Skardu At Bubin the trail splits up: the lower trail goes to Chilim over Deosai into Skardu, 50 km away. The *rest house* in Chilim is occupied by UNO observers. The wooden bridge at this spot used to be dismantled every year for firewood in winter and rebuilt in spring. From Chilim you go up to Chachok Pass, 4595 metres, then to Deosai Plateau, at 4800 metres and about eight square km in area, and from there to Satpara, a distance of 20 km. The distance between Satpara and Skardu is 16 km.

The Deosai Plateau is open from mid-July until mid-September and offers spectacular scenery of the surrounding snow-capped peaks. Keep your eyes open for marmots, and for black and brown Himalayan bears. You may be lucky enough to see some bears fishing in the streams here.

Bubin-Katchura The upper trail from Bubin winds gradually up Alampi-La, 5500 metres high; *campsite* is at 4300 metres. From here to Thlashing Span Hut it's 12 hours through steep, snowy terrain; then a long descent over snowfields for 2½ hours to Barapani, a rocky valley dotted with huts. Just before you reach Satpara, the trail splits, one path going to Katchura.

Note that this is a restricted area, and the majority of people who supplied this information were government officials or scientists on location, who travelled by jeep – none had done this trek on foot. The information concerning distances, names of villages, and time needed to cover the territory – either to Skardu or Katchura – is therefore incomplete.

Astore-Srinagar
There used to be a tral linking Astore to Srinagar via Burzil Pass, at 4500 metres, through Gurais, on the other side of the ceasefire line across Kashmir & Jammu.

BALTISTAN
Satpara Lake-Deosai
This takes two days, a permit is required, but porters or guide are optional. Setting off point: Skardu. Restricted zone. Fairly moderate. Elevation 4600 metres. Time from mid-June until September.

In 1963 Skardu was linked with Diamar via Deosai Plateau by a rough, narrow jeep track, which is open only in summer. The trek up to Deosai Plateau from Skardu usually takes two days, and while this side of Skardu is not a restricted zone, the Deosai-Diamar side requires a special permit from the Ministry of Culture & Tourism.

The route from Skardu to Satpara Lake has been surfaced, but it's just a dirt track up to Satpara Village, 16 km away. The trail continues to Deosai, 20 km further on and 4800 above sea level. You can hire a jeep from the PTDC to take you up to the Deosai Plateau and back, or backtrack it on foot, if you don't have the special permit to cross over into the Diamar region via the Deosai Plateau.

If you wish to go to Deosai Plateau, to be on the safe side, check with the Tourist Officer at K2 Motel in Skardu. Note that there is also an officer here from the Ministry of Tourism, who might be of some assistance.

Skardu-Astore via Alampi-La
This takes six days, and a permit, porter and guide are necessary. Setting off point: Skardu. Open zone. Fairly strenuous. Elevation 5500 metres approximately. Time from mid-June until September.

Get to Kachura from Skardu by jeep – 32 km – then it's a two-hour easy walk to Chakke Village. From the village follow Chakke River which is renowned for trout. A number of villages are scattered along the trail and as you start climbing through summer pastures you will see many yak. On the third day out of Chakke you arrive at Alampi-La at 5000 metres. The ascent is tough and rough, but the view of Nanga Parbat to the south and the Deosai Plateau to the east is magnificent.

From here you descend to the village of Khane at the foot of the pass, then it's another six to eight-hours' walk to Gudhai in the Astore Valley. From Gudhai it takes a few hours to walk to Astore, where there are jeeps available for Gilgit.

Alternative Route

This was recommended by Major Arthur Neve decades ago.

From Skardu to Shigarthang is a two-day walk; Shigarthang-Ordukas, 18 km; easy trail initially, then a steep ascent to a rocky path at 4350 metres; Ordukas to Chumik, 15 km; seven km up a snowy trail, then over Bank Pass, 5350 metres. Be careful – in summer there are crevasses in the glaciers here; steep ascent for eight km up 1500 metres to Chumik. From Chumik to Thingeh it's 17 km; a gradual descent of nine km along the right bank of Herpo Nallah, another two km across a wooded plain, easy going for three km, then a difficult trek to Gutumsar Village. From

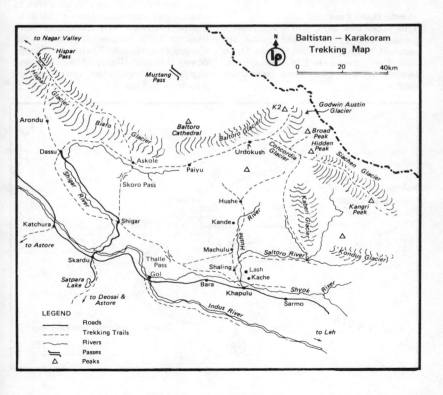

here it's another three km to Thingeh at 2850 metres. There's 23 km between Thingeh and Astore; 12 km easy – going, through hamlets, hard going for 1½ km, reasonable for three km, then a steep ascent. The trail crosses Astore Nallah, ascends and then traverses a ravine into Astore.

Alternative Route
See route via Mendi, Balamik, Baltal above, also recommended by Major Arthur Neve.

Skardu-Shigar
This takes one day and you don't need a permit, but a porter is necessary.

For description see above.

Skardu-Thalle Pass
This takes five days, you don't need a permit, and a porter and guide are optional. Setting off point: Skardu. Open zone. Fairly strenuous. Elevation approximately 5000 metres. Time from June until August.

From Skardu to Balaghar the route is reasonably easy. Ascending to Upper Thalle it becomes more difficult but there are spectacular views of the Karakorams. From there it goes to Brooq and finally on to Thalle Pass at 4877 metres.

If you wish you can continue treeking to Khupulu. See Shigar-Khapulu trek.

Skardu-Skoro Pass
This takes seven days, a permit is not necessary, but a porter and guide are essential. Setting off point: Skardu. Open zone. Fairly strenuous. Elevation 5500 metres. Time from July to September.

From Skardu you go to Dongla, then on to Dassu. From the latter you reach Chakpo along the Braldu River and then trek to Chango and camp or continue to Ashkole. The next section – from Ashkole to Skoro Pass at 5072 metres – goes through villages along the way. Then the trail loops down through Shigar Meadows and continues to Shigar, where you can catch a jeep back to Skardu.

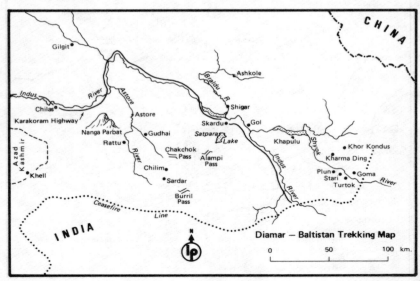

Diamar – Baltistan Trekking Map

0   50   100 km.

Alternative Route

Set off from Skardu to Baha; on to Dassu and Chakpo. From Chakpo the route is via Chago and Ashkole to the base of Skoro Pass. It then goes up to Skoro Pass and finally loops down into Shigar.

Skardu-Masherbrum Base Camp

This takes two weeks. You don't need a permit, but a porter and guide are indispensable. Setting off point: Skardu. Open zone. Strenuous. Elevation approximately 4500 metres. Time from July until September.

Head off to Doghoni from Skardu; then on to Thalis. From here you trek to Khande, Hushe, Wachack and Frozen Lake. Then go straight to the Masherbrum *base camp*.

Returning, backtrack to Khande and from there to Khapulu where jeeps are available for Skardu.

Skardu-Sherpigang Glacier

This takes two weeks. You need a permit and a porter and guide. Setting off point: Skardu. Open zone. Strenuous. Elevation 5500 metres. Time from July to August.

This is in the same valley and along the same route as the preceding trek. But from Doghoni take the trail to Shaling; then on to Thalis; to Khande; Halde; Thagas; Brooq; Latchit; Kharmading; Khor Kondus; and to the snout of Sherpigang glacier. It's an awesome trail.

Return by backtracking to Khande, and from there to Khapulu where you can catch a jeep back to Skardu.

Skardu-Khapulu

This takes five days. No permit, porter or guide necessary. Setting off point: Skardu. Free zone. Fairly easy. Elevation approximately 3000 metres. Time from early spring to early autumn.

This route is along the main jeep track.

From Skardu to Khapula it's 102 km. The ascent along the Indus River between Skardu and Gol is gradual and gentle. Gol is situated at the confluence of the Indus and Shyok rivers. There's a bridge over the Shyok River at Gol and you pass through several hamlets along the way. From Gol to Quresh and on to Karpakhs takes four hours. Between June and July you get a good view of the Masherbrum from Quresh. After Quresh, the first village en route to Khapulu is Barra, which has numerous springs and streams and is a great place for trout fishing. Then on to Khapulu and beyond is Sarmo, 18 km to the east.

SHIGAR VALLEY
Shigar-Dassu

This takes four days and you don't need a permit or a porter or guide. Setting off point: Shigar. Free zone. Fairly moderate, even easy. Elevation approximately 3000 metres. Time from early spring to early autumn.

Shigar is the gateway to Concordia via Dassu, 80 km away. From Shigar the trail goes through a fertile area of grainfields, poplar trees and hamlets, then down an escarpment by the Shigar River. The valley is broad and sandy, and the river is broken into little streams.

The most direct route to Dassu is along the right bank, heading upstream, but there is an alternative approach from the other side of the valley. Just out of Shigar is a track that leads straight down to a bridge, which spans the broad, sandy valley streaked with streams. There are numerous lush areas and quiet little villages with huts of wattle and mud over this side. You will also see a number of women and children, dressed in traditional costume. Even the babies wear the traditional headgear, richly embroidered and embellished with metal buttons and other metal objects.

If you go south the jeep track leads to Katchura, while if you head to the north it finishes at the end of the valley. Near where the jeep track ends is a trail which goes for some distance before branching off in two directions, one track going to Arondu, the other leading to Dassu. At the end of the jeep track across the sandy, river valley are four little bridges, which link it with the main jeep track to Dassu.

On the main track direct from Shigar are some orchards. It begins to get arid and barren again along the escarpment, before ascending to a rather claustrophobic, but lush green valley. From here it descends into a boulder-strewn stream. Jeeps and tractors dive into it, and have to lumber up a steep bank. You can cross the river by foot, jumping from boulder to boulder. There are also two long poles here, which you can use to cross to the other side.

The country around here has abundant fruit trees and terraced grain fields. The *rest house* is clean, modern but basic, with several beds and one western toilet plus local loos. The food is limited to eggs, chappatis and tea.

Close by is the camp of the Gemstone Corporation geologists, who are hospitable and friendly. If you let them know in advance, they will make food available. Don't leap to the assumption that war has broken out if you hear an explosion – they're just blasting for gems. Take a look at the Corporation's collection of unpolished stones – quartz, tourmaline, aquamarine and others.

Crowds of porters are camped, more-or-less permanently, on wooded hillsides, near the road and rest house, as there is a continuous shuttle of mountaineering expeditions and trekking parties going in and out. You'll see tractors, crammed with bright red and orange packs, equipment and supplies, plying back and forth; and loads of liaison officers either paying off or recruiting porters.

The jeep track continues for about eight km past this spot, but treks to Concordia start here. The area has recently been surveyed to see whether it's possible to make it up to Ashkole, which would cut the trekking time to Concordia by three to four days.

Warning It's advisable for individual travellers who wish to join trekking or mountaineering parties to check with the PTDC at K2 Motel, Skardu, before going to Dassu – or at Hushe in the Khapulu Valley. There are chances of getting accepted, but it's essential to have your own camping gear and provisions, and it's necessary to hire a porter for this trek.

Dassu-Ashkole-Concordia

This takes 26 days, and you need a permit, a guide and porters. Setting off point: Dassu. Restricted zone. Strenuous. elevation 2590 to 4267 metres. Time from June until the end of August.

Most trekking parties comprise elderly or middle-aged westerners, accompanied by a few younger people, generally their sons and daughters.

Usual setting off time is 4 am – occasionally earlier – going through until 6 pm or 7 pm.

It's approximately 57 km from Dassu to Ashkole. On the first day you cover the distance between Dassu and Chakpo, which is 15 km and takes about six to eight hours. It's fairly strenuous in sections. The trail goes through barren country across streams and glaciers, but the terrain along the banks of Braldu River is quite gentle with only occasional steep sections over moraines, through gorges and narrow passes. There is a danger of falling rocks or avalanches on this stretch. It's very hot near the Braldu Gorge.

Between Chakpo and Chango is the toughest segment of the entire trek, ascending about 665 metres through desolate, barren country, before descending to a village. It's a six to eight-hour walk.

From Chango to Ashkole it's an easy three-hour' ascent through grassland, farms, mulberry and apricot orchards and irrigation canals, then up glaciers, along sheer precipices and ravines, and past a hot spring. Ashkole is the last village on this trek.

The section from Ashkole to Korofan is where you begin to enter the wilderness of glaciers, deserts and lofty peaks. It's easy crossing the glaciers to the campsite at Korofan, which is on the far side of Biafo Glacier. The site is surrounded by trees and has fresh water spring.

Between Korofan and Bardomal there are numerous small streams to ford and then you will come to a rope bridge in bad repair. This is operated by a *haji* – a Moslem, who has been to Mecca – who charges Rs10 per person plus Rs5 a pack. While this is considered to be excessive by the local government, there is no way they can persuade the haji to bring his rates down as the only alternative to crossing at this spot involves another two or three days' detour via the Dormundu Glacier. Immediately after the bridge the going is difficult for eight to 10 hours.

From Bardomal to Paiyu the elevation is around 3500 metres. There are a few streems to cross and a rocky area to cover on the way to Paiyu, which is on the south side of Baltoro Glacier. The camping area here was once green, wooded area, but is gradually being denuded of trees, and beginning to be littered with campers' rubbish – mostly lavatory paper.

The trek continues from Paiyu to Liliwa, taking about six hours, before crossing Baltoro Glacier. The camp at Liliwa is just off the glacier and offers a view of Paiyu Peak and Trango Towers.

The next *campsite* along is Urdokush at 4350 metres. The going is rough and steep, with many ups and downs. There is also a difficult stream to cross. The *camp* is not far from the glacier on the south side and is rather like an oasis. The view of Paiyu Peak, Trango Towers to the north and Baltoro Cathedral is stunning.

Between Urdokush and Goro there is another tough over stony ground. The **camp** here is at the junction of Muztagh and Baltoro Glaciers. There are spectacular views of Muztagh Tower to the north, Masherbrum Peakto the south, and Gusherbrum 1V to the east.

The elevation between Goro and Concordia is 4665 metres, but the trek to Concordia Valley is fairly easy. The valley itself is hemmed in by K2, Broad Park, the Gasherbrum Group, the Golden Throne and Chogolisa. This is where all the glaciers meet. The **camp** is on a ridge of a glacier and has a view of Masherbrum to the south and Muztagh Tower to the north.

From here you can go on to the **base camp** of Chogolisa – an eight hour trek – or take a side trip to the **base camp** of K2 or Broad Peak.

To return, backtrack over the same route; or when you reach Chogolisa continue to trek south into the Khapulu Valley. See Khapulu Valley treks.

Other

The weather in this area is unpredictable; even in summer there's intermittent snowfall, hail and rain.

Keep your eyes open for rubies, garnets and other semi-precious stones, along the way.

Concordia was so-named bedause it is the junction of Siachen, Baltoro and other minor glaciers like the Godwin Austin, the Gusherbrum and the Masherbrum. The valley itself is broad and surrounded by the white, snowy walls of slopes and peaks. This is the inner sanctum of the Himalayas; the approach to the mighty peaks of K2, the Gasherbrum and the Kangri. Most trekkers are tempted to climb up to the base camps of K2 or Broad Peak. Left of the valley is a grand view of Marble Peak. Once you get to Concordia, it takes another three hours to trek to the Minor Peak **base camp**.

Alternative Routes

Major Arthur Neve gives the following seldom trodden trails, previously used only by the British military explorers and other early 'sportsmen' in the region. These trekking routes are in both open and restricted zones where permits, porters and guides are needed. As well, there's usually a liaison officer detailed to trekking parties. If you intend undertaking a climbing, trekking, rafting or skiing expedition it is best to check with the PTDC for detailed information on formalities before you go.

Shigar-Ashkole

This takes 17 days and you need both permit, porter and guide. Setting off point: Shigar. Restricted zone. Strenuous. Elevation approximately 5000 metres and over. Time from June until August.

From Shigar to Yuno is 32 km, along an easy trail shaded by willow trees; over a sandy, stony plain with streams to be forded. From Yuno to Koshuma – opposite Dassu – it's 19 km along a similar stretch of sandy, stony country; near Wungo, the trail ascends, then follows a canal and crosses the Shigar River to Dassu; between Koshuma and Chukpa there's 16 km of difficult trekking to the rope bridge below Biano. There's a better trail on the right via Dassu; Chakpo to Ashkole, 25 km of rough, stonny trekking. Crossing the stream here takes 1½ hours; another two streams further on take another 1½ hours, four hours from Chukpa altogether. At Pakore use the rope bridge to cross from the left bank of the Braldu River to the right bank.

Alternative Route This was used by British explorers and was completed in three easy stages from the second camp at Thal Brock via the lower route to Ashkole, returning via Skora-La.

When Domordo Nallah can be forded it takes nine hours from Ashkole to Bardomal. If Domordo Nallah can't be crossed on foot, there is a long detour to a bridge. Camp at Korofan. The second day out, there's a six-hour march between Biafo Glacier and Domordo Nallah; from Bardomal to Urdokush it's a 15 km, up over Baltoro Glacier; and from here it takes six hours to get to Liliwa following the bank of the river over boulders, past a small lake; then to Chober Zechen it's three hours over glaciers, before crossing to the other side of the moraine to Urdokush, which is another three hours. There's a good *campsite* here.

Crossing the glacier from Urdokush takes four hours; then you'll get to Muztagh Lunka at Conway's Piale Glacier. Ascending Muztagh over the glacier and getting to Muztagh Spang-La takes 11 hours. On the left banks of Lobsang Blangra is a grassy slope. Follow the glacier at the foot of the pass for four hours. There is a difficult three-hour ascent to the summit at 6335 metres, and particularly difficult descent north of Chang Tong.

Return to Shigar by backtracking over the same route.

Alternative Return Route From Ashkole to Pakore is 3½ hours; Pakore to Hu five hours; Hu to Dassu six hours; Dassu to Simu six hours. In the old days you had to cross the river by raft to get to Shigar, but today there is a trail straight down to Shigar from Dassu. Moreover the river is now shallow and has two bridges spanning it.

Shigar-Baltoro-Muztagh Pass

This is an exploration route undertaken by Sir Francis Younghusband, which takes 16 days. A permit is necessary and a liaison officer is detailed. Porters and guide are essential. Setting off point: Shigar. Restricted zone. Strenuous. Elevation over 6000 metres. Time from June until August.

It's 1½ hours from Shigar to Hashu; head

upstream to cross the *nallah*, from here it takes approximately nine hours to get to the *campsite*, which is about 100 metres above a steep grassy slope, just below the snowline. From the camp to Ashkole is another long trek – 10½ hours – up a 1000-metre high snowy and rocky region; then two hours to the summit of the 5078-metre Skora-La. On the north side of this is a glacier-filled valley; the trail leads through snowfields for three hours, then down to some hamlets and into Thal Brock, 6½ hours from the summit. From here there's a steep drop into scenic Braldu Valley and the rope bridge below Ashkole. This takes two hours.

Shigar-Mango Gussar

This takes 14 days. You need a permit, and a porter and guide are necessary. Setting off point: Shigar. Open zone. Fairly strenuous. Elevation 5073 metres to 6288 metres. Time from June until August.

From Shigar go to Khutti Skoro, then on to Dassu. From Dassu either head for Biano or go directly to Chakpo. On reaching Chakpo, you have a choice of going straight to Ashkole on the same day or going to Chango. The next stage is Mango Gussar Peak.

Return by backtracking to Dassu or the Skoro Pass (5078 metres).

Shigar-Choktai Glacier

This long trek takes a month. A permit is necessary and you need a porter and guide. Setting off point: Dassu. Restricted zone. Strenuous. Elevation between 5407 metres and 5833 metres. Time from June until August.

Trek from Dassu to Chakpo; then to Chango or Ashkole; from here to Korofan, Panmah, Panmah Glacier, Chiring Glacier, Drinsang Glacier. From Drinsang Glacier trek to Nobande; then to Sobande Glacier; to Skam Pass (5407 metres); on to Singang Glacier and Singing Pass (5833 metres); and finally to Choktai Glacier. Backtrack over the same route.

Shigar-Snow Lake

This takes 16 days. You need a permit, and a porter and guide are necessary. Setting off point: Dassu. Open zone. Strenuous. Elevation 5000 metres. Time from June until August.

Along the same valley and route, but when you reach Ashkole take the trail to Drinsang; then go on to Mongo; and from there to Biafo Glacier, Singang Glacier and finally Snow Lake.

Backtrack to Dassu over the same route.

Shigar-Shusbun Glacier

This is a 10-day trek through open zone. You need a permit, and a porter and guide are necessary. Setting off point: Dassu. Strenuous. Elevation 6462 metres. Time from June until August.

Once again this trek is in the same valley, but take the trail to **Hohlungma Glacier** to the base of Ganchen Peak (6462 metres); then to Tsilbu Glacier and on to Shusbun Glacier.

Backtrack to Dassu.

Shigar-Chogolisa

This takes 24 days. A permit is required and a liaison officer is assigned to each party. Porters are also necessary. Setting off point: Dassu. Restricted zone. Strenuous. Elevation 5800 metres. Time from June until August.

From Dassu go to Chakpo; then to Chango or Ashkole; from here to Korofan and on to Bardomal. Then to Paiyu, Liliwa, Urdo-kush, Goro, Concordia and to the foot of Chogolisa.

Backtrack to Dassu or continue down to Dansam Valley or Khapulu Valley. See Khapulu Valley trek.

Shigar-Haramosh

This is a 10-day trek through open zone. A permit is not necessary, but you need a porter and guide. Setting off point: Shigar. Fairly strenuous. Elevation approximately 5500 metres. Time from June until September.

Go to Molto from Shigar, then to Chutran, Arondu, Chogolugma Glacier and to the base of Haramosh Peak 11 (6217 metres).

Backtrack over the same route to Shigar.

Dassu-Arondu

This takes one day and you don't need a permit; porter and guide are optional. Setting off point: Dassu. Open zone. Strenuous. Elevation 4500 metres and over. Time from June until September.

From Dassu to Mendi, the main village in Arondu, it takes five hours to trek along a difficult trail down through a riverbed, then a steep ascent up to a ridge at 665 metres. Another alternative is from Damodas on the Indus to Arondu, which is apparently only two km.

This is a starting out point for the Nagar Valley over Hispar Glacier. Formerly used by British sportsmen, it's an alternative to the Ashkole-Nagar route, but the climb up the Biafo-Hispar Glaciers is extremely difficult.

Shigar-Nagar Valley

This takes two weeks through an open zone. You need a permit, and a liaison officer is assigned to each party. Often, in winter or early spring, they do not go the whole way. Porters are necessary, but high altitude guides generally refuse to do this trek in winter, sometimes even until early spring. Setting off point: Dassu. Strenuous. Elevation over 5600 metres. Time for trekking from early spring in late May until September.

If you are in Shigar take a jeep to Dassu.

From Dassu you go to Chakpo along the same trail to Ashkole. At Ashkole take the trail to Drinsang; then on to Mongo; Biafo Glacier; Hispar Pass (5151 metres); Hispar Glacier; Nagar Valley and on to Ganesh where cargo jeeps and buses are available for Gilgit.

Alternative Treks

This is another of the old British 'marches' of Major Arthur Neve via Shigar's western branch, the Basha. There are trails on either bank, but Major Neve preferred the route along the left bank. It involves crossing the stream to Gulapore, and a three-day walk, climbing all the way. However, there is now a direct route to Dassu from Shigar, and from Dassu it is only two to three days' walk to Ashkole.

At Ashkole the trail splits up with one route heading west to Biafo Glacier, the other branching eastward to Concordia or Muztagh Pass. The Biafo Glacier is northwest of Ashkole and linked to the Hispar Glacier by a snowfield. It is also traversable from the Nagar Valley, but the usual way to go is via the western route.

In the winter of 1978 four Americans skied from Ashkole to the Nagar Valley over the Biafo and Hispar Glaciers, and in the early spring of 1980 an American couple also made this trip. Less fortunate were the 50 brigands from Nagar Valley, who lost their way on this glacier in the mid-19th century and perished as a result.

Between Shigar and Kashomal it's a six-hour trek along fairly flat, but stony ground; and from there it's 1½ hours to Hashu; another 1½ hours to Alchori, and another 1½ hours to Tshildi, and an hour to Kashomal from the latter. There is a magnificent view of the peak of Koasar Gan from Kashomal.

The next stage is an eight-hour trek from Kashomal to Chutrun through a wide valley – confluence of rivers – then it's 1½ hours to Yuno. When you reach the Braldu

River cross the bridge and walk for 2½ hours across the flat, stony plain until you come to another bridge over the Basha River. From here it's 1½ hours to Tisser. High up on the left are some waterfalls, and opposite is the gorge of the Braldu River. There's a sharp ridge here, then trek up Braldu Valley for 1½ hours. The first stage is easy, scenic; the second is over sand and stones to Chutrun. The word Chutrun means 'hot water' and there are hot springs and baths here. You will also notice white marble in this region. It takes three hours to get from Chutrun to Doko Sibri, the first half through cultivated land, followed by an easy walk through walnut groves to Dogoro; then half an hour to Sibri and another half-hour to Doko, 2000 metres above the river. Just beyond the village is a *camping site*. From here it's an easy descent to Gulapore, but below Tisser, the trail is rough and dangerous. Cross a stream into Doko. From Doko to Arondu it's four hours along slopes, 2½ hours up and down, turning left when the valley widens. At first the valley is stony and barren, later it is cultivated. When you get out of the valley it's another two hours to Arondu across a stony, sandy plain and several streams.

Arondu is the last village in the Rondu Valley. About a km west of Arondu is the rather dirty-looking snout of the Chogolungma Glacier. To the south, overhanging the village, is Tipor Glacier Over many years these glaciers have shifted quite a distance, and more recently they have started to recede. The village is at an altitude of 3265 metres.

This completes the first half of the trek to Nagar Valley via the Biafo and Hispar Glaciers. Trekking above Arondu is difficult as it involves technical rock climbing. This is probably why today skiers generally start their trip at Ashkole, and go straight across the glaciers to the Nagar Valley.

Arondu-Nagar Valley

This route via Kiro Nallah goes north out of Arondu to Domak. Follow a narrow trail over the Chogolungma for two hours; and continue to Beg Bransa for another half an hour. There's a campsite at Harimach, which is 2½ hours' ascent over moraines and along a glacier, followed by an hour's walk through a grassy forest of birch trees. Domak, at an altitude of 3835 metres, has some picturesque stone huts. From Domak to Katche Bransa takes four hours along grassy slopes, and another hour to a meadow and polo-ground known as Shagram. From here you go through the junction of Hunches Alchori Glacier and Kiro Glacier, which takes 1½ hours. Beside the moraine is a grassy, hollow region, the *campsite* at Tasuwacha. Wood and water are available at this site. Not far from Tasuwacha is another grassy hollow. Cross the glacier to Katche Bransa at 4664 metres here.

From Katche Bransa trek to Strathu Bransa. It involves a walk of 4½ hours across the middle of the glacier, followed by an hour's ascent of a moraine, then another hour climbing and crossing to Ding Bransa at the foot of a spur to the north. Climb up this spur for 1½ hours, then head down the side of the glacier. From here you trek in a north-west direction – be very careful of crevasses in this area – on a rugged trail up to the next spur. Once you reach this spur it's another two hours to the *campsite* at Strathu. Strathu is perched high on a steep and tiny platform 5335 metres above sea level.

It takes 1½ hours to get from Strathu Bransa to Galefang Bransa. One hour's easy trekking up a snowy valley to Nushik Col where you get a good view of the mountains in Hunza. Backtrack about a hundred metres then turn east up a steep, snowy ridge to some large rocks – very good sheltering place at 5600 metres. Beyond the rocks is a steep, icy slope traversable in an hour, and another easy slope, 160 metres. There are often avalanches in this vicinity, so be careful and keep alert.

The best time to go is in mid-June as

there are lots of snow bridges over Zur Briggan. By early July there's only one snow bridge left and by September, none at all. There are crevasses ranging from three metres to 14 metres wide in this region. If there are snow bridges descend to the side of the glacier, and cross over to Haigutum or Hai Kurum on the left of Hispar Glacier – 1½ hours. There's a snowy lake here. from the glacier to the Hispar Valley takes a day, then it's another day to Nagar about 20 km away. The distance altogether is about 240 km.

Shigar-Khapulu

This takes four to five days, you don't need a permit, and a porter and guide are optional.

From Shigar to Khapulu it's about a hundred km through hamlets. The trekking is strenuous to Thalle Pass, at 5335 metres – hard-going all the way, but the scenery is spectacular.

Just before Humayun Bridge is a trail that veers to the north. It's actually a jeep track which goes all the way to Hushe, but there are very few cargo jeeps in this area. Mountaineering expeditions and large trekking parties on their way to Masherbrum generally go directly to Hushe. Others on foot usually rest up in Khapulu for a while.

From Khapulu head straight up north. This can be difficult as the Shyok River gets swollen in summer. In spring the riverbed is just an expanse of pebbles over two km across. Getting over the Shyok by *zakht* – a raft floated on four or more goatskins filled with air – is an extremely dicey proposition. Once you do get across the river the trail goes through typical Balti settlements, but it's hard to find. There is an alternative route via Humayun Bridge, 40 km from Khapulu – a necessary detour to go through Shaling.

From Shaling the next village on is Machulu, a distance of 18 km. There's a *rest house* here, built in an an attractive spot, which has fairly good food. From here it's half an hour to Asherpe, then on to Hushe across the river of the same name. The further you go along this trek, the more awesome it is.

At 3250 metres, Hushe has only three or four trees – almost nothing grows in this area – a few huts and very friendly inhabitants. You can hire low and high altitude porters and guides in Hushe, and also camping and mountaineering equipment if you need it. There is no *rest house*; you must have your own camping gear and some provisions. From Hushe continue trekking to the Masherbrum area.

To return, backtrack to Khapulu.

Hushe-Masherbrum

This takes one day each way. You don't need a permit and hiring a porter or guide is optional. Setting off point: Hushe. Open zone. Elevation between 3500 metres and 5600 metres. Time from early spring to early autumn.

Hushe is the setting off point to the Masherbrum *base camp*, and the trail to Concordia, which goes over the Masherbrum-La to the Baltoro Glacier. The Masherbrum-La region is covered in snow all year round, and because the marked trails are fading, they now use sticks as markers. This used to be a popular trail, but it has diminished in importance and is hardly used today. Even mountaineers and trekkers scaling the Kangri Group usually take the Dassu-Ashkole-Concordia route nowadays. It takes 11 hours from Hushe to the Masherbrum base camp along this dangerous, difficult, rocky and glacial trail, overhung with ice-cliffs. In summer crevasses crack and cave in. It's a rather daunting trek but porters and guides know it well.

Other Treks

A short distance beyond Humayun Bridge on the Hushe jeep track, there's a branch going east to the Saltoro River, north of Shyok in the direction of the Siachen Glacier and the Kangri Group. Above the

Hushe-Saltoro Nallah are some extra-ordinarily beautiful peaks. The trail along the Saltoro leads to the Muztagh Range at the end of the valley and offers spectacular views.

Around Khapulu

There are a number of short treks in the surrounding area and villages along the Shyok. On a nearby plateau above Khapulu you can get a magnificent view of snowcapped peaks.

Machulu-K6 Base Camp

This takes 18 days through an open zone. You need a permit, and porters and guide are also necessary. Setting off point: Machulu. Fairly strenuous. Elevation approximately 5500 metres. Time from June until August.

If you're in Skardu get a jeep straight to Machulu; jeeps are also available to Machulu from Khapulu. Alternatively it takes three or four days on foot to get from Khapulu to Machulu by Humayun Bridge and then three days across the Shyok River via Shaling. From Machulu cross the Hushe River to Halde; then go to Sinu; and from there to Thang. From Thang trek to Lachit in the Kondus Valley, then on to Lachit Meadow and finally to the K6 *base camp*.

Halde has a *teashop* with beds that you can rent for the night, and at Thagas, near the Kondus Valley, there are some very hospitable and friendly school teachers, who will almost certainly put you up.

To return, backtrack to Machulu.

Machulu-Ghandugurup Valley

This is an eight-day trek through open zone. You need a permit, and porters and a guide are a must. Setting off point: Machulu. Fairly strenuous. Elevation approximately 5600 metres. Time from June until August.

You go through the same valley, but from Machulu trek up to the village of Hushe.

From here go to Ghandugurup Balley via Cholinga Glacier up the Baltora side in the direction of Shigar from Masherbrum. On the same trail going north towards Trinity Peak is Gondoroko Valley. This is a longer route in the vicinity of the Biarechi or Biarchedi Glacier. A detailed map of this trek is indispensable.

Backtrack over the same route on your return.

Machulu-Gharkun Peak

This takes 16 days. You need a permit, and porters and guide are indispensable. Open zone. Strenuous. Elevation approximately 5800 metres. Time from June to August.

Cross the Hushe River to Halde from Machulu; then trek to Paron; Dansam; Unak; Gyang Glacier, and finally to the base of Gharkun Peak (6620 metres).

To return, backtrack to Machulu.

Machulu-Chumick Peak

This is a 24-day trek through an open zone. You need a permit, and porters and a guide are indispensable. Setting off point: Machulu. Strenuous. Elevation approximately 6000 metres. Time from June until August.

Follow the same route through the valley until you reach Unak, where the trail forks. Take the branch leading to Goma; from Goma trek to the snout of Ghayari Glacier; then to the snout of Bilafond Glacier; and on to the base of Chumick Peak (6754 metres).

Backtrack over the same route.

Machulu-K2 Base Camp-Dassu

This is a month-long trek through a restricted zone. A permit is necessary and a liaison officer is detailed. Porters are also a must. Setting off point: Machulu. Strenuous. Elevation 5800 metres. Time from June until August.

In the same valley and over the same

route, but from Bilafond Glacier take the trail to Ali Brangsa; from there to Bilafond Pass; Bilafond Glacier; Siachen Glacier; Sia-La at 5833 metres; Abruzzi Glacier and then to K2 **base camp**. Continue down to Condordia via Baltoro Glacier; and on to Paiyu; Bardomal; Korofan; Ashkole; Gomboro and Dassu.

If you want to continue trekking from Ashkole to Shigar take the trail over Skoro Pass. See Skardu-Skoro Pass trek.

Machulu-K12 Peak
This takes 24 days through an open zone. You need a permit, porters and a guide. Setting off point: Machulu. Fairly strenuous. Elevation approximately 5600 metres. Time from June until August.

In the same valley and along the same route, but after you get to Bilafond Glacier take the trail to Garamcha Valley. From there trek to the *base camp* of K12 at 7468 metres.

Backtrack over the same route.

Machulu-Dansam Peak
This is a 20-day trek through an open zone. A permit is required, and porters and a guide are necessary. Setting off point: Machulu. Strenuous. Elevation approximately 5800 metres. Time from June until August.

In the same region and along the same route, but when you reach Goma take the trail to the foot of K13; then go to Dansam Peak at 6660 metres.

To return, backtrack over the same route.

Machulu-Sherpi Kangri Peak
Another 20-day trek through an open zone. A permit, porters and guide are necessary. Setting off point: Machulu. Strenuous. Elevation 6000 metres. Time from June until August.

In the same valley and along the same route, but from Unak take the trail to

Lachit; from there to Kharma Ding, Khor Kondus; **Sherpigang Glacier**; to the base of Saltoro Kangri Peaks 1 and 11 (7706 and 7742 metres respectively); and on to the foot of Scarpi Kangri and Sherpi Kangri Peak at 7380 metres.

Backtrack over the same route to return.

Machulu-Dassu
This is a one month trek through a restricted zone. A permit is necessary, and a liaison officer is detailed to each party. Porters are also a must. Setting off point: Machulu. Strenuous. Elevation approximately 6000 metres. Time from June until August.

In the same region and along the same route. At Kharma Ding take the trail along the Kondus-Kabiri river valley to the base of Chogolisa Peak; continue from there to Vigne Glacier in the Concordia Valley, then trek towards Ashkole, and finally to Dassu.

Alternative Route
Once again on the same route but branch along the trail to Trinity Glacier from Charaksa Glacier. From Trinity Glacier trek to the foot of Trinity Peak at 6800 metres; then on to Vinge Glacier; Vinge Pass; Baltoro Glacier in the Concordia Valley; Ashkole and then Dassu.

Machulu-K7 Base Camp
A 16-day trek through an open zone. You need a permit, and a porter and guide are indispensable. Setting off point: Machulu. Fairly strenuous. Elevation around 5600 metres. Time from June until August.

Take the trail to Khane from Halde; then go to Hushe; Charaksa Glacier; and the base of K7 at 6935 metres. If you're in Khapulu, cross the Shyok River and walk along the banks of the Hushe River to Halde; then on to Hushe etc.

Backtrack over the same route on return.

Machulu-Dassu

This is a one-month trek through a restricted zone. You will need a permit and a liaison officer will be assigned to your party. Porters are indispensable. Setting off point: Machulu. Strenuous. Elevation 5600 metres. Time from June until August.

From Hushe take the trail to **Chandogoro Glacier**; on to Chandogoro Pass; to the base of Biarchendi Peak at 6705 metres; then to **Baltoro Glacier** in the Concordia Valley; to Ashkole and Dassu.

Alternative route via Masherbrum Pass

Take the trail to **Masherbrum Glacier** from Hushe; then trek to the base of Masherbrum Peak at 7821 metres; over the pass at 5883 metres; on to **Yarmundo Glacier**; then to **Baltoro Glacier** and into Concordia Valley; Ashkole and Dassu.

From Ashkole you can always trek over Skoro Pass into Shigar if you prefer.

Machulu-Mitre Peak

This takes 20 days through an open zone. You need a permit, and porters and guide are necessary. Setting off point: Machulu. Fairly strenuous. Elevation 5500 metres and over. Time from June until August.

From Hushe take the trail to **Aling Glacier**; then trek to the foot of the 6553-metre Daube Peak; on to the base of Itwar Peak (6400 metres); then to the base of Hunch Peak at 6553 metres; and finally to the base of the 5944-metre Mitre Peak.

On your return, backtrack over the same route.

Khapulu-Sia-La

An 18-day trek through a restricted zone. You need a permit and a liaison officer is detailed to each party. Porters are also necessary. Setting off point: Khapulu. Strenuous. Elevation is approximately 5400 metres. Time from June until August.

Take the Khapulu trail east towards a bridge across the Shyok. Then follow the trail along the Hushe River banks; cross the Saltoro River to Halde; from Halde to Tagas and then to Kharma Ding, the last village on the trail. There is a **campsite** in some fruit orchards in the Kondus Valley. This is a very remote and isolated area. The villagers cling to their traditional customs and culture, but are extremely hospitable and friendly. It takes three days to trek to Kharma Ding. From there go to the base of the Kondus Glacier, where the *campsite* is surrounded by the stunningly beautiful peaks of Chogolisa and K12. Cross the Kondus Glacier from there. This is tough in sections and fairly strenuous. On the second day out from the Kondus Glacier you will reach the foot of Sia-La (5665 metres).

The scenery here is out of this world, with superb views of Saltoro Range, Sia Kangri and the **Siachen Glacier**.

Backtrack over the same route on your return.

Warning Never attempt to cross the ceasefire line into Indian Kashmir by following the Indus River into Kargil or Leh. In the summer of 1983 an American, weary of hanging around in Skardu for his flight to Rawalpindi, was caught trying to cross the ceasefire line by UNO observers. He was returned and kept under escort until his plane arrived and departed. If you do make it across, you might end up being shot on the other side or – better, but nonetheless dangerous – having to do a lot of fast talking to explain yourself.

HUNZA VALLEY
Passu-Shimshal

This takes five days through an open zone. No permit is necessary, and porter and guide are optional. Setting off point: Passu. Fairly strenuous. Elevation 2800 metres to 3200 metres. Time from June until September.

You set off in a north-easterly direction from Passu on this 80-km trek to Shimshal. It's a hard trek up and down mountains, across rivers and streams, along dangerous, narrow trails to mountain passes, through a mass of broken rocks, across three old wire-rope bridges, over small outcroppings of glaciers. The largest outcroppings are about 30 metres across, and it's easy to get confused about where to cross over as the trail fades away. The average elevation is between 2125 and 2400 metres.

From Passu, the trail starts just before the Batura Bridge, goes up the Murkhan Pass, which is only open for two months in summer, then along the Shimshal River to Donte for about eight to 10 hours, passing through a few hamlets with stone huts along the way. From Donte to Ziarat takes between five and six hours over rough country, and a few wooded areas around Gurn. The last stretch from Ziarat to Shimshal takes eight to nine hours.

Half-way up the pass is a *rest house*, often closed. Without a detailed map of the area and a reliable compass, it's easy to get lost, especially around the rivers and glaciers for trails fade away here. In winter the streams and rivers are frozen over and the tempreture drops to -20°, and occasionally as low as -35°.

Locals, who use this route in summer to get their supplies, can make this trip in two days, but, without a guide, most trekkers would take four to five days.

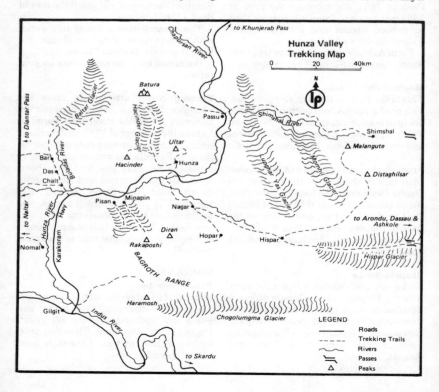

There is no police checkpoint in Shimshal, but a government official checks passports. The village itself consists of about 100 mud-stone huts, housing about a thousand people, who are friendly, honest and hospitable. The main crops are wheat, barley, peas, potatoes and several other kinds of vegetables. They also keep sheep, cattle, chickens and goats. The goats provide enough milk for drinking and some dairy products. Apart from milk, the only fluids available to drink are glacier water and salted tea.

The village is at the foot of a massif with the Shimshal River right below. The elevation is 2400 metres and the weather is pleasant in summer, with warm days and cold nights. It is still quite a distance from here to Shimshal Pass at 5665 metres, and the nearest place to the east is another 80 km. Midway is the village of Darband, and further on is the pass to the Chinese border and the Muztagh Range.

In 1937 Eric Shipton surveyed the Surukwat Basin via Aghil Range, crossing the pass to Zug-Shaksgam, traversing Braldu Glacier, and going over Shimshal Pass into Hunza and Gilgit. On this route packs should not weigh more than 15 kilograms. If you intend to go further a permit and guide are necessary, and the load should not be more than 25 to 30 kilograms.

Side Trip to Malangute Base Camp This is a one-hour walk and you get a great view of Distaghilsar from here.

Passu-Khorodopin Glacier
A 20-day trek through an open zone. Permit, porter and guide are necessary. Setting off point: Passu. Strenuous. Elevation approximately 5000 metres. Time from June to August.

From Passu to Lupgharyaz Glacier; to Momhilsar Glacier; to Ziarat; to the base of Malangute; across Malangute Glacier; to Shimshal Valley; Yazgil Glacier; Yakshin Garden Glacier; and then on to Khoropdopin Glacier.

On return, backtrack over the same route.

Passu-Batura Peaks
This 56-km trek takes one week. This is a reasonably easy trek over the **Passu** and **Batura Glaciers**.

Check with Ibrahim Baig at Diran Hotel, Karimabad for more information on this trek.

Restricted Area
Special permit required.

From Shimshal Valley a trail leads to Kulamudi in the Yarkhund Valley heading north-east towards China. Another trail branches off towards the Pamirs. There are numerous wild yaks and ibexes to be seen. To the north-east are tribes of Pakposhes and Shakshahs, who live at an altitude ranging from 3000 to 3250 metres. Very little is known about these peoples, though it appears likely they are of Aryan descent. They are fair-complexioned and speak the language of the Chagatai Turks.

North of the Hunza Valley is Sirikol Pass. Kilik Pass, at 5000 metres, is wide enough for horse and camel caravans, and is now used by Afghan Kirghiz refugees. Much further up is Mizghar Pass, which now has bridges spanning the rivers

In 1878 Chinese rule was re-established in Kasghar and brigandage on trading caravans to Leh ceased. But towards the end of the century Chinese power declined and brigandage on this route and in Baltistan was resumed, until the British arrived.

To the north-west is the Karumbar River Valley, which is 40 km across. The river joins up with the Ishkoman Valley at Darkot Pass. On the other side of Ishkoman Pass at 4350 metres, is the Oxus River, situated in the Badakshan region or what is now known as the Wakhan, a narrow strip of land which separates Russia from Pakistan by just 16 km. This area is mainly inhabited by the Kirghiz tribes, who sought refuge in Pakistan when the Russians invaded Afghanistan.

Karimabad-Ultar Glacier

A four-day trek through an open zone. No permit is necessary, porters are optional but a guide is indispensable. Setting off point: Karimabad. Fairly strenuous. Elevation 5600 metres. Time from June to September.

Follow the trail that runs on the left of the stream behind the old fort in Baltit. It stops just beyond the bridge, then continues up a very rugged stretch over a gorge to the left. Depending on pace it should take from half a day to a day to climb up to the *shepherds' hut* at 3000 metres. The trail is steep, but very scenic.

If you start early in the morning, it's possible to return on the same day. But you can camp here and climb to the top of **Ultar Glacier** with a guide the following morning. The trail continues to ascend, then forks. Both branches lead to the glaciers, one being easier but taking longer than the other. The more difficult trail goes right to the top of the glaciers – there's a dark mica glacier and a snowclad ridge nearby. After crossing two small glaciers, you have to scale a dangerous cliff. When you reach Ultar Glacier, you're 6000 metres above sea level and the world around you is pristine white. The view of the Hunza Valley from this glacier is magnificent. Guides usually cost Rs70 a day, which you usually have to pay on the spot. Ultar Peak is a towering 7329 metres, but there are other peaks on the same massif that are even higher. The Ultar *base camp* is at 4500 metres above sea level, but Karimabad is situated at 2500 metres up, so it's only 2000 metres further on. Make sure you get acclimatised before doing this trek. Recently, a Japanese doctor on a mountaineering

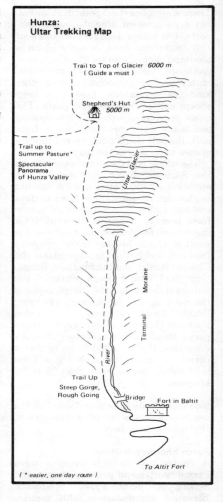

Hunza:
Ultar Trekking Map

Trail to Top of Glacier *6000 m*
(Guide a must)

Shepherd's Hut
5000 m

Trail up to
Summer Pasture *

Spectacular
Panorama
of Hunza Valley

Ultar Glacier

Moraine

Terminal

River

Trail Up
Steep Gorge,
Rough Going

Bridge

Fort in Baltit

To Altit Fort

(* easier, one day route)

expedition died of altitude sickness compounded by pneumonia. There is a flat, grassy patch with a view of some peaks to the north, probably part of the Batura Group.

Be very careful going down. Take it slowly as the going is difficult.

Aliabad-Hacinder Glacier

This trek takes two days through an open zone. A permit's not necessary, and neither are porters or a guide. Setting off point: Aliabad. Easy. Elevation 2800 metres. Time from June until September.

The trail begins at Hasanabad River, 1½ km south of Aliabad on the Karakoram Highway. Follow the Hasanabad River westward, then turn south to Hacinder Valley, an extraordinary region consisting largely of pebbles and boulders, that must once have been a riverbed or the site of a gigantic glacier. There is a trail leading up a slope to Hacinder **base camp**. Other trails in the same region go to Thosdaro and Hicinder Glaciers. Campsites along this route are known as *harabasa*.

(From Khaled Aziz & Akram Huna Baig, Gilgit.)

Sultanabad (Hini)-Passu Peak)

A 14-day trek through a 'deleted' zone. Permits are not issued, but if you are allowed to do it, porters and guide are a must. Setting off point: Aliabad. Strenuous. Elevation approximately 4800 metres; Time from June to August.

From Aliabad go to Sultanabad; Muchichul Glacier; the base of Batura Peak at 7785 metres; Hasanabad Glacier; the base of Shishpare Peak (7619 metres); and then to the foot of Passu Peak at 7284 metres.

On return, backtrack over the same route to Sultanabad or continue along Passu Glacier to Passu Village on the Karakoram Highway. There are wagons and buses going to Karimabad from here.

Chalt-Baltar

This is a seven-day trek through a free zone. A permit is not required, and porters and guide are optional. Setting off point: Chalt. Fairly moderate. Elevation from 2800 to 3200 metres. Time from June to September.

Chalt is 48 km from Hunza and 54 km from Gilgit, where the Hunza River veers southward at a 90° angle to the Karakoram Highway. The bridge here spans two gorges. To the south are the villages of Chaprot and Nilt. The latter, conquered by the British in 1891, was the last fortified village guarding the route to Baltit.

A jeep track from the bridge leads to Chalt. Turn right at the blue signboard – written in Urdu – just before you come to another bridge crossing a tributary. Go past the forest ranger's office, which appears to be permanently closed, and through some apricot orchards. Climb a trail above the stream, then cross the bridge.

From Chalt to Budalas – a long, sprawling village – takes two hours. Near Budalas is a sulphur spring. Continue along the jeep track, and as you approach Das, you'll get a view of Rakaposhi. The section between Budalas and Das takes three hours. Stay on the jeep track after crossing to the left bank of the Bolas Das River: the tributary splits up here, and the stream to the left leads to the Diantar Valley. About a third of the way along is another bridge. Keep to the jeep track. Getting to Bar from Das takes 1½ hours. Bar can also be reached by another route, which branches off about a hundred metres past the bridge. The jeep track ends at Bar, which is a very attractive village. There is a **campsite** here.

About an hour out of Bar on the way to Shunghe, the trail becomes difficult to follow – it seems to fade away. Press on and you'll come to a bridge, and cross over to get to the right bank of the river. It's another hour from here to Shunghe, a shepherd's hamlet consisting of a few mud-stone huts. Getting to **Baltar Glacier** from Shunghe takes another five to six hours.

The next part of the trek is tough going. As Ronald Mis of California puts it, be prepared to 'tighten boot laces and prepare for a really rough trail. Without a guide, good luck!'

Trek right up to where a stream flows out from beneath a glacier, that is covered with scree. Above is a beautiful meadow. There are *shepherds' huts* here. The view is superb and there are plenty of places to *camp*. There is another trail via the left bank of the Baltar Nallah, but it's said to be even rougher. What's more there are no villages along the latter.

It's almost 50 km from Chalt to Baltar Meadow through deep, narrow valleys and across streams. **Baltar Glacier** is steppe-like, about four km long and three km wide. As you climb the snow-clad slopes to the snowline at 4000 metres, the birch forests of the meadow give way to junipers. Above – all around – snow-capped peaks rise up to 6775 metres. The meadow is 2500 metres above sea level, carpeted with flowers and there are numerous vividly-coloured small birds darting about. There are also ibexes and bears up here. To the west is **Kukay Glacier.**

On the return trek, start early in the morning from Baltar Meadow and follow the shepherds. They are so fit they seem to skip, hop and jump over rocks all the way down to Das – for 12 hours! Camp overnight in Das.

Das-Diantar Pass-Naltar

This is a five-day trek through a free zone. A permit is not necessary, but you do need a porter and guide. Setting off point: Das. Fairly strenuous. Elevation 4800 metres. Time from August until September.

The trail drops down to a little bridge between Das and the Diantar Valley; then trek up a slope for 1½ hours, and down to the river again and across another bridge. Keep heading west on the right bank of a stream, up to a long, narrow village. Diantar Village is 3350 metres above sea level and about two hours' walk from the second bridge. It takes about half an hour to get through the village, and 1½ hours to another bridge where the trail branches, one branch going left into a small village, the main trail leading to Korong.

Enquire about the pass here, as it's seldom used and hardly known by the shepherds. Nevertheless, they will ask Rs100 to guide you up, well worth it if they

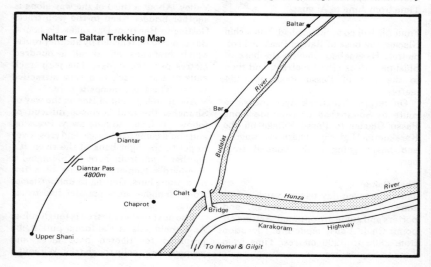

Naltar — Baltar Trekking Map

really know the way.

When you get out the village of Korong, take the left side of the stream, then climb up to a meadow where shepherds graze their flocks. You will notice piles of dry birch twigs here that are gathered by the shepherds for their own use.

The Diantar Pass is in a snowy massif at an elevation of 4800 metres. In early summer it doesn't exist. There are no marked trails over the steep, snowy slopes, and late in July, it is still iced over. Try August when the ice has thawed. Camp in the meadow and early next morning, climb the steep slope for about 350 to 400 metres. Late in the day this is too risky, as there is a danger of avalanches due to the snow thawing, because the sun hits this side of Toloybar early in the morning. It's a six to seven-hour trek up from the valley to the snowy ridge.

On the other side of the Diantar Pass in the Naltar Valley is Upper Shani. The trail splits in Upper Shani, one path going southward to Naltar, the other going north-west to Naltar Pass. From Upper Shani the trail leads down to Lower Shani. See Naltar-Baltar Trek.

Chalt-Naltar

This is a four-day trek through a free zone. A permit is not necessary, and neither are porters or guide. Setting off point: Chalt. Moderate to easy. Elevation 2800 metres. Time from June till September, maybe October.

If there's no sign of the Diantar Pass by early summer or even mid-summer, and you wish to continue westward, go down to Chalt. A little to the south is a trail that follows the Chaprot Nallah to Upper Shani. It is an easier and safer route.

When you get to the Naltar Valley, you can either continue trekking to Ishkoman or return to Gilgit via Nomal. It will take two or three days either way.

NAGAR VALLEY
Nagar-Distaghilsar

This is a one-week trek through a free zone. No permit is needed; porter and guide optional. Setting off point: Nagar. Moderate. Elevation 3800 metres. Time from June until September.

It takes a day to walk the 18 km to Hispar Village from Nagar. If the trek is slow, there is a *harabasa* (campsite) en route. The route involves crossing streams, and trekking over glaciers and down narrow ledges. Hispar Village has an unfurnished *rest house*, a mosque and a dispensary. The next stage is to Bularong – basically just a *harabasa* – through glaciers, and across streams and rocks. The scenery gradually becomes craggier and more glacial. It's only five hours from Bularong to the *base camp* of Distaghilsar at 7885 metres. At 6500 metres the snow is starting to melt revealing dark-greyish glaciers.

Backtrack over the same route.

Malangute

A little further north-west of Distaghilsar is Malangute, which at 7342 metres is not as high as Distaghilsar. It's five or six hours to the base camp from here. There are moraines along this route. The best time to cross the glaciers is early in the morning; it's not slippery then. If you look carefully you will see markhors on the high, sharp ridges. There is vegetation from 3000 to 5000 metres, and there are quite a few of these impressive-looking animals in this area. Some of them are as tall as 1½ metres and have huge horns.

Nagar-Rondu-Ashkole

A two-week trek through open zone. A permit is necessary and a liaison officer is detailed to the party. Porters are also necessary. Setting off point: Nagar. Fairly strenuous. Elevation 5600 metres. Time early spring for skiers; mid-June until September for trekkers.

In the village of Hispar the trail splits up: one branch leads north to the *base camps* of Distaghilsar and Malangute; the other towards the east over **Hispar** and **Biafo Glaciers**, which cover 112 km together. About midway along it forks again, and one trail leads down to Rondu, the other continues to Ashkole. It goes through the 5830-metre Hispar Pass, passes a snow lake, and covers a distance of 240 km altogether. The beauty of this region has been described by Martin Conway as one of the 'wonders of the earth'. See Shigar-Nagar trek.

Nagar-Barpu Glacier

This is a 10-day trek through an open zone. No permit is required, and porter and guide are optional. Setting off point: Nagar. Moderate. Elevation approx 5800 metres. Time from June until September.

The first section between Nagar and Shishken is gentle trekking through apricot orchards and villages. Along the way you get a fine view of the Rakaposhi Range. Shishken is on the other side of **Kapel Glacier** – an easy four to five-hour walk.

From Shishken walk to Lake Rush, where you can *camp* above **Barpu Glacier** at 5000 metres. It's a picturesque area, the water is crystal clear and the green slopes are dotted with flowers. There are views of Malubiting Peak (7292 metres), Golden Peak, Miar Peak at 6824 metres to the Nagar Valley. From Lake Rush trek to Chokotans. It's too hot in summer trek to Chokotans. It's too hot in summer to do this trek during the day; better to start off in the afternoon. Camp at Chokotans, a beautiful area with spring water, streams, flowers and juniper trees. Trek from here to Gridindil. Crossing the Barpu Glacier takes two to three hours. The campsite – at 5800 metres – is known for its wildlife. There are several peaks nearby that are easy to scale.

On return, backtrack over the same route.

Nagar-Malubiting

A 12-day trek through an open zone. No permit is necessary, and porters and guide are optional. Setting off point: Nagar. Moderate. Elevation 5600 metres. Time from June until September.

From Nagar trek to the Buldar Glacier; continue to the base of Diran (7279); Barpu Glacier; Miar Glacier; the base of Miar (6824 metres); and finally to the foot of Malubiting (7292 metres).

Backtrack over the same route.

Nagar-Kanibasar Glacier

This is a 14-day trek through an open zone. A permit is not required, but porters and guide are necessary. Moderate. Elevation 5200 metres. Time from June until September.

Go to Hispar from Nagar; then on to **Hispar Glacier; Kunyang-Pak Glacier; Pumarikish Glacier; Jutmaru Glacier;** and finally **Kanibasar Glacier**.

Backtrack over the same route.

Nagar-Hopar (Hopakhund)

A one-day trek in an open zone. Permit not necessary; and porters and guide not required. Setting off point: Nagar. Elevation 3200 metres. Time from June until October.

From Nagar the trail leads southeastward to Hopar, eight km away. There's an unfurnished *rest house* here. From Hopar, it's a steep uphill trek across streams. The trail tapers off on a slope where there are some *shepherds' huts*. You can get milk and curd from here.

Hopar Glacier is slowly becoming smaller, and eventually will only be a moraine. On the left side of the junction towards the direction of Hopar is the former mir's palace. Further up **Barpu Glacier** you can get a view of Diran in the Rakaposhi Range.

Backtrack over the same route on return.

Nagar-Pisan

A one-day trek through a free zone. Permit not required, neither are porters or guide necessary. Setting off point: Nagar. Moderate almost easy. Elevation 2800 metres. Time from early spring until October.

The main jeep track which leads to Hunza is a circuitous route to this place, backtracking towards Ganesh, then turning south. Apparently there is a trail which leads straight through to Pisan from Nagar via narrow valleys – like Shahyar – and other villages. It climbs steeply, along narrow ledges, then descends into Minapin.

From Minapin to Pisan the trail follows a shelf above the Hunza and then crosses a stream. It's only a half-hour walk. There's an unfurnished *rest house* here, and the man who runs it is helpful and friendly. This village is only about five km from the bridge on the Karakoram Highway if you're coming from Gilgit by bus. There are two glaciers – the **Minapin** and **Pisan glaciers** – on this slope of the Rakaposhi Range.

Nine km to the south of the Karakoram Highway Bridge is the village of Dudimal. This is on the same shelf as Pisan, and is interesting because of its packed mud-stone huts which are huddled along narrow ledges.

Minapin Glacier Trek

This is a four-day trek through a free zone. No permit is necessary, nor is a guide, and a porter is optional. Setting off point: Minapin *rest house*. Moderate. Elevation 4600 metres. Time from early spring until September.

About a km up, turn right to Taghafari, a beautiful meadow just below Diran. The trail follows the glacier to Rakaposhi *base camp*. Better to do this in the late afternoon as it's too hot during the day in summer. There are settlements at Hapkhund and Tagaya, but from here to

Taghafari the trail gets narrower and more difficult. Turn up to Kacheli, another wooded meadow. There are lots of flowers here and no snow until you reach the 4500-metre level. From the top of the moraine of **Minapin Glacier** you get a stunning view of the 5200 and 7700-metre icy walls of Rakaposhi and Diran that stretch to around 30 km in length.

The following day cross the glacier in the middle. Follow the glacier, which is flat, until you reach another green, wooded meadow, closely surrounded by mountain peaks. There seem to be continual avalanches on these mountains, so be very careful. You will also see Rakaposhi, seamed with glaciers, towering above the rest, its slopes covered in pines, fir trees, willows, alpine scrubs and flowers.

It's possible to climb further up to another meadow – 3554 metres altitude and be transported to a world of ice, snow, stones, rocks and streams. There is a *campsite* slightly above Kacheli at 3600 metres. Backtrack over the same route on return.

Trekkers can continue to the Rakaposhi **base camp** from here, or the **base camp** of Minapin Peak (7279 metres). There are tremendous views of surrounding valleys from these camps.

Around Minipan

Pisan Trek This is basically just a gentle stroll. There is a trail leading out of the nearby village of Pisan, which goes up the glacier to a meadow. It's a gentle climb. The meadows on this side are lower than those on the Minapin side. There are lots of flowering plants, trees, medicinal herbs and butterflies here.

GILGIT

Gilgit-Bagroth

A five-day trek through an open zone. No permit, porters or guide are necessary. Setting off point: Gilgit. Easy. Elevation not over 3000 metres. Time from early spring until early October.

Bagroth is 46 km east of Gilgit, through deep, scenic valleys that are lushly green and have flat, terraced ridges and precipitous cliffs. The jeep track from Gilgit is paved in sections, generally easy going, and finishes at Bagroth. The trail continues through meadows, ascending gently to grain fields. Cargo jeeps ply this route, but if you're trekking all the way, go from Gilgit through Danyor across the Chinese Bridge to Oshikhandas. From there it's eight km to Snakar, three km to Datuchi. Away to the right is Oshikhandas, and right of Datuchi is Farfu, 1½ km away. Nearby is a fresh water spring. Then it's 2½ km to Chirah, and on to the unfurnished NAWO *rest house*.

Cross the bridge then climb up to the edge of the valley. There's a grey-black glacier to the left, and right in front is Diran, capped with snow.

Note that off the main jeep track there are other trails across the grain fields to the rest house.

Follow a narrow trail up a steep slope, then descend to Chirah; around the mountain is Gasunder. There are glaciers and pine forests around this region. To the left is the dark-grey Henerchi Glacier, and nearby is Bulchi. Left of Gasunder is Gutmi Glacier – also slate grey – beyond is a bridge and just after the bridge is Buyofor Glacier. Continuing to the right is Chargo Glacier, to the left is a footpath to Barchi Glacier. At the foot of the glacier is the village of Barchi. Further on is the Kardi Glacier. The trail takes you back to Gasunder, Farfu and the rest house from the latter.

It's possible to explore the valleys in more depth by following the trail from Henerchi Glacier. This leads to the Nagar Valley and there are wooded areas along the way were you can **camp**. It's

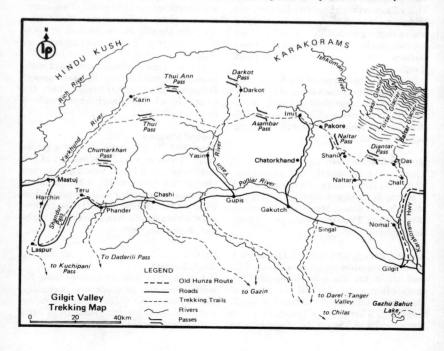

Gilgit Valley
Trekking Map

LEGEND
– – – – Old Hunza Route
———— Roads
- - - - Trekking Trails
~~~~ Rivers
≣≣≣ Passes

0   20   40km

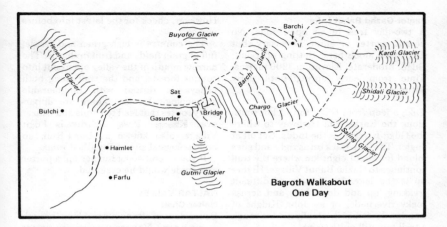

**Bagroth Walkabout
One Day**

advisable to get hold of a detailed map of the area before you set out. There are lots of semi-precious gems around in this region – mostly aquamarines. Accommodation is possible with villagers, but don't count on it. Take camping gear and provisions with you.

If you decide to go to Bagroth, check at the Tourist Cottage in Jutial, Gilgit before you set off. You may be able to hitch a lift on a tractor – occasionally tractors go there for a day or two in spring, summer and early autumn. If you manage to hitch a ride, be prepared to rough it. Take a warm jacket and a scarf, especially during the cold season.

Gilgit-Haramosh

This is a 10-day trek through an open zone. A permit is not necessary, and porters and guide are optional. Setting off point: Gilgit. Easy. Elevation 3200 metres. Time from June until September.

Take a jeep from Gilgit to Jaglot, or a bus up to Sassi. Trek to Shah from Sassi; then on to Bahut, **Ishkapal Glacier**; and to the base of Haramosh (7406 metres).

Backtrack over the same route on return.

Gilgit-Phuparash Glacier

An 18-day trek through an open zone. A permit is not necessary, but porters and guide are essential. Setting off point: Gilgit. Moderate. Elevation 5600 metres. Time from June until September.

Get a jeep from Gilgit to Jaglot where the trek to Hanochol starts. From there you trek to Sassi; Dache; Ishkara; **Mani Glacier; Baskai Glacier;** the base of Laila Peak (6218 metres); the base of Malubiting Peak (7452 metres), and finally to **Phuparash Glacier**.

Backtrack over the same route on return.

Gilgit-Rakaposhi Base Camp

This takes 10 days through an open zone. A permit is not necessary, and porters and guide are optional. Setting off point: Gilgit. Moderate. Elevation 6000 metres. Time from June until September.

Take a jeep to Danyor from Gilgit; then trek to Bilchan; the base of Dobani (6143 metres); the base of Diran (7279 metres); and finally to the *base camp* of Rakaposhi.

Backtrack over the same route on return.

Jaglot-Gazhu Bahut Lake

A two-day trek in an open zone. No permit, porter or guide necessary, but don't trek alone here. Setting off point: Gilgit. Moderate. Elevation 3200 metres. Time from early spring until early autumn.

Take a jeep from Gilgit for 43 km south along the Karakoram Highway to where the Gilgit River joins the Indus. Get off at Jaglot. The jeep track turns right and goes inland for about eight km where the trail continues to Gazhu Bahut Village. Higher up is the lake. It's 18 km of difficult trekking, up and down hills and across rocky riverbeds, or as John Knight of London describes it, 'Really not too rough a trail but still quite tough'.

This trek is particularly suitable for anglers for the lake is well-known for golden trout.

Darel-Tanger

This is three days through an open zone. No permit, porter or guide necessary, but do not trek alone in this area, neither should you camp. Setting off point: Chilas. Easy. Elevation not above 2400 metres. Time from early spring until early autumn.

Follow the trail beyond the bridge at Chilas. But check with the superintendent of police at Chilas before setting off as this area has a long-term reputation for being dangerous: the feuding among native tribes is continuous. At one time even archaeologists could not work here without being accompanied by a police contingent. The houses are all fortified with tall towers and, like the Pathans and Kohistanis, the men are armed. The local inhabitants appear to actively spurn progress, though there are now government offices – mostly for the departments of forestry and agriculture – and *rest houses*. The villagers' attitude towards foreigners has apparently softened and they are reported to be quite friendly.

However, check for the latest info before you go.

The country is lush green and fertile, full of grain fields and fruit orchards. The narrow mouth of the valley opens out into conifer forests, and the trail along both valleys is dotted with innumerable archaeological ruins. There are apparently routes that lead to Gupis and Ghizer over Khanjer Pass. Nearby is Fogit Village, also known as Dar-I-Run, an archaeological site of Buddhist ruins.

If you intend going further up, a porter and guide would be essential.

NALTAR VALLEY
Naltar-Chalt

Seven days of strenuous trekking through an open zone. No permit necessary, porter optional but guide indispensable. Setting off point: Naltar. Elevation 4800 metres. Time from mid-July until September.

If you're in Gilgit and there is no cargo jeep service available to Nomal or Naltar, take the Hunza or Passu bus. Tell the driver to drop you off at Rahimabad, also known as Maltum Das, on the Karakoram Highway. There is a little *inn* here where you can get bed and breakfast for Rs16. Early next morning cross the river by raft; the fare is Rs1.50 per head to Nomal.

From Nomal it is 16 km to Naltar, up a gentle trail to an altitude of 3222 metres. Go to Dominal on the south side and Jaglot on the north; continue to Bichgari at 3400 metres; and Shingobar at 3745 metres. The bridge is a little difficult to find, but it's just behind a small wood. Naltar is a ski-training area with a *rest house*, which requires advance booking in Gilgit, and a tiny *hotel*. There is also a small shop here.

From Naltar to Naltar Lakes along the the river of the same name is 12 km or four hours' trekking through pine forests. You will see numerous species of birds along this trail including the snowcock, monal pheasant and Himalayan pika. There are also ibexes in this area. You will come

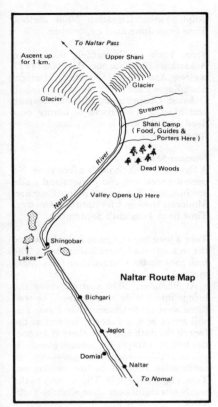

Naltar Route Map

Lower Shani to Upper Shani. A small, dark glacier is on the left, and after about two km the trail forks, with one branch going north-east to Diantar Pass, the other east to Chaprot and Chalt.

There are two ways to get to Chalt. The first is via Chaprot from Upper Shani; the second via Diantar Pass. Set up *camp* at Upper Shani, a beautiful spot which offers a good view of Khatta Peak. There are numerous ibexes around here.

The trail from Chaprot to Chalt is fairly easy from early spring till early autumn. But the route via Diantar Pass is tough-going, and, generally, is used by trekkers continuing to Baltar Meadow. Trek up to Distar-Bar and camp overnight. From Distar-Bar go towards Diantar Pass (4800 metres), an extremely difficult section, which calls for stamina and a good guide. Guides are available in Lower Shani or Diantar Village on the other side for Rs100 to Rs150. Once you get over the pass, you descend to summer pasture land, 300 metres above the village of Diantar. From here you go down to Budalas River, then turn south towards Chalt; or north to Baltar Meadow and Glacier.

Take the bus along the Karakoram Highway for Gilgit on return.

Naltar-Pakore
Seven days through an open zone. No permit is necessary, and porters and guide are optional. Setting off point: Naltar. Moderate. Elevation 4500 metres. Time from June until August.

In the same valley and along the same trail north, but out of Upper Shani on the third day of the trek, the trail splits, with one branch leading to Diantar Pass, the other to Naltar Pass at 5150 metres. Take the one to Naltar Pass. From here there is a gradual ascent over rather rocky and glaciated terrain to Khori Bort. There is a good *camping* spot here with commanding views of Rakaposhi, Dobani and some of the peaks of Nanga Parbat in the far

across nomads who will sell you milk and butter.

The lakes are 4675 metres above sea level, and there are *shepherds' huts* nearby that are primitive but dry. The lakes are full of trout, so take some fishing gear with you. From the lakes the trail ascends gradually for six to eight hours up to Lower Shani, a scenic wooded area with a view of the peaks of the Hindu Raj to the north. There is an ideal *camping* spot in a wooded area in Shani. There are also hamlets here where porters and guides can be hired, and milk and eggs are available. The trail climbs gently from distance. From Khori Bort to Pakore the trail is easy-going for two days. From here the trek to Chatorkhand is only one hour via Hayul Gol (5250 metres).

There are jeeps going to Gilgit from Chatorkhand, but you can continue trekking to the Valley of Yasin via Asambar Pass if you wish.

YASIN VALLEY
Ishkoman-Yasin

A five-day trek through a 'deleted zone'. No permits are issued, and if you are allowed to go porters and guide are optional. Setting off point: Chatorkhand. Moderate. Elevation 4500 metres. Time from June until September. The Darkot Pass is described as a 'deleted' zone, restricted and off-limits because of the situation in Afghanistan and the influx of Afghani refugees. It also overlooks Badakshan in the Wakhan area. The Thui Ann is hardly passable even in high summer because it's too slushy. But between late August and September it clears up.

Take a jeep from Gilgit to Chatorkhand, which has a *teashop* and a tiny bazaar. Then go from Chatorkhand to Asambar Aghost (4432 metres); Muduri; Sandhi. From the latter it is eight km or 2½ hours' trek to Yasin.

There's a jeep service from Yasin to Gilgit.

The trekking route from Yasin continues towards Darkot Pass – at 4690 metres – into the northern region of the Chitral Valley. Another trail leads to Thui Ann Pass at 4500 metres and drops right down into Mastuj in Chitral. There is a third route via Naz Bar Pass (4977 metres) into the Ghizer Valley and over Chumarkhan Pass or Zagar Pass (5009 metres) into Mastuj.

Yasin-Mastuj

Ten days' of strenuous trekking through an open zone. No permit is necessary, and porters and guide are optional. Setting off point: Yasin. Elevation 5000 metres. Time from June until September.

From Yasin to Nazbardeh; then on to Askarthan; Shikhan; Naz Bar Pass (4977 metres); Ano Pass (3483 metres); Haringal Shal; Zagar Pass (5009 metres); Anoshal; Dakshal; Chapchirgah; Shiashi; Chapali; and Mastuj. This route is hardly ever used, and the area is uninhabited except for shepherds.

Phander-Mastuj

A three-day trek through a free zone. No permit necessary, and porters and guide are optional. Setting off point: Phander. Moderate to easy. Elevation 5000 metres. Time from June until September.

Take a jeep from Gilgit to Phander where the trek into the Ghizer Valley starts. The trail goes via the Chumarkhan Pass (5009 metres).

At Phander, 3030 metres, cross the bridge into a wide open valley. The trail turns west up to Chumarkhan Pass. You will arrive at a shepherds' hamlet at the foot of the path and from there it's a one-day trek into Mastuj for younger people. If you're middle-aged it's necessary to acclimatise yourself before moving on. Take a light pack only. The scenery to the north is magnificent. See Chitral-Yasin Trek.

Ghizer-Darel-Tanger

A six-day trek through an open zone. Permit and porters not necessary, but a guide is required.

About 15 km before Teru is a small hamlet called Ghizer. There is a trail from here that goes through narrow valleys into Siazin or alternatively through the Darel-Tanger Valley.

Ghizer-Kalam

See section on Swat Valley treks.

Teru-Laspur

A one-day trek through a free zone. No permit, porters or guide necessary. Setting off point: Teru. Easy. Elevation 3720 metres. Time from early spring until mid-November.

This trek via Shandur Pass (3720 metres) is only 25 km.

From Laspur the trek can be continued to Harchin 10 km further on, or 2½ hours along an easy route. You can get jeeps to Mastuj from there. Alternatively you could head off in the direction of Ustur, Koghozi and Madaghlast. See Chitral Valley treks.

CHITRAL VALLEY

Chitral trekking regions are usually restricted zones, but generally all trekking permits are obtainable from the Deputy Commissioner's officer in Chitral.

Kalash Valleys

The traditional setting off point for any of these treks is always Chitral. But treks can start in any of the three valleys, or even Ayun. Trek to Bhishala, 45 km away in the Birer Valley; and from there to Bumburet, then Rumbur. Backtrack to Bumburet where you can catch a cargo jeep to Chitral. Or take a jeep to Bumburet and go to Rumbur from there, returning to Bumburet before setting off to Birer. Alternatively you can start at any point along the jeep track to Bumburet. There is a trail along the northern tributary of the river – near where it forks – which leads to Rumbur; then up to Bumburet, Birer and back to Chitral.

Below are some of the more popular treks to do between early spring and early autumn around the Kafiristan Valley, where the elevation does not exceed 3500 metres. Many of them are fairly easy walks. 'Living-off-the-land' is almost possible, but it's best to bring along extra provisions.

Birer-Bumburet-Rumbur

Six days through a restricted zone. Permit is necessary, obtainable from the Deputy Commissioner's Office in Chitral. No porter or guide needed.

Take a cargo jeep from Chitral to Birer, 45 km away. From Birer trek up the massif into Bumburet. It's only nine km up, but it takes four to six hours to get there because the trail is so steep. There are several *places to stay* here. From Bumburet to Rumbur is 11 km, or three to four hours' easy walking. You can either backtrack to Bumburet or take a jeep, then trek up to Birer, the third of the Kalash towns. See section on Kalash above.

On return, catch a jeep back to Chitral.

Garam Chasma-Birmughlast

A two-day trek through a restricted area. A permit is necessary, but no guide or porters are needed.

Take a jeep into Garam Chasma where the trek to Birmughlast starts, then head back to Chitral. This is a scenic trek but not particularly spectacular.

Be careful not to stray across the border into Afghanistan.

Shugur-Barn

A 10-day trek through a restricted zone. Permit and guide are necessary, porters optional.

Take a jeep to Garam Chasm, get off at the bridge and trek into Shugur, where they still distil 'Hunza Water'; then on to Ojhore; Orin and finally Barn. The area is dominated by Tirich Mir so the scenery is breath-taking.

Backtrack over the same route.

Alternative Routes Interconnected valleys that are good to trek through are Ludkho, Turikho and Mulikho in Upper Chitral. There are extensive treks in this region.

Chitral-Reshun-Mastuj

An eight-day trek through a restricted zone. Permit necessary, porters and guide optional.

An easy trek, which follows the jeep track most of the way. There are a number of small *inns* along this route. The track to Mastuj forks off midway up, and you can trek northward to the last village, Barenis.

Either backtrack along the same route on return, or there are several other ways you can take. Be sure to acquire a good map if you attempt this trek without a guide.

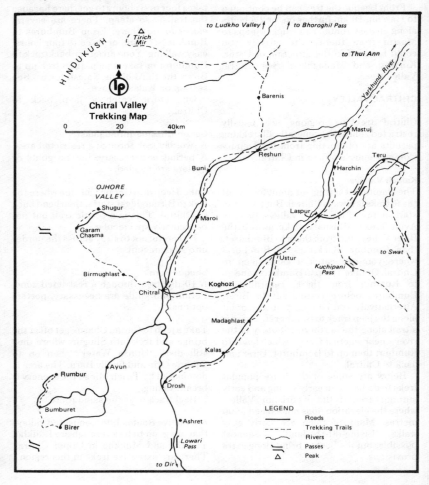

Chitral Valley Trekking Map

0   20   40km

LEGEND

——	Roads
- - -	Trekking Trails
∿	Rivers
≈	Passes
△	Peak

Chitral-Laspur

A five-day trek through a restricted zone.

One way to go is along the jeep track via Koghozi, but you need to take provisions and camping gear. The more popular route is via Chitral-Mastuj by jeep all the way to Harchin. The last stage of the trek between Harchin and Laspur takes three to four hours to walk.

The usual route to Chitral from Laspur is also via Mastuj. It's a trekkable distance, but most trekkers catch a jeep into Chitral for the more scenic and spectacular routes in the valley.

Laspur-Kalam

See Swat Valley treks.

Warning Whether you hire a guide or not, before heading off on a trek, check with the tourist officer in Skardu, Gilgit and Chitral for more information. The situation in these areas is in a constant state of flux, which means changes are inevitable and should be anticipated.

Always ask about availability of supplies, distance between villages, hamlets, towns etc., fares or rates, and border situations.

Bishala (Birer Valley) – Birmughlast

A six-day trek through restricted territory. Permit necessary, porters and guide optional. Setting off point: Chitral. Moderate. Elevation 2400 to 4500 metres. Time early spring until September.

Take a jeep from Chitral to Bishala in the Birer Valley – this Chitral-Bishala jeep track is seldom trekked. Then from Birer the trail goes up to Chumbai Pass (1150 metres), before descending rather steeply to the Bumburer Valley. From here you walk through a long, narrow valley and across a footbridge, which consists of a single pole, into Brumbutu, where there is a *rest house* with very little choice in food.

There is more choice when you get to Bumburet. Continue northward; the trail south leads to a tiny village known as Krakal, and beyond Krakal is the Afghan border. Between Bishala and Bumburet there is a six to eight-hour trek.

You can continue to trek to Rumbur from Bumburet passing through hamlets along the way. It only takes about three hours. From Rumbur go down to Bashagan, over Utak Pass (4647 metres), and then to Birmughlast.

At Birmughlast the trail splits, one branch leading to Chitral, the other to Garam Chasma.

Bumburet-Garam Chasma

Hire a local guide or porter for this trek.

At the south end of Bumburet is a small village called Brumgram or Burumgram, which has a *teashop* and a tiny general store. There's a trail leading north-west from here through uninhabited valleys along the banks of the Chumarsan River. It climbs up to the 4647-metre Utak Pass, which is open from mid-June until mid-September, then down into Putrik Village and into Garam Chasma.

After a day's trek, the trail forks, one branch leads to Garam Chasma, the other loops down into Rumbur. The Brumgram route is stunningly beautiful, but the area is not inhabited so it's easy to get lost or confused. If you haven't been able to get hold of a detailed map or compass, hire a local guide or porter. It's only a day's trek over two low passes from here to Rumbur. This is a variation on the route to Rumbur via the Burumgram trail. From there you can either go to Birmughlast, Garam Chasma or Chitral.

Be careful not to stray across the border into Afghanistan.

SHISHI VALLEY
Chitral-Laspur

A seven-day trek through a restricted zone. Permit necessary, porter or guide optional. Setting off point: Chitral.

Moderate to strenuous. Elevation 4800 to 5525 metres. Time mid-June until mid-September.

Madaghlast-Koghozi Take a jeep for 86 km to Madaghlast from Chitral. In fact, if you wish, you can take a jeep all the way to Koghozi, a jeep terminus with *teashops* – or further, to Laspur. The trek starts in Madaghlast and goes through meadows and forests in the Shishi Valley. Then it's a three-day climb to Dok Pass at 4500 metres and on to Golen. From the third *campsite* it's 5½ km or two hours' walk through scenic country to Koghozi.

From Koghozi there's a 25-km trail back to Chitral, so don't go any further if you wish to return to Chitral. However, the same trail is an alternative trek from Chitral via Koghozi to Laspur. It's a breathtakingly beautiful trek through lush meadows in sharp contrast to the surrounding snowfields and glaciers.

Koghozi-Laspur Alternatively you can continue all the way to Laspur from Koghozi. The first stage is to Ustur, then from Ustur it is 48 km to Laspur. The trail goes through the village of Rahman, over Farghan Pass at 5525 metres then down into Laspur. There are magnificent views of the towering peaks of the Hindu Raj Range along the way.

Laspur-Kalam

A strenuous, seven-day trek through restricted territory. Permit, porters and guide essential. Setting off point: Laspur. Elevation 550 metres. Time from mid-July until mid-September. There is a police warning on this route to lone trekkers and small parties.

Get the early morning jeep from Chitral to Laspur. It's a seven to eight-hour trip. **Camp** either at Laspur or Sorlaspur and start trekking early nex morning. It is 16 km to the first **camp**, which is at the first stream crossing you arrive at. After this it is a 10-hour trek up to the base of Kha on

the edge of Shandur Valley, a rugged, barren region. You spend the third night at Metha Uth, and there's fresh, spring water there. The trail then wanders gradually over screes, glaciers and snowfields to Kachi Khani Pass at 3600 metres – open from late June until mid-September. On the fourth night *camp* at Kruederi; and the next morning glissade down the snowy slopes, then trek up to Falaksher *base camp*. Camp here. From there go to Matiltan via Lake Mahodand; and from Matiltan it is a six-hour trek to Kalam.

Ustur Junction On the Madaghlast-Laspur jeep track is the junction of Ustur. From the junction a trail leads up to Resun, a village on the Mastuj-Chitral jeep track. You can either trek up to Mastuj from Resun and back to Chitral, or go to Mulikho Valley, Ludkho Valley, Turikho and around the Valley of Yarkhund into Yasin.

LUDKHO VALLEY
Shugur-Dirgol Glacier

This takes eight days through a 'deleted' zone. No permit is issued, but if you are allowed to make it, a liaison officer is detailed. Porters or guide are optional. Setting off point: Chitral. Moderate. Elevation approximately 5200 metres. Time from June until September.

Take a jeep from Chitral to Shugur where the trek starts. From there you go to Momi; Shahi; Arkari; and finally Dirgol Glacier. This trek is both colourful and spectacular with Tirich Mir dominating the whole region.

Backtrack over the same route.

Shugur-Susum

Four days through a restricted zone. Permit necessary, porter and guide optional. Setting off point: Chitral. Easy to moderate. Elevation approximately 4800 metres. Time from June until September.

Take a jeep from Chitral to Shugur or further on to Susum Valley. If you get off at Shugur the trek goes to Susum via Ovir; then on to Kosht. It's a scenic trail with views of Tirich Mir along the way.

Backtrack to Shugur or catch a jeep back from Susum to Chitral on return.

Shugur-Purisht

A relatively easy four-day trek through a restricted zone. Permit necessary, porters or guide optional. Elevation approximately 4800 metres. Time from June until September.

Through the same valley and along the same trail, but take a jeep to Garam Chasma from Chitral. The trek goes through attractive country to Purisht.

Backtrack to Garam Chasma on return.

MULIKHO-TURIKHO-YARKHUND VALLEYS

Chitral-Turikho-Yasin

A long 26-day trek, ranging from moderate to strenuous, through restricted territory. Permit, porters and guide essential. Setting off point: Chitral. Elevation 4400 metres. Time from June until September.

Take a jeep from Chitral to Drasan or Parpich. The latter is 57 km north of Chitral, Drasan is only 14 km from Kosht in the Mulikho Valley or Lower Kho. In the village of Rain you can hire porters and guides for expeditions to the peaks in the west of Turikho Valley. It's a two-day trek from Rain to Shagram.

Alternatively you can get a jeep from Chitral to Warkup Village, and then it's a two to three-day trek to Rua, at 3000 metres, on the west bank of the Turikho river valley. There are villages and streams along the trail, and the tributaries to the north-west lead to glaciers. Notice the ibexes in the upper reaches. At a village six km from Warkup there is a rock carving of a Buddhist stupa.

Up towards Turikho Valley via Zani Pass (3000 metres) there is a flat ridge, 24 km long, which offers a view of Tirich Mir and other mountain peaks. *Camp* here. Not much further on is Moghland and a shepherds' hamlet. Beyond Khot Pass (4600 metres) is the Khot Valley, which leads into Yarkhund Valley. The best route is to the north through Lasht Khot Village.

Once you get out of the valley the route becomes confusing as there are trails leading in all directions. You need a local guide to take you through this extremely scenic section.

From here you go down the valley through another village and across a stream into Brep, a village which has a *teashop-inn*. To the south is Mastuj, but at Gazin you can go to Yasin Valley via Thui Ann Pass (4499 metres), and into Shotaling, Mushk, Harph and then Yasin.

Another route is from Mastuj via the Chumarkhan Pass (5009 metres) or Zagar Gol, just off Chapali Village, 12 km north of Mastuj, across a bridge, up a gradual ascent to the pass at 1150 metres. Once you reach the Yasin Valley go either to Shiahsi or Phander in the Ghizer Valley.

Another variation of this trek is from Warkup to Mastuj in the Turikho-Yarkhund valleys which takes eight to 10 days.

Chitral-Shah Jinali-Yasin

A 24-day trek through a restricted zone. A permit and porters are necessary and a liaison officer or mountain guide is detailed. Setting off point: Chitral. Elevation 4400 metres. Time from June until August.

Take a jeep to Istaro from Chitral. It's possible to get a jeep all the way to Uzhnu via Shagram in the Mulikho Valley. Note that there is another *shagram* – polo ground – in the Turikho Valley.

From Uzhnu go to Phurgram; Shah Jinali; over Shah Jinali Pass (4300 metres); and then to Ispru; Shosht; Lesht;

Dobargar; Gazin; and Brep in the Yarkhund Valley. From Gazin there is a trail over the Thui Ann Pass into Shotaling, Mushk and Harph in the Yasin Valley.

This trek to Yasin is a variation of the preceding one. There are many different trails going from Chitral to Shah Jinali, but all of them end in Mastuj – see above. You can trek back to Chitral or catch a jeep from Brep or Mastuj all the way. Another variation is to go to Yoshkist Village, just north-east of Shah Jinali Pass. Here the trail forks off east to Darkot Pass, or alternatively, to Brep and Mastuj.

Warning Darkot Pass has been classified as a 'deleted' zone because of the Afghanistan situation. Also Thui Ann is inaccessible in early summer, and sometimes through high summer, because of deep slush. This is therefore a more difficult trek than the Mastuj-Chumarkhan Pass route.

Note The trekking region up here is vast and in preparing this section it has not been possible to personally cover all the trails which have been written up in this book. However, careful research has been undertaken both from books, brochures *et al* and from other trekkers. The former includes trekking brochures put out by the PTDC, literature on trekking and mountaineering published by the Ministry of Culture & Tourism in Pakistan, and books on anthropology, history, archaeology, geology and on general exploration of the region.

Index

Map references in **bold** type

Lonely Planet travel guides

Africa on a Shoestring
Australia – a travel survival kit
Alaska – a travel survival kit
Bali & Lombok – a travel survival kit
Burma – a travel survival kit
Bushwalking in Papua New Guinea
Canada – a travel survival kit
China – a travel survival kit
Hong Kong, Macau & Canton
India – a travel survival kit
Japan – a travel survival kit
Kashmir, Ladakh & Zanskar
Kathmandu & the Kingdom of Nepal
Korea & Taiwan – a travel survival kit
Malaysia, Singapore & Brunei – a travel survival kit
Mexico – a travel survial kit
New Zealand – a travel survival kit
Pakistan – a travel survival kit kit
Papua New Guinea – a travel survival kit
The Philippines – a travel survival kit
South America on a Shoestring
South-East Asia on a Shoestring
Sri Lanka – a travel survival kit
Thailand – a travel survival kit
Tramping in New Zealand
Trekking in the Himalayas
Turkey – a travel survival kit
USA West
West Asia on a Shoestring

Lonely Planet phrasebooks

Indonesia Prasebook
Nepal Phrasebook
Thailand Phrasebook

Lonely Planet travel guides are available around the world. If you can't find them, ask your bookshop to order them from one of the distributors listed below. For countries not listed or if you would like a free copy of our latest booklist write to Lonely Planet in Australia.

Australia
Lonely Planet Publications, PO Box 88, South Yarra, Victoria 3141.
Canada
Milestone Publications, Box 2248, Sidney British Columbia, V8L 3S8.
Denmark
Scanvik Books aps, Store Kongensgade 59 A, DK-1264 Copenhagen K.
Hong Kong
The Book Society, GPO Box 7804.
India & Nepal
UBS Distributors, 5 Ansari Rd, New Delhi.
Israel
Geographical Tours Ltd, 8 Tverya St, Tel Aviv 63144.
Japan
Intercontinental Marketing Corp, IPO Box 5056, Tokyo 100-31.
Malaysia
MPH Distributors, 13 Jalan 13/6, Petaling Jaya, Selangor.
Netherlands
Nilsson & Lamm bv, Postbus 195, Pampuslaan 212, 1380 AD Weesp.
New Zealand
Roulston Greene Publishing Associates Ltd, Box 33850, Takapuna, Auckland 9.
Papua New Guinea
Gordon & Gotch (PNG), PO Box 3395, Port Moresby.
Singapore
MPH Distributors, 116-DJTC Factory Building, Lorong 3, Geylang Square, Singapore, 1438.
Sweden
Esselte Kartcentrum AB, Vasagatan 16, S-111 20 Stockholm.
Thailand
Chalermnit, 1-2 Erawan Arcade, Bangkok.
UK
Roger Lascelles, 47 York Rd, Brentford, Middlesex, TW8 0QP.
USA
Lonely Planet Publications, PO Box 2001A, Berkeley, CA 94702.
West Germany
Buchvertrieb Gerda Schettler, Postfach 64, D3415 Hattorf a H.